RESHAPING THE LABOUR MARKET

Regulation, Efficiency and Equality in Australia

The outcomes of the labour market have become the major economic and social problems of OECD countries over the past decade. Inflation has virtually disappeared, material standards of living on average are high, but 35 million people remain unemployed, inequality of earnings is rising and the establishment of regular employment is increasingly difficult for young people. In this book, a team of leading economists take Australia as a case study in which to examine whether regulation of the labour market assists or detracts from the achievement of desirable labour market outcomes. Attention is focussed especially on the provision of adequate incomes and jobs for low-skilled workers, because this is the area in which labour markets around the world, including Australia, have failed most seriously in the past two decades.

Sue Richardson is an Associate Professor in the School of Economics at the University of Adelaide, and a Fellow of the Academy of the Social Sciences in Australia. She has been a member of various Ministerial policy committees at state and national levels advising on technological change and energy policy and a Director of several companies in related fields. Between 1995 and 1997 she was an Associate Commissioner with the Industry Commission. She is the co-author of *Living Decently* (1993) and is currently co-editor of *The Economic Record*.

RESHAPING AUSTRALIAN INSTITUTIONS

Series editors: Geoffrey Brennan and Francis G. Castles, Research School of Social Sciences, Australian National University.

Published in association with the Research School of Social Sciences, Australian National University.

This program of publications arises from the School's initiative in sponsoring a fundamental rethinking of Australia's key institutions before the centenary of Federation in 2001.

Published in this program will be the work of scholars from the Australian National University and elsewhere who are researching and writing on the institutions of the nation. The scope of the program includes the institutions of public governance, intergovernmental relations, Aboriginal Australia, gender, population, the environment, the economy, business, the labour market, the welfare state, the city, education, the media, criminal justice and the Constitution.

Brian Galligan *A Federal Republic*
    0 521 37354 9 hardback   0 521 37746 3 paperback
Patrick Troy (ed.) *Australian Cities*
    0 521 48197 X hardback   0 521 48437 5 paperback
Ian Marsh *Beyond the Two Party System*
    0 521 46223 1 hardback   0 521 46779 9 paperback
Elim Papadakis *Environmental Politics and Institutional*
    Change
    0 521 55407 1 hardback   0 521 55631 7 paperback
Chilla Bulbeck *Living Feminism*
    0 521 46042 5 hardback   0 521 46596 6 paperback
John Uhr *Deliberative Democracy in Australia*
    0 521 62458 4 hardback   0 521 62465 7 paperback
Mitchell Dean and Barry Hindess (eds) *Governing Australia*
    0 521 58357 8 hardback   0 521 58671 2 paperback
Nicolas Peterson and Will Sanders (eds) *Citizenship*
    and Indigenous Australians
    0 521 62195 X hardback   0 521 62736 2 paperback
Martin Painter *Collaborative Federalism*
    0 521 59071 X hardback
Julianne Schultz *Reviving the Fourth Estate*
    0 521 62042 2 hardback   0 521 62970 5 paperback
David Peetz *Unions in a Contrary World*
    0 521 63055 X hardback   0 521 63950 6 paperback
Moira Gatens and Alison Mackinnon (eds) *Gender*
    and Institutions
    0 521 63190 4 hardback   0 521 63576 4 paperback

'The business by which a person earns his livelihood fills his thoughts during by far the greatest part of those hours in which his mind is at its best: during them his character is being formed by the ways in which he uses his faculties at work.'

– Alfred Marshall, *Principles of Economics*, pp. 1–2

RESHAPING THE LABOUR MARKET

Regulation, Efficiency and Equality in Australia

EDITED BY

SUE RICHARDSON
University of Adelaide

PUBLISHED BY THE PRESS SYNDICATE OF THE UNIVERSITY OF CAMBRIDGE
The Pitt Building, Trumpington Street, Cambridge, United Kingdom

CAMBRIDGE UNIVERSITY PRESS
The Edinburgh Building, Cambridge CB2 2RU, UK   http://www.cup.cam.ac.uk
40 West 20th Street, New York, NY 10011–4211, USA http://www.cup.org
10 Stamford Road, Oakleigh, Melbourne 3166, Australia

First published 1999

Printed in Australia by Ligare Pty Ltd

Typeface New Baskerville (Adobe) 10/12pt. *System* QuarkXPress® [PH]

A catalogue record for this book is available from the British Library

National Library of Australia Cataloguing in Publication data
Reshaping the labour market: regulation, efficiency and
equality in Australia.
ISBN 0 521 65281 2 hardback
ISBN 0 521 65424 6 paperback
1. Labor market – Australia. 2. Labor policy – Australia.
3. Unemployment – Australia. I. Richardson, Sue, 1946 –.
(Series: Reshaping Australian institutions).
331.120994

Library of Congress Cataloguing in Publication data
Reshaping the labour market: regulation, efficiency, and equality in
Australia/edited by Sue Richardson.
    p.   cm. – (Reshaping Australian institutions).
A collection of 7 original essays by Australian scholars.
Includes bibliographical references and index.
ISBN 0-521-65281-2 (alk. paper). – ISBN 0-521-65424-6 (pbk.: alk. paper)
1. labor market–Australia. 2. Full employment policies–
Australia. 3. Wages – Government policy–Australia. 4. Minimum
wage – Australia. 5. Wages and labor productivity – Australia.
8. Public welfare – Australia. 9. Labor supply – Effect of education
on – Australia. I. Richardson, Sue, 1946 – . II. Title: Reshaping
the labor market. III. Series.
HD5850.A6R467 1999   99-30802
331.12'042'0994–dc21

ISBN 0 521 65281 2 hardback
ISBN 0 521 65424 6 paperback

Contents

Tables

Figures

Contributors

JEFF BORLAND is Associate Professor, Department of Economics, University of Melbourne. Between 1996 and 1998 he was Visiting Fellow, Centre for Economic Policy Research, Research School of Social Sciences, Australian National University.

BRUCE CHAPMAN is Professor and Director, Centre for Economic Policy Research, Research School of Social Sciences, Australian National University and Fellow of the Academy of Social Sciences in Australia.

BOB GREGORY is Professor and Head, Economics Program, Research School of Social Sciences, Australian National University, and Fellow of the Academy of Social Sciences in Australia.

KEITH HANCOCK is Honorary Fellow, National Institute of Labour Studies, the Flinders University of South Australia, and School of Economics, the University of Adelaide and Fellow of the Academy of Social Sciences in Australia. During 1997 Keith Hancock was a Visiting Fellow, Economics Program, Research School of Social Sciences, Australian National University.

ANN HARDING is Professor and Director, the National Centre for Social and Economic Modelling, University of Canberra, and Fellow of the Academy of Social Sciences in Australia.

EVA KLUG is a Research Assistant, Economics Program, Research School of Social Sciences, Australian National University.

YEW MAY MARTIN is a PhD student, Economics Program, Research School of Social Sciences, Australian National University.

DEBORAH MITCHELL is a Fellow, Economics Program, Research School of Social Sciences, Australian National University.

SUE RICHARDSON is Reader in Economics, University of Adelaide. During 1997 Sue Richardson was a Visiting Fellow, Economics Program, Research School of Social Sciences, Australian National University. She is a Fellow of the Academy of Social Sciences in Australia.

GRAEME WOODBRIDGE is an economic adviser, Australian Competition and Consumer Commission.

NIA

BK Title: *Preface*

ed

The twentieth century has seen great advances for workers across the developed Western world. Real wages have risen to levels never before experienced, and generally become more equally distributed. Hours of work have diminished and extended paid holidays and sick leave have been introduced. Child labour is banned, death and disablement from work have fallen greatly. Employers are prohibited from discriminating on the basis of irrelevant characteristics such as sex, marital status and religion and are obliged to prevent sexual harassment in the workplace. Workers are much more educated and the existence, in most countries, of government income support for unemployed workers makes the possibility of unemployment less fearsome.

But this optimistic tale has acquired a prickly edge over the past two decades. Unemployment has become a disturbingly persistent problem in most OECD countries. The average level of real wages has grown only slowly if at all, and inequality in its distribution has grown in all the English-speaking countries. The last two developments have combined to produce a fall in the real level of earnings of workers in the lower end of the wage distribution, and has raised increasing concerns about the emergence of a class of 'working poor' – i.e., people who are working full-time but earning an income which places them well below average standards. Many other workers are unable to find steady full-time work, and manage on the income from casual, contract and part-time jobs.

Both the long run optimistic and shorter run pessimistic stories apply to the Australian experience. All developed countries regulate their labour markets, but Australia has 95 years of experience with a unique approach to regulation, in the form of a comprehensive system of federal and state industrial tribunals. These tribunals have set minimum wages, hours and other conditions of work for about 80 per cent of the employee workforce. The intent of the system has been to produce more favourable outcomes for workers than they were able to achieve for themselves; to provide a means whereby notions of fairness in the distribution of pay may have some expression; and to ameliorate the extent of direct industrial conflict in the relations between employers and employees. This system has never been without controversy, but the last ten years have seen a sustained and effective challenge to the role of the tribunals, in the name of deregulation.

The English-speaking world has experienced a sea-change in public policy attitudes to the roles of the market and the state over the past two decades. Specifically, the power of the market and of competition has been celebrated and the proper role of government has been seen to have shrunk, so that much tougher tests have now generally been set before intervention in the market is deemed to be justified. The move to deregulate the Australian labour market is thus part of a much broader trend – one which extends into other spheres of the economy and across national borders.

Since labour is used in every economic activity, the functioning of the labour market is inseparable from that of the whole economy and each of its parts. One argument for deregulation of the labour market is that the economy would be more productive if employment relations were determined by employers, constrained by the forces of competition but not by restrictions imposed by government, tribunals or unions. A second argument is that a less regulated labour market would be fairer, since employers would not be inhibited by high regulated wages or other terms of employment from taking on people who otherwise would be unemployed.

This book is a collaborative effort to explore many, but not all, of the issues surrounding regulation of the labour market. It has an Australian focus. But because much of the Australian experience is shared with other developed, especially English-speaking, countries, the stories told have a relevance beyond Australia's shores. The structure of the book and its evolution has been collaborative among the authors, but they have not sought to come to a common mind on every contentious point. The collaborative process, whereby each author has looked over the shoulders of the others, has been designed to promote cohesion in the content of the book and to capture the benefits of having many intelligent minds reviewing each chapter. The review process was facilitated by a conference at which each author presented a draft of her or his chapter for discussion. The authors are mostly labour economists, mainly based in the Research School of Social Sciences at the Australian National University. The common background in labour economics has influenced the themes of the book and the approaches taken.

The book begins with a discussion of the reasons for regulation of the labour market, the changing economic environment within which that regulation operates and recent changes to the way in which the Australian labour market is regulated. The opening chapter finishes with a summary of the main findings of the subsequent chapters and draws some conclusions from these.

Chapter 2 does two things. The first is to tell the story, in some detail, behind the changes to the role of the industrial tribunals as regulators of the Australian labour market, which have been wrought by legislation over the past 10 years. The second is to evaluate the arguments that have been put forward to justify those changes. Particular attention is paid to the arguments that deregulated labour markets are more efficient, and that this is a sufficient justification for their adoption.

The focus on the role of the industrial tribunals is continued in Chapter 3. There the difficult question is asked, and answered: have the tribunals made a difference to the wage structure and if so, what are the consequences for inequality in the dispersion of pay and for unemployment? This is an important question, because a major justification of the system of industrial tribunals is to promote fairness in the wage structure. The fairness theme is continued in the following two chapters. These explore, in the short run and for people followed over a period of years, the characteristics of low wage workers and whether receipt of low wages is strongly linked with living in a low income household. If the tribunals, in their wage setting decisions, do affect the structure of wages, does this have an overall equalising effect on the distribution of household income?

Those who challenge the efficiency and fairness of a regulated wage structure often do so on the grounds that high minimum wages generate unemployment and that the unemployed are worse off than low wage workers. Chapters 3 and 4 explore these propositions. Chapter 6 looks at the question the other way round. If the reduction of wages is one way to create extra jobs because it brings down the wage to the level of productivity of the unemployed worker, can this process be reversed? Can the unemployed workers have their productivity raised to match the level of the minimum wages?

The protection of low wage workers can be achieved, more or less effectively, by regulation. But it can also be achieved indirectly by the provision of an alternative source of income which means that people who are offered harsh terms of employment can refuse to accept them. The final chapter examines whether the welfare state in Australia plays this role, as a support for or an alternative to the active regulation of wages at the bottom end.

The authors are all economists. Nonetheless, the arguments are presented in English rather than mathematics and all the chapters are intelligible to readers who have no formal education in economics.

Acknowledgements

The authors have been greatly assisted by a number of people who have read and commented on their work. These include the discussants at a conference at which the contents of this book were first publicly aired, namely Grant Belchamber, Guy Debelle, Denise Doiron, Peter Forsyth, Michael Keating, John Quiggin and Glenn Withers. Braham Dabscheck, Peter Gahan, Bob Goodin, Suzanne Hammond, Joe Isaac, Simon Lambert, Philip Pettit, John Piggott and Barbara Pocock have all provided valuable assistance with specific parts of the book and we thank them for their time and for their most helpful contributions.

The project was conceived and much work for it done while Sue Richardson and Keith Hancock were Visiting Fellows in the Reshaping Australian Institutions program in the Research School of Social Sciences at the Australian National University. The support of this program was crucial and is warmly acknowledged.

Abbreviations

ABS	Australian Bureau of Statistics
ACTU	Australian Council of Trade Unions
AGPS	Australian Government Publishing Service
AIRC	Australian Industrial Relations Commission
ANU	Australian National University
AWA	Australian Workplace Agreement
AWIRS	Australian Workplace Industrial Relations Survey
BCA	Business Council of Australia
CAI	Confederation of Australian Industry
CPD	*Commonwealth Parliamentary Debates*
CEDA	Committee for the Economic Development of Australia
EMTR	effective marginal tax rate
EPAC	Economic Planning Advisory Commission
GDP	gross domestic product
NATSEM	National Centre for Social and Economic Modelling, University of Canberra
OECD	Organization for Economic Cooperation and Development
SER	standard employment relation
TCF	textiles, clothing and footwear
TER	transitory employment relation

CHAPTER 1

Regulation of the Labour Market

Sue Richardson

Regulation of the labour market has been a feature of Western economies since it was proposed as an amelioration of some of the worst abuses of workers experienced during the Industrial Revolution. This chapter rehearses the main reasons for regulation and describes how the Australian labour market has been and is now regulated. It looks briefly at the changing economic and social environment that provides some understanding of why dissatisfaction with historical forms of regulation has been loud. It concludes with a short summary of the findings of each of the chapters to follow, and argues that on the basis of their evidence, the case for retaining active regulation of the labour market is strong.

The outcomes of the labour market have become the major economic and social problem of OECD countries during the 1990s. Inflation has virtually disappeared, material standards of living on average are high, but 35 million people are unemployed, inequality of earnings is rising and the establishment of regular employment is increasingly difficult for young people. For people of working age, employment is both their major source of income and a major use of their time and their abilities. The labour of the workforce is also the main productive resource for the economy. The way in which work is allocated, organized and rewarded has large consequences for the economy and for society. In recognition of this, regulation of the terms and conditions of employment is ubiquitous among Western nations. The employment relationship is not just a private matter. But the role of regulation and its optimal design are under challenge. Regulation of the employment relation has evolved over time in response to changing social values about the rights and equality of ordinary people, the nature of the economy and the consequences of the tussle for power between labour and capital. It continues to evolve, with contemporary pressure for fewer restrictions on the

1

employers' rights to determine the terms and conditions of employment, often referred to as deregulation.

The authors of this book take Australia as a case study in which to
examine whether regulation of the labour market assists or detracts from
the achievement of desirable labour market outcomes. Attention is
focused especially on the provision of adequate incomes and jobs for
low-skill workers, because this is the area in which labour markets
around the world, including Australia, have most seriously failed in the
past decade or two.

Australia has an unusual and extensive history of regulation of the
labour market. Within three years of the establishment of the Commonwealth of Australia in 1901, a federal industrial tribunal had been
established to assist in the peaceable resolution of disputes between
workers and employers. In 1907 this tribunal established a minimum
wage for an unskilled adult man, and higher minima for skilled workers,
in a decision known as the 'Harvester Judgment'. A system of industrial
tribunals, at both the federal and state levels, has thus prevailed in
Australia for the whole of the twentieth century. Among other things,
these tribunals have set wages and conditions of employment, embodied
in 'awards', which are binding on employers. These awards have covered
up to 80 per cent of the employee labour force. The desirability of this
structure of awards has been seriously challenged over the past decade.

When we speak of 'the labour market' we speak of an abstraction. But
it is a useful abstraction. It encompasses a vast range of transactions of
which the one common feature is the payment of people to provide
services. The functions which would generally be ascribed to the labour
market include:

- allocation of workers between alternative employment;
- providing work for those who want it;
- generation of different levels and types of skills;
- engendering high productivity from employees;
- providing a dignified and safe work environment and tasks that
  enhance rather than shrivel workers' human capacities; and
- generation of income for those who work and the people who depend
  on them.

The success of the labour market will be judged by reference to its
performance of these functions.

Labour markets are regulated because people have judged, rightly or
wrongly, that regulation will enhance their performance in terms of the
above criteria. Even those who are least attracted to interference think
that a market economy requires a framework of law within which transactions can take place – for example by enforcing contracts. Much

regulation, however, goes beyond this minimalist purpose. Most of the additional regulation has derived from an intention to improve the lot of people who are, or might be, employed. There has long been recognition that the competitive pressures of supply and demand may generate inefficiently low wages and investment in the development of worker skills. But even if unregulated labour markets were efficient, they need not thereby be fair. As the economist and Nobel Laureate Amartya Sen put it so pithily, market outcomes may be both perfectly efficient and perfectly disgusting.

What do we mean by 'regulation'? The term accommodates various alternatives, but the common element is some form of intervention by the state. That intervention may take the form of direct requirements imposed on labour market participants, with legal consequences attached to non-compliance. Minimum wages and occupational health and safety codes are examples. Alternatively (or additionally) the state may alter the power relations between participants, thereby influencing market outcomes. Laws relating to trade unions are an obvious example. Again, the state may shape outcomes by altering the environment. Policies for education and training, taxation, social welfare, government employment and foreign trade are all likely to impinge on the labour market. The chapters of this book do not constitute an encyclopedia of labour market regulation. While the topics discussed do reflect the diversity of types of intervention, they focus particularly on the role of the labour market and its regulation in generating adequate incomes for workers.

Regulation involves the imposition of restraints on the actions of employers and/or their workers. The acceptability of such restraints and the purposes for which they are legitimate vary with the intellectual and ethical climate of the time, as well as with the reality that is being experienced. Throughout the Western world, the twentieth century has seen a remarkable rise in the belief in the equality of people as citizens.[1] Australia largely rejected the European structure of social class and its notions of superior and inferior stations in life. But certain categories of people were nonetheless denigrated and often excluded from full citizenship. These social inequalities, which ranked people according to sex and race and social background and, often, religion, have prevailed for most of the recorded history of Western civilization. They remain in the hearts of many people today. But now the (radical) official, public and legal position is that all adults are equal in their citizenship and have a right to be treated as such. This right extends beyond formal relations with the state to include rights as customers, spouses and workers.

Historically, economic inequality, including the subordination of the employee to the employer (or servant to master), reinforced social inequality, which in turn was seen as proper and necessary for a stable social order. Today, a high degree of economic inequality and sub-ordination disturbs and confronts the challenging new ethic of social equality. What is more, 'this movement to greater equality has necessarily interfered with freedom of contract, for it has involved the overriding of the free choice of contracting parties in the interests of socially proclaimed values' (Atiyah, 1979: 633). In the context of this book, it is important also to note Atiyah's conclusion that 'freedom of contract naturally suits the strong, and is disadvantageous to the weak' (ibid.: 648). Inevitably, these movements of opinion have had a profound influence on ideas about freedom of contract, free choice, and the importance of consent in exchange relationships.

In the twenty or so years since Atiyah wrote, the weight given to egalitarian values and the perceived unfairness of relying on market-based exchange seem to have dwindled in public discourse, at least that about economic policy. And the environment has changed, so that the price paid for overriding the market in the interests of fairness and of more egalitarian outcomes is perceived to have risen.

OECD countries have faced a combination in the past one or two decades of growing inequality in the distribution of earnings, often accompanied by falls in the real earnings of the low-paid, and falls in employment – often but not only manifest in growth in unemployment. The rising inequality has led to renewed interest in the usefulness of legally binding minimum wages and other forms of regulation as instruments to redress this (see Fernie & Metcalf 1996; Freeman 1994). The high unemployment has led to a renewed interest in removing restrictions on the terms of employment, in the hope that this will increase employment and reduce unemployment.

Have the costs of protecting vulnerable workers by regulation become too great, in terms of lost productivity and increased unemployment? Can and do regulators affect the structure of wages in the interests of the low-paid? Have low wages ceased to be strongly linked with low family income, so that increasing low wages is an ineffective instrument of redistribution? Is it the case that the least skilled cannot achieve pro-ductivity levels that enable them to command an adequate wage in their own right? Is the welfare system a hindrance to egalitarian outcomes, or an essential complement to the labour market, or an alternative? These questions are all carefully scrutinized in the chapters of this book.

In what follows I pause initially to reflect on the experiences of early labour markets that led to the emergence of forms of regulation that were intended to make them more humane and less brutal. I then discuss the particular Australian approach to regulation of the labour market, and how this has changed over the past decade. Recent changes have gained momentum from changes in the economic environment within which firms operate. I provide a brief summary of these environmental forces for change. Finally, I summarize the main findings from subsequent chapters, and draw conclusions from them on whether and how the labour market should be regulated.

The Origins of Regulation

Harsh treatment

With the emergence of the market as the principal form of economic life came an awareness of the harsh consequences of a system that relies on the competitive pursuit of profit as its energy source. The experience of the Industrial Revolution, a mere 150 years ago, provides graphic reminders of just how savage the consequences can be for the losers in the competitive struggle. Children as young as four, and most commonly seven or eight years old, were employed to operate the machines and mines that drove the Industrial Revolution in England and elsewhere in Europe. Evidence given by factory workers to the Committee on Factory Children's Labour (1831–32) gives a stark picture of the condition of children:

Q: At what time in the morning, in the brisk time, did those girls go to the mills?
In the brisk time, for about six weeks, they have gone at 3 o'clock in the morning, and ended at 10, or nearly half past at night.
Q: What intervals were allowed for rest or refreshment during those nineteen hours of labour?
Breakfast a quarter of an hour, and dinner half an hour, and drinking a quarter of an hour.
Q: Was any of that time taken up in cleaning the machinery?
They generally had to do what they call dry down; sometimes this took the whole of the time at breakfast or drinking, and they were to get their dinner or breakfast as they could; if not, it was brought home.
Q: Had you not great difficulty in awakening your children to this excessive labour?
Yes, in the early time we had them to take up asleep and shake them, when we got them on the floor to dress them, before we could get them off to their work; but not so in the common hours.
Q: What was the length of time they could be in bed during those long hours?
It was near 11 o'clock before we could get them into bed after getting a little victuals . . .
Q: What time did you get them up in the morning?
In general, me or my mistress got up at 2 o'clock to dress them.
Q: So that they had not above four hours' sleep at this time?
No, they had not.
Q: Were the children excessively fatigued by this labour?

Many times; we have cried often when we have given them the little victualling we had to give them; we had to shake them, and they have fallen to sleep with the victuals in their mouths many a time.

Q: Did this excessive term of labour occasion much cruelty also?
Yes, with being so very much fatigued the strap was very frequently used.
Q: Have any of your children been strapped?
Yes, every one;——
Q: Had your children any opportunity of sitting during those long days of labour?
No; they were in general, whether there was work for them to do or not, to move backwards and forwards till something came to their hands.
(Cited in Bland, Brown & Tawney 1914: 510–13)

The plight of children whose youth and health was lost in endless toil is particularly poignant. But the conditions under which adults worked were equally horrific. These included wages that hardly sufficed to keep workers and their families alive, extremely long hours of work, factory conditions that were both dangerous and intensely stressful, arbitrary and severe penalties for breach of work rules, such as reducing the day's pay by one quarter for arriving a minute or two late for work (in an age when only the employer had a timepiece). The pressures of competition, when there was unemployment, led employers to extract the maximum output they could from their workers. The motivation of employers – callous indifference, greed, or the fear of being uncompetitive – may have varied, but the consequences for workers of an unregulated, competitive labour market did not: they were truly terrible.

Compassionate people of the time could see no remedy for the plight of the working poor that was superior to regulation. Even those who were more hard-hearted were concerned at the deleterious effects on the health, stature and spirit of the working class; among other things, it made them less fit as potential soldiers. Over time, and with a struggle, regulation was indeed enacted. Such regulation included limits on working hours and prohibition of the employment of very young children and of women underground in mines. The Children's Employment Commission, Mines, 1842, concludes:

That instances occur in which children are taken into these mines to work as early as four years of age . . . while from eight to nine is the ordinary age at which employment in these mines commences.

That although this employment scarcely deserves the name of labour, yet, as the children engaged in it are commonly excluded from light and are always without companions, it would, were it not for the passing and re-passing of the coal carriages, amount to solitary confinement of the worst order . . . In some districts they remain in solitude and darkness during the whole time they are in the pit, and, according to their own account, many of them never see the light of day for weeks together . . .

One of the most disgusting sights I have ever seen was that of young
females, dressed like boys in trousers, crawling on all fours, with belts round
their waists and chains passing between their legs . . . (Cited in Bland, Brown
& Tawney, 1914: 517)

According to observers at the time, the regulations, where they were
enforced, had clearly beneficial effects on the health of children.

We see in this history a prime reason for regulation: to prevent
employers from imposing intolerably harsh conditions of employment.
The Factory Acts were 'imposed not as a means of class domination; but
with the purpose of defending the weak, and especially children and
mothers of children, in matters in which they are not able to use the
forces of competition in their own defence' (Marshall 1930: 751). In the
absence of external constraint, there seemed to be no natural limit to
how far employers would go to extract maximum output from workers at
minimum cost. Marx was scarcely exaggerating when he claimed that

in its were-wolf hunger for surplus . . . labour, capital oversteps not only the
moral, but even the merely physical maximum bounds of the working day. It
usurps the time for growth, development, and healthy maintenance of the
body. It steals the time required for the consumption of fresh air and sun-
light. It higgles over a meal-time, incorporating it where possible with the
process of production itself, so that food is given to the labourer as to a mere
means of production, as coal is supplied to the boiler, grease and oil to the
machinery. It reduces the sound sleep needed for the restoration, reparation,
refreshment of the bodily powers to just so many hours of torpor as the revival
of an organism, absolutely exhausted, renders essential. It is not the normal
maintenance of the labour-power which is to determine the limits of the
working day; it is the greatest possible daily expenditure of labour-power, no
matter how diseased, compulsory, and painful it may be, which is to determine the limits of the labourers' period of repose. (1932: 291)

The 'free' labourer . . . is compelled by social conditions, to sell the whole of
his active life, his very capacity for work, for the price of the necessaries of life,
his birthright for a mess of pottage. (1932: 297)

That Marx was not exaggerating is clear from the ample evidence not
only of extreme hours of work, of the employment of women if they were
cheaper than men and of children if they were cheaper still, but also of
the serious damage to health, physique and life expectancy that work in
the factories produced during the 100 years either side of 1800.

It disturbs the order of nature, and the rights of the labouring men, by
ejecting the males from the workshop, and filling their places by females, who
are thus withdrawn from all their domestic duties and exposed to insufferable
toil at half the wages that would be assigned to males, for the support of their
families . . . The wife can do nothing for her husband and family; she can

neither cook, wash, repair clothes, nor take charge of the infants; all must be
paid for out of her scanty earnings, and, after all, most imperfectly done.[2]

My boy, Edwin he was a proverb for being active and straight before he went
[to the factory]; there is a portion of ground of considerable extent . . . in our
neighbourhood, and that boy would run seven times round that piece of
ground and come in without being much fatigued; but when he had gone to
the mill some time, perhaps about three years, he began to be weak in his
knees; I had three steps up into my house, and I have seen that boy get hold
of the sides of the door to assist his getting up into the house; many a one
advised me to take him away; they said he would be ruined and made quite a
cripple; but I was a poor man, and could not afford to take him away, having
a large family, six children, under my care; they are not all mine, but I have to
act as a father to them. (Cited in Bland, Brown & Tawney 1914: 514)

There is no reason to suppose that, one and a half centuries later, the
forces of competition left to themselves have been transformed so that
they would deliver only benign outcomes for workers. That we do not
see frequent contemporary examples of such abuse of workers is in part
a tribute to the effective protections provided by regulation and the
existence of a social welfare system that obviates the need to accept such
desperate conditions. Because the employment of workers on very harsh
terms is prohibited by regulation in Australia, evidence on the extent of
such employment is hard to obtain. The textile, clothing and footware
industry is often cited as an area where there are harsh conditions
of employment, because many workers work from home, are immigrants
with limited command of English and are employed on piece rates. The
Industry Commission, in its draft report on the textile, clothing and
footware industries (1997a), reports a number of examples of very low
pay and other misuse of workers. 'Vietnamese women are working for
less . . . maybe 60c per dress whereas I get $2 . . . The prices haven't
changed in ten years.' The Commission notes that this implies an hourly
rate of pay of between $1.20 and $4 (in 1997 dollars) (1997a: D 18).
They go on to add that 'payment for holidays and other entitlements as
specified in the awards is said to be a rarity, although it seems that some
employers do attempt to create the appearance of providing paid
holidays. "Two months before every holiday they reduce the price per
piece, and then they say they are giving me paid holidays but actually it's
all paid through my work. If I have a day sick leave, then they take 260
dresses instead of 240, and this is how they pay sick leave." ' (ibid.: D 19).
   The report of the employee ombudsman in South Australia in 1998
states that he finds 'some employers forcing people to work for sub-
standard pay and conditions, well aware that their employees won't
complain because there are many more looking for work and the people
that have the work do not want to lose it because even the small amount

of money that they earn is better than no money at all. We therefore have outworkers, casual workers that are not paid according to the award' (Office of the Employee Ombudsman 1998: 4).

While less formally documented, there are other contemporary stories that show that harsh and demeaning experiences still occur in the workplace. For example, there is still sexual abuse of subordinates. Young people are enticed to work for weeks or even months for no pay, by the promise that they may eventually get a paid job or apprenticeship. In a contemporary example of the employment of children as cheap labour, children as young as 8 are today being employed for up to nine hours a day selling sweets door to door, for an hourly rate of pay of between $1.40 and $2.10 (Ibid.: 12). We cannot know how much more of such ill-treatment there would be if regulation were greatly diminished, but the experience of the last time there was little regulated protection of workers – the Industrial Revolution of 150 years ago – suggests we should not be sanguine.

Subordination

There is a second reason for regulation that has more force in an egalitarian and democratic culture than it did for the Europe of several centuries ago. This reason is personal freedom and dignity. It means the ability of the worker to look the boss in the eye and expect to be treated with respect. The idea is captured in the union slogan 'United we bargain, divided we beg'.[6] 'The employment relationship is not equal in that one party has the duty to obey, and one party has the right to direct. One party is subordinate to the other. A relationship which is based on subordination and domination restricts the "freedom" of the subordinate party' (Hammond & Harbridge 1993: 17).

Workers are not free if employers are in a position of dominance over them. This may be understood to mean that employers, in setting the conditions of employment and in their daily relations with their workforce, are in a position to consult only their own opinion or judgement and can ignore the interests or opinions of their workers (Pettit, 1997a: 5). To a society that values the equal dignity of all its members, such dominance is an affront even if workers are not treated harshly. The freedom and dignity of workers is compromised if employers have the power unilaterally to impose harsh conditions on their workforces, even if this power is not exercised. Workers employed by benevolent employers have to rely on continued benevolence, which may be withdrawn. Decent treatment then is not a right but a gift in the hands of the employer. This is a relation of subordination, not of equality: 'Ten years of experience have taught me that avarice and cruelty are not the peculiar and inherent qualities of any one class or occupation – they will ever be found where the means of profit are *combined with great and, virtually, irresponsible power.*'[3]

Where the employer has unilateral power over the employee, the worker has to live with apprehension, to placate in order not to be harmed. It is this demeaning need to ingratiate that is itself an evil, even if the employer does not in fact act in a harmful way – perhaps because the ingratiation worked. One suggested remedy from an earlier time was 'to appoint certain grave and discreet persons to view the straitness of works, [and] to assess rates for wages according to the desert of their works'.[4] The Australian industrial tribunals can be seen as the contemporary embodiment of such grave and discreet persons.

Appropriate legislation, or regulation, is a means by which freedom and dignity may be enhanced: such regulation restricts the capacity of one individual or group unilaterally to exercise power over another. This includes the capacity of employers unilaterally to fix the terms and conditions of employment.[5] It may also include the capacity of unions to coerce employers.

Employers have power over workers when the worker needs the job more than the employer needs the worker. This will always be the case when there are many other workers available for employment who are good substitutes, in the eyes of the employer, for the individual worker in question. In recognition of this, over the centuries there have been sporadic attempts by workers to act collectively. If employers cannot find ready substitutes for individuals (because all the potential workers have banded together or are able to prevent outsiders from taking the jobs), then their power is diminished. This move to group action by workers was formalized in Australia in the second half of the nineteenth century in the form of the union movement.

Collective action by workers is intended to limit the extent of employer power by confronting it with worker power. The subsequent clashes of two powerful groups can be costly and even dangerous, not only to the parties involved but to citizens at large. As with any locus of power, that power is constantly at risk of being abused, and in the case of both employers and unions, has been abused. Regulation is a means of protecting workers from the consequences of unequal power that does not require them to collect equivalent power in their own hands.

The efficacy of both collective action and regulation in enhancing the rights of workers and their conditions of employment is substantially influenced by the general excess of workers, of particular kinds and in total. The best protection for workers always is to be in excess demand.

Why accept such work?

Why did workers accept conditions such as those which prevailed in the factories and mines of the Industrial Revolution? The simple answer is that they had no alternative; there were no other employments available that were not equally harsh. And the alternative to employment was starvation. Indeed, many did starve, or emigrate, when workers were displaced by machinery or when demand for their product was low. In some cases desperation may have been reinforced by ignorance of the physical harm done by the conditions in which they and their children worked. But as the father of Edwin quoted above makes plain, even when they did know the consequences, they saw no alternative but to accept them. This is an example of what is known as a 'desperate exchange'. It is voluntary, in the sense that the workers know and consent to the conditions under which they will work. But it is not thereby fair or unproblematic because the 'consent' arises from the fact that they have available only desperately awful alternatives. A proper use of the power of the state is to prevent the need to accept desperate exchanges.

When workers were uneducated and unskilled and pitifully poor, they had no bargaining power. The tasks were routine and made more so by the introduction of machines, and productive effort could be coerced through supervision and punishment rather than induced by generating within workers some commitment to the well-being of the enterprise or pride in their work. Thus workers could indeed be treated as 'factors of production' where it was not necessary to engage their voluntary cooperation. They did not have to want to be productive. The employer need only ensure that they were fearful of being judged unproductive, and hence of being beaten, fined or fired. It was not necessary to treat workers in a humane and respectful way in order to extract maximum productivity from them.

The stories from the past provide an understanding of the circumstances in which workers today are vulnerable both to domination and to harsh terms of employment. This vulnerability arises when there is no alternative, superior, work available; when there is no alternative source of income other than work; when the skills required are widely available, in excess supply, and high productivity can be achieved through coercion and close supervision; and when workers have inadequate information about the consequences for them of the work they are accepting. The more these conditions are present, the more is regulation or some other restriction on the freedom of employers necessary to ensure a humane and dignified work environment.

The Australian Approach

Whether by design or by evolution, during the course of the twentieth century Australia developed a system for the protection of workers' incomes and other interests which, with hindsight, appears to have been integrated and quite effective. The system has been characterized by Castles and Mitchell (1993) as 'the workers' welfare state'. Its key features were:

- legal minimum wages that varied with the demands of the job (and, for much of the period, with the sex of the worker);
- hours of work and other minimum conditions of employment determined by independent tribunals;
- a substantial positive role for trade unions;
- tariff protection, which provided an opportunity for firms to pay these wages and remain profitable;
- wages that were sufficient to enable a full-time male employee to maintain himself and his family adequately according to the standards of the day (but were inadequate to enable a woman to maintain a family);
- basic levels of support through the social welfare system for those who were unable to provide for themselves due to old age, unemployment or disability; and
- with the exception of payments for dependent children, those in employment and those in receipt of social welfare payments were seen to be distinct groups.

For those in employment (especially full-time males), this system produced a relatively fair and adequate pay structure, restrictions on the employers' rights to command, and the employee self-confidence that came with a robust trade union movement. The trade unions, among other things, played an important role in ensuring that regulated pay and other conditions of employment were enforced in practice. This, together with the expansion of the social welfare system, removed two major sources of harsh treatment of workers. One was the 'race to the bottom', whereby firms that adhered to award conditions might be put out of business by those that breached them. The other was the need for workers to accept any terms, legal or not, because they had no alternative source of income: the welfare system increasingly came to provide a 'reservation wage', below which workers need not sink.

Over the past twenty years there have been four significant developments that have altered the system described above. The first is the reduction in the protection of capital and product markets from international competition, and an increase in competitive pressures in domestic markets. Employers have responded by seeking to reduce the regulated restraints on the terms on which they employ their workers. The second is the blurring of the distinction between unpaid work done in the home and paid work done in the workplace. Many activities once done in the home are being 'contracted out' by households and by government. Examples are childcare, elder care, housework, cooking and gardening. In addition, some of this work is now attracting an implicit payment (from government) if still done in the home, such as childcare and housework done by a dependent spouse. The third is the blurring of the distinction between households that rely on earned income and those that rely on social welfare payments. Government financial support for children, students and the costs of rental housing has been extended to families that rely mainly on earned income. This intersection has been enlarged by the fall in the real earnings of low-wage, fully employed men over the past twenty years.[6] Working families are increasingly finding themselves eligible for means-tested social welfare benefits, partly because their incomes have been falling and partly because the range and eligibility conditions of social welfare benefits have been expanding. The fourth is the decline in the strength and coverage of trade unions and the expansion of employer prerogative in the determination of the conditions of employment.

One result of these changes has been the gradual replacement of the wage determination system by the social welfare system as the instrument for protecting the living standards, if not other conditions of employment, of low-paid workers.

The Changing Environment of Regulation

It is outside the scope of this chapter to provide a satisfying explanation of why discontent with the traditional Australian system of regulation via the industrial tribunals has been loud and influential in recent decades. But it should be helpful nonetheless to describe briefly the major changes in the economic environment that undoubtedly are part of such an explanation.

Around the world, the last quarter of the twentieth century has seen great change in the nature of employment and the social and economic environment in which it is carried out. The main forces for change in the developed world have been the emergence of women from the home and into paid employment, microelectronics-based technologies, a shift in consumption patterns away from goods towards services, and increased internationalization of product and capital markets. In Australia, which is not alone, these exogenous forces have been reinforced by policies to increase competition in product markets, through reduced

Table 1.1 Comparative levels of GDP per hour worked, selected OECD
countries, 1870–1992 (index)

Country	1870	1913	1929	1938	1950	1973	1992
United States	100	100	100	100	100	100	100
Canada	71	82	69	61	77	81	87
Japan	20	20	24	25	16	28	69
Germany	70	68	58	56	35	71	95
France	60	56	55	62	45	76	102
Italy	46	41	38	44	34	66	85
United Kingdom	115	86	74	69	62	68	82
Australia	147	103	86	83	69	72	78
Belgium	94	57	44	39	32	65	83
Netherlands	103	78	84	72	51	81	99
Denmark	67	66	68	61	46	68	75
Sweden	54	50	44	49	56	77	79
Finland	37	35	34	36	32	57	70
No. higher than Australia	0	0	1	1	2	5	9

Source: Adapted from Maddison 1995; quoted in Industry Commission 1997b: 64

tariff protection, deregulation of financial markets and the transfer of a
range of economic activities from the public to the private sector. In
addition, migration, including from non-English-speaking countries, has
continued strongly.

Australians are constantly reminded that over the course of this
century Australia's position in the ranking of countries according to
GDP per capita has been slipping – from right at the very top at the turn
of the century to about seventeenth today. This relative decline was
accelerated by a period of quite low relative rates of growth in productivity that started after the Second World War. Australia's relative
position among thirteen rich countries is shown in Table 1.1.

By 1994 Australia's GDP per capita had fallen below the OECD
average (at 98.6 per cent) and was exceeded by that in fourteen of the
OECD countries. The modest gains in productivity in Australia have
been associated with a dramatic decline in the size of the manufacturing
sector, from a quarter of GDP in 1970 to a mere 15 per cent by 1993
(Industry Commission 1996: 104). Employment in manufacturing has
declined – from 1 478 000 people in 1974 to 1 120 000 in 1994 – as total
employment has grown by 36 per cent (OECD 1996b).[7] Not surprisingly,
people have asked why we have not done better.

The past quarter-century has seen a number of other major developments in the national and global economy, each of which may be
expected to have consequences for the labour market and the way in

which it is best regulated. The Australian economy is today more open to the rest of the world than it has been historically. Although the share of exports and imports in GDP has not increased much in the postwar period, the decade 1978–88 saw the sum of capital inflows and outflows rise fivefold, to around 11 per cent of GDP (Bora 1995: 93–4). This resulted from a combination of technological change and deliberate changes in policy – the latter motivated by the judgement that economies which were more open to trade and capital flows were performing better than those that were more inward-oriented. The technological change has greatly reduced the costs of information and capital flows across international borders. 'With open capital markets, arbitrage and the flow of information between Australian and foreign asset markets is now rapid and continuous' (Gruen 1995: 129). Technological change, a floating exchange rate, deregulation of the financial system and reduced tariffs have all combined to increase substantially the exposure of Australian firms to international competition and the need to change old ways of doing things. Lansbury and Kitay conclude that 'All OECD countries are experiencing intensified pressure to adapt their traditional [employment] practices to increased global competition and changing technologies' (1995: 171). And 'countries that have traditions of tight job control or Tayloristic forms of job regulation (Australia, Canada, UK, US), or were more highly centralised in structure (Sweden), have experienced more fundamental changes or transformations in their industrial relations systems' (ibid.: 172).

In common with other OECD countries, Australia also experienced the effects of the oil price shocks and episodes of high and intransigent inflation. Unlike many of the other developed countries, Australia also has experienced a sustained decline in its terms of trade.

There are two conclusions to be drawn from this brief account of recent economic history. One is that Australian firms now find themselves in a more competitive and more challenging environment. Firms are having to deal with greater exposure to international competition, the uncertainty of a floating exchange rate, unrestrained international capital flows and rapid technological change. It is probable that managers in such an environment feel they would benefit from greater autonomy in their relations with their workforces. They thus argue for a reduction in the extent to which these relations are regulated by tribunals or legislation, and for a reduction in the power of collective labour in favour of greater power and autonomy for individual employers.

The second conclusion is that the Australian economy has underperformed over a long period, starting in the 1950s. The evidence for this is the slide in relative productivity, the conclusions of a number of studies that compared the performance of specific industries and even firms in Australia with their counterparts in other developed countries, and the evident inability of the manufacturing sector to prosper in a competitive world environment (Gaston 1998). It is sensible, when looking for causes of Australia's relative underperformance, to look for distinctive attributes of the Australian economy. The way in which the labour market is regulated is one such attribute.

But it is not only firms that have had to deal with large and difficult changes. The environment for workers has also altered substantially, and in ways that are detrimental to many of them. The outstanding changes, which have affected many workers, are: the rise in unemployment, and in particular, long-term unemployment; the rise in the participation of married women in paid employment and the decline in the participation of men; the growth in levels of formal education; a sizeable growth in the proportion of part-time or casual jobs; an increase in the inequality of pay among men and among women, with a fall in real pay for men at the bottom and a substantial rise for men at the top; a rise in the pay of women relative to men; a fall in job security; a rise in inequality in the number of hours worked.[8]

While broadly similar trends are to be observed in most OECD countries, there are also notable differences. The most striking difference is in the recent US experience. During the 1950s and 1960s, the United States had levels of unemployment that exceeded the OECD average. It shared the OECD experience of rising unemployment during the 1970s and 1980s, though in somewhat muted form.

But the 1990s have seen a remarkable turnaround, in which unemployment in the United States has fallen to levels below those that prevailed in the 1960s and the employment-to-population levels have reached record levels.[9] This is in marked contrast to the other major OECD countries and Australia, most of which have seen persistent high unemployment, including long-term unemployment, and falling or static employment ratios. The fall in the employment-to-population ratio of adult males is a trend almost as disturbing as the rise in unemployment, since it is mostly interpreted as being a reluctant response by men to the absence of employment opportunities.

The reasons for this remarkable recent US performance are not well understood, but people have not failed to notice that the United States has a relatively unregulated labour market, that inequality in pay levels and the distribution of earnings has risen sharply, that pay levels for relatively unskilled and uneducated workers have fallen in real terms over a long period – up to twenty years – and are now considerably below comparable wages in Australia and in many European countries. This rising inequality has not occurred in most of the continental European countries, though it is apparent in the United Kingdom, another country that has recently been quite successful in reducing recorded unemployment.

It is not surprising, then, that an argument has developed along the following lines. Major changes in the environment that faces firms have occurred in the past twenty years, caused by globalization and skill-biased technological change. These have reduced the relative demand for unskilled workers, increased the relative demand for highly skilled workers, and caused substantial changes in the structure of the economy, including reductions in employment in declining areas. Countries that do not try to interfere in the market's responses to these changes (in particular, job losses and declining pay for unskilled workers and rising pay for skilled workers) have avoided the worst effect of these exogenous shocks, namely unemployment. They have experienced instead rising inequality. Countries that have tried to protect low-skilled workers from declining wages and rising job insecurity have avoided much of the increased inequality in pay but at the expense of increased unemployment, including substantial long-term unemployment. Put at its simplest, if you prevent price adjustments, then you get quantity adjustments.

The implicit view that price adjustments are better than quantity (or quality) adjustments in the labour market has been reinforced by evidence, especially from the United States and the United Kingdom, that the people who receive low wages are generally not the major bread-winner for the household and live in families that often are not among the poorest in the country. Thus a rise in their wages, perhaps via a legislated increase in the value of the minimum allowable wage, is an ineffective and inefficient way of reducing measured poverty.

In my opinion, the view that the superior employment growth and recent low levels of unemployment in the United States can be attributed chiefly to its greater acceptance of the outcomes of market forces in the labour market is simplistic.[10] This is not the place to justify that opinion. But the view is a coherent and intelligible one and assuredly has given impetus to those who express dissatisfaction with Australia's traditions of labour market regulation.

The Changing Form of Regulation[11]

While the extent and form of regulation of the Australian labour market has not been constant over the course of this century, discontent with its central features has been especially loudly articulated over the past fifteen years.

The main instruments for regulating the Australian labour market are legislation, the common law, and the industrial tribunals. The last of these are peculiar to Australia in the extent of their reach and influence on the terms of employment, and it is the role of the tribunals that has been most under attack. There has also been criticism of legislated restraints on employers, such as those directed to the prevention of unfair dismissals. But when people talk of deregulation, they mainly have in mind a reduction in the unique role of the industrial tribunals in setting the wages and other terms of employment of the majority of Australian workers. And such deregulation has indeed occurred. The process of change and the arguments surrounding it are discussed at length in Chapter 2. It is appropriate here to outline the ways in which the arrangements in 1998 differ from those in existence before deregulation began.

We refer, for simplicity, to the earlier arrangements as the 'traditional system'. Industrial relations in Australia, including labour market regulation, have evolved over the whole of the country's history since white settlement in 1788, though the speed of change has been uneven. There is thus a degree of abstraction in speaking of a 'traditional' system, but it is a convenient abstraction and will be readily understood by those who are familiar with Australia's regulatory history. By chance, the system as it stood on the eve of deregulation was reviewed by a government-appointed committee (known as the Hancock Committee) which reported in 1985 (Hancock, Fitzgibbon & Polites 1985). The committee, in general, could find no reason to recommend abandonment of the system, but proposed various measures to 'fine-tune' it. 'Deregulation', in the Australian context, describes the partial dismantling of the traditional system and proposals for its further dismemberment.

The traditional system – as would be expected of a set of arrangements produced by long evolution – was complex and messy. At its heart, however, was the provision of conciliation and arbitration by tribunals empowered to resolve industrial disputes by certifying agreements and making awards. Such tribunals were the creatures of both federal and state law. The system enshrined a preference for collective representation of employers and employees, especially the latter. It provided for the registration or recognition of unions and employers' associations and discouraged the formation of rivals. Registered unions and associations were subject to legal requirements and recurring scrutiny intended to promote democratic relations between members and leaders and to avert corruption. Awards and certified agreements usually governed the terms of employment of employees who were not members of unions, as well as those of union members. In round numbers, the overall coverage of the employee labour force was about 80 per cent. The wages and conditions prescribed in agreements and awards were minima in the sense that employers were legally free to 'improve' on them, and employees and their unions were ordinarily free to seek better-than-award terms.[12] Formal agreements, certified by the tribunals, covered a small minority. At the same time, many of the terms of awards, especially as to matters of detail rather than larger topics such as wages and working hours, were 'consent' provisions negotiated between the parties.

Compulsory conciliation and arbitration originally had two main objectives: enforcing terms of employment superior to those which some employees could secure by their own efforts (collective or individual), and averting strikes and lockouts. As it developed, the system became the imperfect mechanism of 'wage policy', concerned with both absolute and relative wages and conditions and formulated with regard to evidence of the state of the economy (see Hancock 1979). It was imperfect because bargaining forces periodically took charge and obliged the tribunals to bow to 'realities'. This occurred, for example, in the early 1980s, when the Australian Conciliation and Arbitration Commission could not avert a 'wage explosion' caused by union activity in the workplace and took part in the diffusion of wage increases to groups with less bargaining power. Late in 1982, the first steps were taken to reimpose a degree of wage restraint. With the election of a Labor government early in 1983, wage policy was underpinned by accords between the government and the Australian Council of Trade Unions (ACTU). As to the prevention of industrial disruption, various approaches, including legal prohibitions, had been deployed, all with questionable success. The widely accepted view is that the system succeeded in discouraging protracted disputes, associated elsewhere with formal collective bargaining, but failed to avert disputation evident in a proliferation of short-term stoppages.[13] In the mid-1980s, however, the incidence of disputation was low. At the time this was widely interpreted as a by-product of the accords and the terms of national wage case decisions. Unions that wished their members to receive the available wage increases were obliged to commit themselves to making 'no extra claims'. Such commitments nullified one of the functions of industrial action.

The Hancock Committee described in the following terms the 'fundamental characteristics' of the mechanisms then in existence:

> First, they assign important roles to representative organisations of employers and employees. In doing so, they have encouraged the development of those organisations. Secondly, they offer the service of conciliation to industrial disputants. The Acts under which they operate generally accord a priority to the voluntary settlement of disputes and hence to conciliation over arbitration. Thirdly, they provide for arbitration when the voluntary resolution of issues is not achieved. Finally, they lend the force of law to terms of employment. This applies both to negotiated agreements which are given formal status by the conciliation and arbitration authorities and to the outcomes of arbitration. (Hancock, Fitzgibbon & Polites 1985: 211)

The Committee proceeded 'to consider whether a system having these attributes should be retained and, in the course of doing so, to evaluate proposals for change'. Having done so, it expressed its firm conviction 'that Australia should retain a conciliation and arbitration system having the basic characteristics described in [the above passage]'.

In 1999 there still exists a network of awards made by federal and state tribunals – some occupational, some industrial, and some specific to particular enterprises or parts of them. Some have wide geographic spread and others are more local. The changes described in Chapter 2 have led to a situation where perhaps half of the employee labour force depends on these awards. This group comprises both workers whose employers adhere strictly to award wages and those who are subject to awards but receive over-award payments. In the 1998 safety-net wage case conducted by the Australian Industrial Relations Commission (AIRC), the 'joint governments' (the federal government, all state governments except New South Wales, and the two territory governments) estimated that 30 per cent of employees were in receipt of award rates without additional over-award amounts (AIRC 1998: 19). Whereas in the traditional regulatory system most employees on over-award rates would have received the wage increases awarded by the tribunals (maintaining their over-award margins), it is uncertain to what extent this now occurs. Award wages and conditions, much more so than in the traditional system, now have the character of a safety net rather than a base to which actual terms of employment, even if superior, are related and with which they move.

Under the arrangements which prevailed in 1998, the relationship between an employer and an employee may lawfully take one of a variety of forms:

- the employer is bound by an award and adheres to its terms;
- the employer is bound by an award but provides more generous pay and conditions;
- the employer is bound by a collective agreement to which one or more unions are parties;
- the employer is bound by a collective agreement with its employees to which there is no union party;
- there is a formal agreement between the employer and the individual employee made in accordance with the provisions of a federal or state Act; and
- none of the above applies, with the effect that the relationship is regulated by a common-law contract.

There are, in each of these cases, additional legal constraints, such as those pertaining to health and safety and to discrimination in the workplace. Which of the alternatives applies to any employer depends on numerous factors: there is no suggestion that the employer normally has a free choice, though a few may do so. As we move down the list, however, two tendencies are apparent: the likelihood that the relationship will reflect enterprise-specific circumstances increases, and the employer's capacity to influence its terms also grows. Those tendencies are constrained by the existence of 'no disadvantage' tests or (in Western Australia) minimum conditions of employment imposed by legislation.

In Chapter 2 there is an account of the changes in the industrial relations system whereby more emphasis is now accorded to formal agreements between employers and their employees. (They are formal in the sense that they have the force of law and displace inconsistent terms of awards.) In the main, these are agreements to which unions are parties. Probably 20–25 per cent of the employee labour force worked under the terms of such agreements in 1998. Recent legislation has provided for collective agreements to which unions are not parties and agreements between employers and individual employees. The number covered by individual and collective non-union agreements is, as of 1998, small.

The ability of the tribunals – in particular, the AIRC – to manage aggregate wage levels has been diluted by the growth in formal agreements and, probably, a lessening of its influence over the over-award sector. As a result, the focus of wage policy, as administered by the AIRC, has shifted somewhat, but not entirely, from the macro-economic effects of its decisions towards the management of the safety net of award rates on which a minority of employees now depends. The AIRC must have regard to a priority, specified in the statute, for bargaining rather than award prescription. It has construed this to mean that safety-net terms should not generally match in generosity to employees what unions achieve in negotiations. Although uncertainties attach to the interpretation of the available statistics, there is little doubt that those who depend on award wages have fared badly in the 1990s. In real terms their wages have fallen, while those under union agreements have grown quite strongly. It is impossible to predict whether the gap that has emerged between the agreement and the award sectors will continue to grow, be stabilized or diminish.

The movement away from regulation by arbitration and towards formal agreements was instigated to a significant degree by the trade union movement and its political ally, the Australian Labor Party. It has occurred, however, at a time when the proportion of employees who are union members has fallen substantially. Increasingly, there are enterprises that are wholly or virtually union-free. Some employers who have for long dealt with unions and still employ union members have been attempting to diminish the unions' influence. Thus although the shift from award prescription to bargaining appears to have operated to the benefit of employees represented by strong unions, the majority of the labour force faces the prospect of working under wages and conditions determined by employers, constrained only by the market and the safety net. It is difficult to foresee the future of the safety net. Subject to that uncertainty, employers will have regained much of the control which a 'free' market allows them.

The shift in the balance of power in favour of employers that has been facilitated by deregulation has occurred at a time when changes in the economic environment have been harsh on many workers, especially men and the relatively unskilled. This provides a reason for re-evaluating the contribution that specific forms of regulation may make towards ameliorating some of this hardship. The rise in unemployment (especially long-term unemployment), the decline in manufacturing, the decline in union membership, the rise in the proportion of workers employed in casual, contract, part-time and low-paid jobs and rising job insecurity all make workers more vulnerable in their relations with their employers, and thereby in increased need of some protection by independent third parties, or some other means. There have been some offsetting factors that reduce the vulnerability of workers, including the reduced reliance of the average family on the income of the male breadwinner, the substantial backstop still provided by social welfare, and for young people the willingness of the family to accommodate them at home. At the same time, the move from centralized determination of wages and conditions of employment to individually determined conditions makes workers more vulnerable, especially as it has coincided with a fall in union coverage. Enterprise bargaining and individual workplace agreements come in many forms, but clearly they can leave individuals in a very unequal bargaining position, as these interviews testify:

> I had my interview with the boss. He said to me this is the deal for you. This is the amount you get . . . if you don't like that . . . go out and look for another job. So here's me sitting in the Board Room. I'm stuck, I don't know what to do . . . So I say I'll keep the $273 because I don't want to lose my job. . . . At first I didn't agree with it, but then I agreed because I was a little bit scared.
>
> We are supposed to get an adult pay for starters, and that's the reason I asked for a pay rise, because what we get paid is really pathetic. I can't survive on it. I've got too much bills to pay off. I want another job, that's what I want to do, but I can't, I've got no experience. (Peter)
>
> That's the way it is in retail. As a shop steward I see it all the time. People are just scared of losing their jobs. They don't know what their rights are, they

don't know what they're entitled to. They're too scared to put their neck out. (Barry)

Where I work most of them are migrants. They hardly even speak English and most of the time they'll be given more rooms [to clean] and eventually they find out after talking amongst each other and they'll come to me and then I have to jump down the boss's throat. But if I wasn't there what would they do? These people are scared, this is their livelihood and they've got to do whatever because they don't even know they have rights. (Sallie) (Brotherhood of St Laurence 1996: 56–8)

Regulation, Wages and Welfare

The objectives of labour market regulation on which this book focuses are the provision of adequate pay and levels of dignity for the less skilled worker. It is widely accepted that, whatever the efficiency properties of the market, it cannot be relied on to generate a distribution of earnings (or other income) that is fair or that enables those who receive the lowest earnings to live adequately according to the standards of the day. Nor does it ensure that the domain of employer command over the employee is acceptable in a socially egalitarian society.

There are many other aspects of the economy and society that bear on outcomes in the labour market, for example the system of education and training, levels of investment, the skills and culture of management, demographic changes and levels and types of immigration and the general commitment to competitive processes in product markets. The strategy for this volume has been to eschew a broad review of all the dimensions that can affect the labour market, and all the roles that regulation may play. Instead it looks in original detail at the issue of whether regulation of the labour market has a justifiable role to play in enhancing the economic well-being of low-skilled members of the workforce, and as a corollary, enhancing their standing as employees. The main conclusions of subsequent chapters are summarized in this section.

Chapter 2 describes the forces behind the deregulation of the Australian labour market which had occurred up to 1998. The arguments put forward by the most vigorous proponents of deregulation are carefully assessed. In most cases they are found to depend either on a controversial set of values or to make claims to efficiency properties that do not withstand close scrutiny. The chapter concludes that if there is a compelling efficiency or equity case for deregulation of the labour market then it has not yet been made by Australian protagonists.

It should be noted at this point that much of the work of the industrial tribunals has concerned not the big questions of pay and hours, but rather details of the conditions of employment. Many of the disputes over such conditions have been resolved by conciliation, with the solutions agreed between employer/s and workers then embodied in awards of the tribunals. In hindsight, the prescribed conditions of employment in many awards that have accumulated over time as a result of this process look unjustifiably restrictive on employers, and it is these that have been the target of much of the push for deregulation. There is almost no evidence on the practical effects of these award conditions on overall productivity. There have, however, been some case studies which suggest that they can indeed inhibit productivity at the level of the firm.

A major criticism of regulation of the labour market is that it imposes a set of restrictions which make it difficult for firms to respond rapidly and in innovative ways to changes in the product market. Despite the wide support for this view, there is in fact very little evidence to support it as an important phenomenon. Among OECD countries there is no correlation between degree of regulation of the labour market and overall economic performance. Guy Standing's views on this matter apply, in our opinion, with equal force to Australia:

> An influential variant of the supply-side school has postulated that Europe has been suffering from a virulent disease known as 'Eurosclerosis' – a tightening of the arteries, a flabbiness of the muscles and an inability to move caused by excessive security and protective regulations. This delightful imagery has sunk deep into the European policymakers' psyche. The mildly odd fact is that after a decade and a half of explicit and implicit erosion of protective and pro-collective labour regulations, unemployment is much higher than when the disease was diagnosed and the treatment started. One is constantly reminded of medieval quackery and the leeches: the patient has not recovered, so suck more blood. (1997: 16–17)

One reason why regulation of wages and other conditions of employment does not have the devastating efficiency costs predicted by the economist Friedrich Hayek and his supporters is that there are many ways in which labour markets adjust to imbalances in supply and demand for particular skills. These have been termed 'wage-like adjustments' by Blandy and Richardson (1982) and include variations in the quality and experience of the worker employed, in the extent of on-the-job training provided, in rates of promotion and in the extent of job search.

Chapter 3 essays the ambitious task of establishing the effects that the traditional Australian system of regulation has had on the structure of pay. It establishes a systematic framework with which to identify the various ways in which the structure of pay may be viewed and through which regulation may affect those structures. It is not possible to be definitive. Nonetheless, a careful review of the evidence produced to date supports a number of conclusions. The strongest one is that the system of wage determination had a powerful influence on the gender differences in pay, at first by keeping female wages substantially below those of males doing comparable work and later by largely removing this bias. Where the tribunals have explicitly sought to alter the structure of pay, it has usually been to compress that structure, especially at the bottom end. It seems that they have had some modest success in this, and greater success in improving the wages and conditions of particular vulnerable groups, such as part-time and casual workers (many of whom are women). They do not seem, however, to have affected the structure of pay across industries. Nor have they prevented a fall in the real pay of low-wage men employed full-time. The tribunals' decisions have at times been outrun by wage changes generated in the market. But at other times, such as during the period of the Accord, in the 1980s, the tribunals and the Accord partners together seem to have exercised a noticeable effect on wage outcomes, both in terms of compressing the wage structure and of reducing the average real level of wages. The wage restraint which resulted has been credited with much of the above-average growth in employment that occurred over this time.

A controversial dimension of the effects of the tribunals is whether, by excessive compression of the wage structure, they have caused unemployment among the unskilled and among youth. The various Australian estimates of the wage elasticity of demand for labour, both in aggregate and for particular groups, all find it to be positive, but the range of estimates is large and no single result can be accepted with confidence. Even if the relatively high elasticity estimate of −0.75 is adopted (and many would argue that this estimate is too high[14]), the chapter concludes that adoption of US-style minimal regulation of wages would increase employment of low-wage workers by only 25 000 to 50 000 (at a time when unemployment stood at 800 000).

There is more agreement among empirical studies that the elasticity of demand is higher for youth than it is for adults. This information, combined with the evidence of later chapters that many low-wage youth live with their parents, supports the view that wages for youth should be kept low so long as unemployment for this group remains a major social problem. Low wages for youth are not demeaning because of the well-accepted idea (embodied in apprenticeship) that they are learning as they work. And in terms of well-being, it is a safe bet that for most young people, a chance to enter fully into the adult world of work is more important than is the level, within limits, of income received.

Chapters 4 and 5 explore the relationship between low wages and material standard of living. Chapter 4 describes who receives low wages. Low-wage workers are evenly divided between men and women; the men are frequently young and living at home, but not students; the women are typically married and prime-age and many have dependent children; they tend to work in sales, clerical and labouring jobs or in personal services. It finds that low-wage workers are not strongly (though they are somewhat, and the more so the lower the wage) concentrated in households with low annual equivalent post-tax incomes. One reason is that single full-time workers who receive even the minimum adult wage have a middling level of equivalent income, because that wage has only to support one person. The second main reason is that many low-wage workers have an employed spouse and the two incomes together provide an income that takes them out of the lowest deciles. A substantial cut in the value of low wages would most severely hurt households in the lowest decile of the income distribution and have least impact on those at the top. Its effects are evenly spread across the middle 70 per cent of households. Only about one-third of the impact on household disposable income is offset by the tax and welfare system, with most of the offset coming from reduced tax liability.

Both chapters support the conclusion that there are several types of low-wage worker. One type has her or his foot on the bottom of the wage ladder and is preparing to climb it; these tend to be young people who are in the process of becoming established workers. A second type is on the snake coming down. These workers are often middle-aged and male, and many have trade qualifications. They are likely to have lost relatively well-paid jobs in manufacturing and to have accepted low-wage jobs as better than nothing at all (others of their type have indeed found nothing at all and have left the workforce). The third type of low-wage worker (probably the majority) is on the merry-go-round. They are of prime age, not very well educated and are not going anywhere, in a wage sense. They are typically, but not exclusively, married women.

The first group may seem to be unproblematic, and to need the protection of regulation not for their wages but only to inhibit other manifestations of employer abuse of power. They can be seen as acquiring valuable work skills in addition to their wage such that the pay plus the training provides a fair return for their efforts. We cannot be completely sanguine even about this group, however. There is some evidence of a growing problem of young people not being able to earn enough to take the important steps into independent adulthood, such as setting up their own household. Chapter 4 identifies a large number of young men, in particular, who are earning low wages, are not students and still live at home with their parents. Casual and part-time employment is likely to contribute as much as low wages to this continuing dependency. And such jobs are less likely than are regular full-time jobs to provide compensating levels of skills development.

Those on the merry-go-round and those on the snake are unlikely to be receiving skills on the job that enhance their future earnings prospects. For them, the level of wages for the sort of jobs they do determines their present and future levels of financial independence and contributions to the income of the family. They can look forward to more of the same. They comprise a sizeable majority of low-paid workers. We cannot be indifferent to the level of low wages on the grounds that all who receive them are on the first rung of the ladder, for this quite misrepresents the nature of the low-wage labour force.

It does seem to be the case, however, that an increase in low wages does not have a strongly egalitarian effect on the distribution of household disposable income, even if we ignore any effect that such a wage increase may have on increasing unemployment. If (as seems unlikely) it should have a substantial effect on increasing unemployment, then a wage rise may even be regressive, as unemployed people typically live in much poorer households than do low-wage earners.[15]

The argument for sustaining or increasing low wages rests on grounds other than that it is strongly equalizing in its effects on the distribution of household income. Some of these grounds are considered next.

The household is not the only appropriate perspective from which to view the standard of living. Even in the best of circumstances, households are not stable in the long run. Members of the household come and go, including income-earners. A person who relies for her standard of living on someone else's income is vulnerable to suffering a sharp drop in that standard of living should the supporting income be withdrawn. The high levels of poverty among female sole parents attests to this.

The level of a person's well-being is affected, *inter alia*, by her or his material standard of living, degree of personal autonomy and level of respect, in the society and within the family. The current level of each of these matters, and so too does the degree of security with which each is held.

Wages contribute to each, in different ways. People can have a very high standard of living while having no wages of their own. They may live in a household where others receive a high wage, and share in the goods and services which that income buys. Their high standard of living would generally not be matched with high levels of autonomy or social standing since these would be derived from the gift of another – the income-earners in the households. It would be contingent, subject to withdrawal if they should offend, or for any other reason that their financiers should conclude is a sufficient ground on which to withdraw that support.

Social mores can be a powerful constraint on the withdrawal of support
by the breadwinner, but where they are they can be expected to constrain the dependent family member even more. Love and compassion
can also constrain the breadwinner, but these too may change unilaterally. The only ways for a person to secure her or his standard of living,
and autonomy, are either to be indispensable to the breadwinner or to
receive her or his own income. That income can either be earned, or
received as a benefit from government. Does it matter which?

There are strong reasons for thinking that the source of income does
matter. Income that is a reward for work done brings not only purchasing power but an independent measure of the worth of that work.
Income that is received as a 'gift' from charity or government has no
such affirmation. Indeed, it conveys the opposite message, that you are
not capable of doing anything sufficiently worthwhile that others will pay
you for it. The centuries-old discussions of the shame and personal
diminishment associated with receiving charity or welfare attest to that.
A low wage implies that a person's efforts are of little value. It is an
offence to the dignity of workers to pay them degradingly low wages.
What constitutes a degradingly low wage will, of course, be affected by
the standards of the time; it is a relative as much as an absolute idea. In
a society that values the equality of the person, very large differences in
the levels of wages will be offensive in their own right. There is no reason
to suppose that the wages which would emerge in an unregulated labour
market would avoid being degradingly low.

A floor to wages can be accomplished in one of three ways. Wages may
be regulated. Or workers may be sufficiently productive that the market
will generate wages that are above the floor. Or the social welfare system
may provide an alternative source of income that enables workers
to refuse to accept wages that are below the floor. Chapters 6 and 7
examine the last two options.

Chapter 6 looks closely at whether, through targeted skills enhancement of the unemployed or through an extension to their general
education, it is possible to increase their employment substantially, within the prevailing wage structure. Some labour market programs work
better than others. When the most effective programs are used, they can
make a substantial difference to total unemployment and employment.
A program targeted on the long-term unemployed could feasibly halve
their number. But labour market programs are unlikely on their own to
provide a full solution to delivering jobs to the unemployed, especially to
the long-term unemployed. It is inescapable that the overall level of
demand for labour has a strong impact on the job prospects of the
unemployed. When there is a large excess of the supply of workers over
the demand for workers, then the displacement and deadweight costs of

labour market programs, including general education, are unavoidably high. Well-designed labour market programs can make a valuable contribution to returning the unemployed to employment within the prevailing wage structure, but they cannot do the job on their own.

If everyone of working age was able to receive an acceptable income regardless of whether or not they were employed, then employers would not be able to entice anyone to work for less than this income (unless substantial skills development was offered as part of the employment). Such an alternative income would provide an effective floor below which wages would not fall, even if there were no external regulation of wages. Does the social welfare system in Australia provide such a floor? Chapter 7 answers this question. It concludes that for some groups of workers, specifically parents on medium-level wages with dependent children, the interaction of the personal income tax and the income tests on social welfare payments are such as to make the disposable income of the family almost independent of the level of wages earned. The range of earnings for which this is true encompasses that received by a full-time low-wage worker. On the one hand, this makes the worker indifferent to the level of wage received, within a range: a fall in payment from the employer is almost fully offset by a rise in payment from the government. On the other hand, the worker is indifferent to working a few hours more or less, in terms of the income received. Both these effects have important implications. In the first case, an employer can reduce the wage offered in the knowledge that the obligation to provide an adequate income will be picked up by the taxpayer. This will effect a redistribution from the taxpayer to the owners and customers of such firms, which in turn are likely to multiply as a result of competition in the product market. In the second case, the disincentive to work more than modest part-time hours may engender resentment in taxpayers, welfare dependency in the worker, and intrusive, expensive application of work tests by the social welfare system.

It should be noted that the simulated wage cuts reported in Chapter 4 conclude that a cut in the value of low wages is by no means fully offset for individual wage-earners by a fall in tax liability and/or a rise in the level of social welfare payments received by their family. To the extent that it was offset, most of the effects came not from a rise in welfare payments but from a reduction in liability for personal income tax. The aggregate result can be reconciled with the existence of some very high effective marginal tax rates (EMTRs) in the following way. First, the very high EMTRs apply only to a relatively small subset of low-wage workers (specifically, those with dependent children and modest assets: people with dependent children comprised one-third of low-wage workers, as identified in Chapter 4). Second, perhaps many who face very high

EMTRs have responded by not seeking employment, and so are not captured in the simulations of Chapter 4. Third, the level of weekly earnings at which the EMTRs are at their most severe, for families, is generally higher than for the workers defined as low wage in the simulations of Chapter 4.

For some people, an effective floor to their material standard of living is provided by the willingness of other members of the family to support them. But family support is not available for everyone, and where it is, it carries implications of dependency and obligation. The social welfare system can provide an alternative or complement to the family welfare system, in providing workers with the option of refusing to work for unacceptably low wages and poor conditions. One major advantage of reliance on the welfare system to provide an effective floor to what workers will accept from employers is that it obviates the need for enforcement of employer compliance with regulation of their wage and conditions offers. Employers may be left largely to themselves, in the knowledge that no one is forced to agree to unacceptably harsh employment terms 'through necessity or fear of a worse evil', as the papal encyclical *Rerum Novarum* (1891) put it. This is an important point in the current environment, when trade union membership is in decline. Australia has traditionally relied on (privately funded) trade unions to enforce industrial law, or at least to bring breaches of such law to the attention of the authorities. Regulation that is not enforced is worse than no regulation at all.[16]

The role of regulation

Growing wage inequality is gradually changing the nature of Australian society and challenging our understanding of the links between wages, employment and labour market institutions. It is also placing increasing stress on the social welfare system. On the one hand, the lower that real wages fall at the bottom end, the more the incentive to work rather than receive welfare is diminished. This is sharply highlighted in the results presented in Chapter 7. On the other hand, the more that the welfare system compensates workers for diminished wages, the greater the strain on the government budget. It would simply not be workable, for these reasons, to combine the Australian social welfare system with the US wage distribution. As Chapter 7 concludes. 'the income distribution implications of wage deregulation are likely to be substantial, so substantial relative to employment gains that it seems unwise to place the policy emphasis on wage deregulation to solve the Australian unemployment problem' (p. 221).

The chapters of this book provide a strong case for the benefits of active regulation of the labour market, on a number of grounds. These include maintenance of the integrity of the wage/welfare system; protection of workers from abuse of employer power as the changing work environment makes workers increasingly vulnerable; the maintenance of a vehicle for the expression of notions of fairness; and the absence of a robust theoretical or empirical case that there would be large efficiency gains from deregulation.

But it is not enough to conclude that regulation is desirable. We need also to say something about what shape it should take. In designing the best plausible set of regulations for the labour market it would be pleasing to be able to adopt the physicians' dictum 'first, do no harm'. In practice, this is a very tough hurdle for any public policy to clear. Regulation that prohibits employment on harsh or demeaning terms may prevent some people from obtaining jobs that they would willingly have accepted. Even regulation to prevent people from being unfairly dismissed, or unreasonably exposed to risk of physical injury, may do harm by reducing the number of jobs on offer. But at least in the latter case, the overall good has been judged to exceed any potential harm.

The challenge is to protect workers from harsh employers while enabling good employers to flourish. One valuable path to pursue is to take advantage of the antiseptic properties of light. The conditions of employment at each workplace should be comprehensively exposed to the public gaze. The conditions should include not just wages and hours actually worked, but also average days of leave actually taken, accident rates, the rate at which workers quit, the rate at which workers are fired, any successful actions for unfair dismissal or sexual harassment, average tenure in the job and so on.[17] This information should be posted on the equivalent of the employer's front door, to inform both the public and potential employees. These disclosure requirements would be comparable to those imposed on companies to disclose financial information if they wish to raise money from the public. The public display of such information is likely to have a strong salutary effect on its own; people mostly do not like to be seen as public pariahs. In addition, a requirement that it be provided to all actual and potential employees would help overcome the large information asymmetry that otherwise exists between employer and employee, and which in part justifies a role for trade unions in the employee relationship. In this regard, it is highly regrettable that individual terms of employment determined under Australian workplace agreements, and state equivalents, are kept secret, revealed only to the workplace advocate. It is also regrettable that employee ombudsmen and advocates can, at least in some jurisdictions, act only on the complaint received by an individual.

Libertarians and some economists argue that a contract freely entered into by adults is always efficient and fair because if there was not gain to both parties then the bargain would not be struck. Regulation that inhibits such bargains diminishes the freedom of action of the people involved and prevents mutually advantageous arrangements. It is thus patronizing and inefficient. But the force of this argument depends crucially on the starting position of each party. Justice Higgins put the point succinctly when he interjected in the Harvester Case of 1907 to describe freedom of contract in the workplace as being 'like the freedom of contract between the wolf and the lamb' (McCarthy 1969: 23). The papal encyclical *Rerum Novarum* of 1891 made the same point at slightly greater length:

> Let it be granted, then, that as a rule workman and employer should make free agreement, and in particular should freely agree as to wages; nevertheless there is a dictate of Nature more imperious and ancient than any bargain between man and man, that the remuneration must be enough to support the wage-earner in reasonable and frugal comfort. If through necessity or fear of a worse evil, the workman accepts harder conditions because an employer or contractor will give him no better, he is the victim of force and injustice.

The employment relationship is one of the most important and complex of economic relations. We cannot be confident that the uninhibited forces of supply and demand, constrained only by the laws of contract, will produce efficient, let alone humane and just, employment relations. And it is one of the more damaging myths of conventional economics that equity and efficiency objectives can, and indeed should, be pursued separately.[18] The other damaging myth is that equity can only be achieved at the expense of efficiency. If we look across all the OECD countries, there is no convincing evidence that those which have more regulated labour markets or more compressed wage structures have done less well on output and productivity growth, on employment and unemployment and on inflation than have countries which are less regulated. But regulation of the labour market, through some combination of direct wage setting, a strong social safety net and a significant role for trade unions, is clearly correlated with less inequality in earnings.[19]

Less regulation of the labour market is almost certainly associated with (and most probably causes) more inequality in earnings and lower relative wages for those at the bottom of the pay distribution and those who are not mainstream workers. Its consequences for employment, unemployment and productivity are most uncertain. Deregulation thus involves a very probable increase in inequality and a very uncertain gain in efficiency and employment. For this reason alone, regulation can be, and in my view is, justified. It may well be justified even if it could be shown to reduce efficiency, because the distribution of the dividend as well as its size is to be taken into account in assessing the consequences for overall welfare. To repeat, market outcomes can be perfectly efficient and perfectly disgusting.

But the employment relationship is about more than wages. A second reason for regulation is to enhance the dignity of the employee, by reducing the extent of the employer's power to direct. The master–servant relationship, or one where the employer has a wide domain over which arbitrary power may be exercised, has no place in a decent and socially egalitarian society.

The means of regulation

The principal instruments for affecting the distribution of pay and power are the tax and social welfare system, trade unions, and industrial tribunals. In our view, each of these has an important role to play, and they are complementary. There is a strongly put argument that the market should be left unconstrained and the protection of worker income and avoidance of the need to accept desperate exchanges should be placed in the hands of the tax/welfare system. The tax/welfare system clearly has a vital part to play, but it cannot successfully sustain the whole burden of ensuring fairness. There are three reasons for this.

First, suppose that removal of wage and other restraints on employers caused a noticeable fall in wages paid to all or certain classes of low-wage workers (such as non-English-speaking, casual, young and/or female workers). If the elasticity of demand for such workers is low, as seems likely, then there will be a fall in the total costs of employment for firms that are large users of such labour, and in the incomes of workers in these categories, with only a small gain in employment. Should the incomes of the affected workers be largely maintained by the welfare system, there would in effect be a transfer of the responsibility for providing an adequate rate of pay from the employers and their customers to the taxpayer. Each option has efficiency consequences. A reliance on the employer may cause some loss of jobs. A reliance on the tax/welfare system imposes deadweight losses from collection of the tax and from disincentives to work. It is an empirical matter as to which set of losses is the greater, but estimates of the deadweight costs of raising tax revenue, including compliance costs, are as high as 30 per cent; the reduced incentives to work must be added to this.

Second, a person's reliance on the tax/welfare system for an adequate income means a reliance on the willingness, both in political and in compliance terms, of the taxpayer to be taxed. Such transfers are contentious and contested and attract less legitimacy than do wages earned. These payments are at risk because they are based on 'needs' rather than on 'deserts'. It has not been possible to produce a measure of 'needs' that commands wide assent and is enduring over time. The very notion of what constitutes need is constantly open to reassessment. Further, any measure of need will always embrace people who are more needy than are the best-off people so classified. It will thus always make the distribution of income more equal to take from the better-off 'needy' recipients of welfare and give to the worst-off, as it improves distribution to take from low-wage earners and give to the unemployed. The only end to this logic is when those defined as being in need are homogeneously the very poorest.

Third, the social safety net could provide an effective 'reservation wage', and prevent unjustly harsh terms of employment by the simple device of providing an alternative so that firms find that no one applies for such jobs. But in order to play this role, access to the safety net must be widely available (e.g. including to single people) and it must be acceptable to refuse a job on the grounds that the terms are too harsh. As with simple versions of negative income tax schemes, moral hazard problems are likely to be severe in such circumstances. It seems unlikely that in the long haul Australian taxpayers would continue willingly to support people who consistently rejected jobs, even if the pay of those jobs was low.

The second leg of the regulation tripod is trade unions. They continue to play an important part, as voice, as *de facto* industrial inspectorate and as countervailing power. The first two roles are essential, but the last is contentious. Power has its own dynamic and will not only be used in a countervailing manner. Even where it is, it is likely to damage uninvolved third parties, as when strikes and secondary boycotts are used. The ideal that underpinned Higgins' industrial tribunals, that reasoned argument adjudicated by an impartial observer would replace punch and counterpunch between employers and unions, still has great merit. With or without tribunals, unions have an important part to play in desirable regulation of the labour market. They identify and articulate workers' interests. They police labour law. They provide strength and dignity to the individual worker who may otherwise be without either. They also abuse their power, to the cost of those outside. Good regulation will enhance union voice and reduce union punch.

The final leg of the tripod is regulation of the labour market, via legislation and/or industrial tribunals. Regulation has a role because it establishes rights for workers: the right not to be discriminated against, not to be sexually harassed, not to be sacked unfairly, not to be exposed to hazardous conditions of employment, not to be unfairly paid or overworked. Rights are different from equivalent terms provided at the discretion of the employer. They cannot legally be taken away, and they reduce the degree of subordination of the worker.

Australia has a unique set of 'institutions of government' in its industrial tribunals. These are largely outside the parliamentary, executive and judicial arms of government and have established a legitimacy through their longevity and performance (a legitimacy not granted by everyone, as Chapter 2 makes clear). The other institutions of government, especially the social welfare system and direct parliamentary regulation, have evolved around the existence and role of these tribunals. Australia has looked to the tribunals to assist in sharing the risks and rewards of the changing market economy, including the benefits of economic growth and the costs of recession. They have from time to time played an important role in managing the macro-economy.

The Harvester Judgment in 1907 implicitly placed the primary responsibility for ensuring a minimum standard of living with the market rather than the state. The community of interest here was 'breadwinners' (not all wage-earners, because women were not included), no matter the industry, craft or location. In this way, the Harvester decision built into the wages system (in theory at least) an explicit poverty avoidance margin that elsewhere was to become the responsibility of the state. Subsequent decisions about appropriate margins for skill established a mechanism through which ideas of equity could be expressed more broadly.

Once this precedent was set in train, all other interested institutions (government, the executive, the unions) realigned their roles and expectations around this decision. As the state increasingly diversified, especially in the post-Second World War period, its newer functions were built around this basic building block. The consequences include the establishment of a minimum wage that contained a secondary purpose (anti-poverty) and that obviated the need for the creation of redistributive mechanisms found elsewhere, the use of home ownership as a form of social insurance in old age, and reliance on the tribunals as the sole instrument for affecting inequality in earned income.

If the tribunals shrink to a residual status in the repertoire of government, then the functions they have evolved to serve will be less well met, or alternative institutions will need to be devised. In my judgement, the case for such a shift has not been made.[20]

Over the past twenty years the rising tide of economic growth has not lifted all boats. The big ones have risen fastest of all and many little ones have remained stuck in the mud – swamped, not lifted, by the incoming tide. We are unconvinced that the tide has risen faster for those countries with less regulated labour markets. What is clear is that the uneven tide has propelled forward the biggest and fattest boats the fastest. Economic growth that rewards the already affluent with still higher incomes, while diminishing the incomes, dignity and prospects of many at the bottom, is not worth sacrificing important social values for. The purpose of the economy is to enhance the well-being of the people. It is not the purpose of the people to provide the lowest cost inputs for the economy. An already rich nation should give a high purpose to ensuring that work is adequately paid, is not physically harmful, and enriches the human capacities of the people who do it. It is not progress to have a workforce in which increasing numbers are paid too little and are afraid, insecure, and treated as readily disposable.

Good institutions will not substantially inhibit growth. But they will pay attention to who is benefiting from that growth. There is nothing in unregulated markets which ensures that the gains from growth are reasonably fairly distributed or that the costs of change are tolerable for those who lose. That has been the function of the industrial tribunals. Ill-treatment of workers must not be allowed to become profitable, or the forces of competition will ensure that it spreads. The economic environment has not changed so much that the best we can do to enhance the well-being of the workforce is to stand by and watch the market at work. The market alone will not remove unemployment and nor will it ensure that the distribution of its product is fair and that the experience of work is enriching rather than shrivelling for the workers. The market needs a hand.

Notes

1 Referring to the United Kingdom, Atiyah (1979: 631) claims that 'after 1870 one of the most significant influences on society and law was the growing strength of the egalitarian ideal'.
2 Lord Ashley, House of Commons in Committee on the Factories Bill, March 15, 1844, cited in Bland, Brown & Tawney 1914: 601.
3 Ibid., emphasis added.
4 A Petition to Fix Wages Addressed to the Justices by the Textile Workers of Wiltshire, 1623, cited in Bland, Brown & Tawney 1914: 357.
5 In a recent judgement of the House of Lords, Lord Nicholls observes: 'An employment contract creates a close personal relationship, where there is often a disparity of power between the parties. Frequently, the employee is vulnerable'. Quoted in the *Financial Review*, 26 August 1997.
6 This trend is to be found in many OECD countries. See OECD, 1998.

7 For an analysis of employment changes in manufacturing in Australia, see Gaston, 1998.
8 For a more detailed discussion of these developments, see Richardson, 1998.
9 The employment to population ratio expresses the number of people employed as a proportion of all people aged 15 to 64 (the traditional age span of employment). It is a more reliable indicator of the state of demand for labour than is the unemployment rate.
10 The main alternative, or complementary, explanations are the unusually long boom in aggregate economic activity which the US has experienced since 1990, and the very meagre social welfare system, which provides little continuing support for out-of-work workers. Note that Gregory 1996, and Gregory et al. in this volume have shown that the growth in employment in low wage jobs has been as fast in Australia as in the United States, despite the fact that low wages have not fallen as far in Australia.
11 Pages 18–21 were written by Keith Hancock, for which I thank him.
12 Some awards, described as 'paid rates' awards, are constructed on the basis that their terms will be observed as both maxima and minima. Even so, employers are legally free to provide better terms.
13 This evaluation is accepted in the 1985 report (see fn 2), vol. 2, pp. 134–6.
14 In its cross-country examination of this issue, the OECD produced estimates of the wage elasticity of demand for teenagers of between –0.01 and –0.58, with a typical figure of around –0.35. The inclusion of Spain and Portugal in the estimations produced estimates that were not significantly different from zero. They concluded that 'negative employment effects for young adults are generally close to or insignificantly different from zero' and 'for prime-age adults, the most plausible specifications suggest that minimum wages have no impact on their employment outcomes'. They add, 'There is also little evidence that negative employment effects are larger in relatively high minimum-wage countries as compared with relatively low minimum-wage countries' (OECD 1998: 47–8).
15 For more extensive evidence on this point, see Harding and Richardson 1998.
16 The Employee Ombudsman for South Australia (1998) claims that 'one explanation for the increase in award breaches, underpayment of wages and ill-treatment of workers that appears to have occurred in recent years, could be the perception that only serious breaches of the legislation will be prosecuted' (p. 7). Both unions and regulatory agencies have diminished resources to enforce compliance. 'As a result, unscrupulous employers can underpay or otherwise ill-treat their employees secure in the knowledge that their offences will remain undetected' (p. 5).
17 My thanks to Nick Gruen for raising these ideas.
18 See Stiglitz 1994 for an informed affirmation of this point.
19 Support for this position is found in OECD 1996c, for example. One relevant conclusion from this publication is 'Employment and unemployment rates for low skilled workers do not appear to be strongly correlated with the incidence of low paid work' (p. 76). Factors other than relative wages, such as the overall level of aggregate demand or the amount of training received, may be more important for determining labour-market outcomes' (p. 94).
20 I am grateful to Deborah Mitchell for her help in developing these ideas.

CHAPTER 2

Labour Market Deregulation in Australia

Keith Hancock

J58

L51

J31   K31

We have seen that regulation of the labour market is both a way of enhancing fairness and a way of preventing abuse of the employer power to command the employee. But high unemployment and relatively low productivity growth rates have led to questioning in Europe and in Australia of whether the price of providing these protections has become excessive. This chapter looks in detail at the steps that have been taken to deregulate the Australian labour market over the period 1985 to 1998. It then assesses step by step the arguments that have been put most strongly in the Australian debate to advocate deregulation. In no case does it find a compelling case that deregulation is necessary in order to increase the productivity of the Australian economy.

The deregulationist program, as I understand it, entails the following: removing or reducing the legal prescription of wages and other conditions of employment; reducing, by law or otherwise, the power of trade unions to affect wages and conditions; and as a corollary of these two features, enhancement (subject to the constraints of competitive forces) of the capacity of employers to determine the wages and conditions observed in their own enterprises or workplaces. Underlying this chapter is a judgement that Australia has moved some distance toward a deregulated system. But the concept is not unambiguous. Where the impact of legal prescription diminishes, but the role of unions is increased (as occurred, arguably, in Australia in the early 1990s), the direction and extent of movement along the deregulatory scale are matters for judgement. There is also a possibility of 'deregulation' by 'regulation'. That occurred in the United Kingdom, where, after 1979, a succession of laws restricted the behaviour of unions, reducing their capacity to impose their will on employers and to resist employer decisions.[1] In Australia, Sections 45D and 45E of the Trade Practices Act operate with similar effect by limiting the power of unions to take industrial action. More fundamentally, calls for labour market deregulation are invariably pleas to locate decision-making powers in the enterprise or sections of it.

The structure of the chapter is as follows. Section 1 describes briefly the forces of deregulation which have operated in Australia since the mid-1980s. Section 2 is a discussion of arguments for regulation and deregulation. Section 3 has the premise that some involvement of the law in the operation of the labour market is inevitable and, with reference to the contents of Section 2, discusses alternative models. I conclude, in Section 4, with a brief speculation about the implications of a continued deregulatory momentum.

My agenda has two limitations. One is its Australian focus. There is an international tendency to deregulate labour markets, and the commonality can hardly be accidental. I do not attempt to locate what has happened in Australia in the wider experience; but I accept that, in further inquiry, this ought to be done. The other limitation is that I do not attempt (except superficially) measurement of the effects of the changes which have occurred to date. This constitutes a major research agenda. Desirable though it is, however, that research will not eliminate dispute. The passage of time may allow more confident judgements than can now be made, but the 'counterfactual' uncertainties which bedevil inquiry about causation will never be fully overcome.

The Forces for Change

The partial deregulation of the Australian labour market is the product of three forces. First, there was a generally supported move in the late 1980s to dilute the uniformity of wage increases stemming from national wage cases so as to encourage cost reduction and productivity enhancement. Second, from 1990 onwards the trade union movement and the federal Labor Government sought to alter the system of wage determination by creating an area for collective bargaining alongside that of arbitration. Third, a growing body of opinion among employers' representatives and in the political Right was aligned behind an objective of reduced interference – whether from arbitrators or from unions – with the control by management of employee relations within enterprises. In the early 1990s the second and third forces yielded a temporary coalition in support of 'enterprise bargaining'. The long-term objectives differed, however. The ideas and arguments of the opponents of interference were developed during the period of the Labor Government; with the change of government that took place in 1996, they moved to centre stage.

Wage policy and productivity

Wage policy in the first years of the Accord era (as in the centralized system introduced in 1975) embodied the adjustment of award rates for movements of the Consumer Price Index. It was thought that constancy of real wages would allow the growth of productivity to redress a compression of profits that had occurred since the early 1970s and that was seen as a cause of the lapse from full employment. In 1985, however, this assumption was challenged by a depreciation of the Australian dollar, which was widely perceived as requiring a reduction of real wages. The government reached an agreement with the ACTU for a reduced level of indexation, compensated by tax concessions. In 1986, when the future of wage adjustments was under review in the Conciliation and Arbitration Commission, an understanding emerged that increases would be linked, in part, to cost reduction and productivity improvement.

The national wage case decision of March 1987 provided for two tiers of wage increases. A general increase of $10 plus a deferred 1.5 per cent constituted the 'first tier'. The 'second tier' – increases of up to 4 per cent – was accessible in different ways; but the main path, in practice, was the negotiation of cost offsets. Many of those negotiations occurred at an enterprise level. This element of the 1987 decision was known as the 'restructuring and efficiency' principle. The Commission, in its national wage case decision of August 1988, foreshadowed a 'structural efficiency principle'. Its terms were discussed between the Australian Industrial Relations Commission and industrial parties during 1989, and the national wage case decision of October 1989 contained detailed prescriptions. Among these was the availability of wage increases of up to 6 per cent (in two instalments) subject to agreement about award alterations that would remove obstacles to higher productivity. The structural efficiency principle did not explicitly require enterprise-level negotiations, but as many larger enterprises had either their own awards or their own sections within awards, much negotiation was at that level.

The restructuring and efficiency and structural efficiency principles were not seen, at the time, as deregulatory. Nevertheless they were a basis of the significant shift that occurred after 1990.

Enterprise bargaining

The wage increases made available by national wage cases from 1983 until 1989 were subject to a 'no-extra-claims' requirement. As a condition of the variation to an award to provide for a wage increase, the applicant union had to commit itself to making no further demands, award or over-award, for a prescribed period. The no-extra-claims commitments, which were inserted into the awards, were generally honoured. Accord VI, negotiated by the Labor Government and the ACTU in February 1990, proposed the inception of enterprise bargaining, which it linked to the productivity-related aspects of the existing wage principles. To this end, the no-extra-claims commitments in minimum rates awards would be modified 'to provide the opportunity for claims based on achieved increases in productivity and profitability'. Increases in wages would be monitored by the Accord partners and the Commission to ensure consistency with an aggregate wage outcome agreed between the Accord partners; 'where practicable', unions would negotiate with employer organizations about 'the framework within which enterprise bargaining may occur'.

This alteration in the Accord partners' position occurred at a time of growing support within employer ranks for a less controlled wage system (a support probably fortified by resentment of the special relation between the ACTU and the government). Discussions during 1990, under the Commission's auspices, led to an agreement to which the ACTU, most employer representatives and the Federal and State Governments were parties. This said that 'the Commission should establish a framework of general guidelines for enterprise/workplace negotiations'; that 'negotiations should focus on the implementation of the Structural Efficiency Principle at the workplace'; and that wage increases would be conceded 'for achieved increases in productivity or efficiency arising out of the Structural Efficiency process'. (A 'disagreed matter' was the availability of wage increases for increases in profitability.) In a closing statement to the national wage case of 1990–91, the Commonwealth Government asserted the continuity of the enterprise-bargaining proposal with previous wage policy:

> Scope for enterprise bargaining . . . is a major innovation being proposed . . . Most parties and interveners see this as a necessary extension and logical development of wages policy pursued over recent years. In our view, enterprise bargaining would provide the scope for greater flexibility which most parties have been seeking but within an overall framework of stable award wage fixing arrangements and commitments. It would give additional incentive for applying structural efficiency to its maximum potential at the enterprise and workplace level. . . . In that context, the Commonwealth sees enterprise bargaining not as a radical change in direction but as the next logical step in the structural efficiency process.

Despite the breadth of the articulated support for enterprise bargaining, the Commission declined to make provision for it (AIRC 1991a).

There were several reasons for this. The first was a perception that the 'consensus' was superficial. The Commission discerned 'a marked divergence of opinion as to how enterprise bargaining should proceed, the means by which [wage] increases would be available and how wage outcomes should be expressed'. Second, it was afraid, because of earlier experience of bargaining about over-award payments, of inflationary wage increases. Third, it was reluctant to relinquish the principle that the benefits of productivity growth should be distributed to all wage-earners and not concentrated on those who happened to work in firms and industries where productivity growth typically occurred.

The decision was met with expressions of outrage by both the ACTU and ministers. In the words of the secretary of the ACTU, it was 'vomit'. The Treasurer (Paul Keating) deplored the Commission's conservatism in clinging to 'the pre-eminent role of the national wage case' and postponing 'a more flexible system of enterprise bargaining'. Only through enterprise bargaining, he said, could Australia 'obtain the great productivity advances available from changing workplace arrangements and conditions'; and only through enterprise bargaining could the wage system become 'more responsive to the changing conditions of demand and supply or to different skills in different regions' (*CPD*, 1991: 3067). Another theme of ministerial criticism was that the Commission had misconceived its role in regarding itself, rather than the Accord, as the source of wage policy.[2]

In October 1991 the Commission retreated (AIRC, 1991b). It instituted a 'principle' under which enterprise agreements might be approved by the Commission, using either the mechanism of consent awards or the certification of agreements. The principle did not limit the amounts of negotiable wage increases, but it did impose conditions. These included a requirement that increases be 'based on the actual implementation of efficiency measures designed to effect real gains in productivity'. Such a stipulation had teeth because of a then existing provision of the Industrial Relations Act whereby the Commission could decline to certify an agreement whose terms were contrary to the public interest. The teeth were drawn in 1992. An amendment of the Act deprived the Commission, when dealing with single-enterprise agreements, of its 'public interest' discretion.

The thrust to overturn the traditional system gained momentum. In August 1992, Paul Keating, as Prime Minister, addressed delegates to a congress of the International Industrial Relations Association in Sydney. He said the system that had developed during the century had served Australia 'quite well', but it was 'finished'. In the period of the Accord it was always recognized 'that we could not indefinitely focus all wage movements in a uniform movement':

We had always recognised that the price of bringing inflation down and employment up through adjusting wages in a single national decision would be some loss of flexibility which we would later wish to recover. So a few years ago we began putting in place a transition to a much more flexible system, under which the vast majority of decisions over wages and working practices would be made at the workplace level, often within an industry framework ... The AIRC queried us at first but late last year it cleared the obstacle, and this year we have amended the Act to encourage the making of workplace bargains throughout the country.

After the government was re-elected, the Act was more comprehensively amended (by the *Industrial Relations Reform Act 1993*, which came into effect in 1994). The law that emerged defined an emphatic priority for collective bargaining. It restructured the Industrial Relations Commission in a manner reflecting that priority, and it promulgated a code for the negotiation of certifiable agreements. For example, parties to negotiations were permitted (subject to meeting procedural requirements) to take industrial action. Awards would be a 'safety net'. This had two purposes. One was to provide a standard for the application of a 'no disadvantage' test to agreements submitted for the Commission's certification or approval. The other was the protection of employees who, for whatever reason, were not subject to agreements. The Commission would periodically adjust the safety net in a manner consistent with criteria that included a preference for bargained outcomes.

The 1993 Act introduced a new class of agreements: 'enterprise flexibility agreements'. These were collective agreements between employers and their employees, intended for enterprises with no or few union members. As originally proposed, they were strongly resisted by the ACTU. In a compromise, provision was made for a union that had any members subject to the agreement to elect to be 'bound' by it (thus acquiring rights of involvement in subsequent proceedings).

Employer freedom

Although there have always been critics of conciliation and arbitration, they were a minor group until the mid-1980s. None of the major interest groups that made submissions to the Committee of Review of Industrial Relations Law and Systems in 1983 and 1984 recommended abandonment of the traditional system. Within a short time, however, spirited criticism emerged. Indeed, it was probably stimulated by the Committee's report and the prospect of legislation consistent with it.

A notable absentee from the list of submissions to the Committee of Review was any from the Business Council of Australia (BCA). Its executive director, however, presented a paper to a conference sponsored by the Committee. He said that the tribunals' adherence to comparative wage justice 'creates severe rigidities in the allocation of labour and other resources, creates unemployment and exacerbates economic pressures on struggling industries'. A growing number of business decision-makers did not believe that the fundamentals of the current system were 'appropriate to the demands of a more open – more competitive – economy'.[3] These remarks were prophetic. The BCA in 1987 appointed an Employee Relations Study Commission, chaired by F. G. Hilmer. Generously funded, the Study Commission produced three reports, which are discussed in the next section of this chapter.

The H. R. Nicholls Society was formed, in direct response to the Committee of Review's report, in 1986. Its founders (members of a steering committee[4]) noted, in a letter of invitation to join the Society, that 'within the Federal Opposition, moves to push for the deregulation of the labour market have gained momentum, and John Howard's elevation to the Leadership of the Opposition is significant in that context'.[5] H. R. Nicholls was a newspaper editor who in 1911 criticized the conduct of H. B. Higgins as president of the Commonwealth Court of Conciliation and Arbitration. Nicholls successfully defended a charge of contempt of court. The use of his name signified a view about 'the system', as did the title of the Society's first publication, *Arbitration in Contempt*.[6] An examination of the many papers published by it shows that the dominant themes are hostility to unions and work practices for which they are blamed, contempt for the arbitral tribunals, support for the involvement of 'real' courts in industrial relations disputes, affirmation of the right of management to make decisions about workplace operations, and belief in the virtues of a free labour market. Many leaders from the conservative side of Australian politics have spoken at the Society's gatherings.[7]

An important indicator of a shift in employer opinion was the decision of the Confederation of Australian Industry (CAI), forerunner of the Australian Chamber of Commerce and Industry, to abandon its support for the traditional system. This decision, taken in 1991, followed a change in the CAI's leadership in 1989. Its chief executive, Ian Spicer, told the H. R. Nicholls Society in September 1991 that the CAI had adopted 'a quite radical agenda for industrial relations reform'. The traditional industrial relations system had 'nothing whatsoever to do with the productivity or efficiency of either individual enterprise, or the nation'. People were paid 'essentially for turning up at work, rather than what [they] did while [they] were at work'. Australia had established conditions of employment that were 'the envy of the world' but that became unsustainable 'when the lucky country bubble burst'. The standard of living could be maintained only if Australia were as efficient and competitive as other countries. For that, industrial relations policies 'must turn from the social objective of the distribution of wealth and start to play their part in the creation of a productive and efficient economy'. The new CAI policy included the removal (with limited exceptions) of *compulsory* conciliation and arbitration. *Voluntary* conciliation and arbitration would be available to parties who agreed to use them and to accept the outcomes. There would be no more national wage cases or general test cases, though the AIRC would fix a minimum hourly wage and minimum annual leave entitlements. The emphasis of the new system would be on reaching voluntary agreements between employers and employees. These would be filed with the Commission and given the force of law, provided that they met the minimum wage and leave requirements and contained grievance procedures.[8]

In the conservative political parties support was emerging for legislative reform to promote agreements between employers and employees without union involvement, for depriving unions of their 'privileged' position (for example by outlawing closed jobs and forbidding award clauses that gave employment preference to union members), and for exposing them to the rigours of the common law and related statutory sanctions against industrial action (such as Sections 45D and 45E of the Trade Practices Act).

I pass over developments at the state level that reflect this body of opinion. The federal Opposition developed policies for industrial relations in advance of successive elections. John Howard, whether as leader of the Opposition or as shadow minister for industrial relations, had much influence over these policies. In 1990, shortly before the March election, Howard said in a speech to the H. R. Nicholls Society that 'the debate about changing our industrial relations system has moved a long way over the last six or seven years (despite enormous opposition from quarters that should have known better) and I think we are finally beginning to win the argument'. There was still far to go, however, because 'the only way you will really begin to dismantle the centralised wage fixing system in this country is to have full blooded agreements outside the Industrial Relations Commission'.[9]

The Opposition went to the 1993 election with a radical industrial relations policy set out in *Jobsback*, published in October 1992. 'The Coalition', it said, 'believes that our future lies not with industrial institutions or systems but the working men and women of Australia'. There would no longer be compulsory arbitration. Award regulation would continue 'only where both an employer and one, some or all of its employees desire it' and would apply only to the parties who so agreed. With that exception, awards would terminate automatically on the next anniversary of their commencement. Certified agreements (to which unions were parties) would cease to be available. Employers and employees would have the opportunity – and be encouraged – to negotiate formal agreements. Such agreements could be concluded 'only between individual employers and one, some or all of their employees'. Neither employer organizations nor unions could be parties to them, but 'employers and employees may use the services of anyone they wish, including a trade union or an employer organisation, to assist them in formulating and negotiating a workplace agreement'. Workplace agreements had to meet minimum standards for pay and conditions: 1) minimum hourly rates for adults equal to the ordinary time rates in awards or agreements formerly in force; 2) minimum hourly rates for youths: $3 at ages 15–17 and $3.50 at ages 18–20; 3) four weeks' annual leave; 4) two weeks' non-cumulative sick leave; and 5) unpaid maternity leave after twelve months' service. It *may* have been implicit in the document (but was not explicit) that an *existing* employee could not be dismissed for refusing to enter into a workplace agreement. No impediment, other than the minimum standards, was implied that would prevent an employer from making it a condition of engagement that the *new* employee sign a workplace agreement in terms prescribed by the employer. An Office of the Employee Advocate would be created. The advocate would 'advise, and where necessary, act on behalf of employees, in relation to grievances arising from workplace agreements'. Employees not covered by agreements would 'continue to enjoy the terms and conditions which applied under the award prior to its termination'.

The position of unions would be altered in various ways, all adverse. As already noted, they would lose their standing as award parties (through the cessation of awards) and as parties to agreements. Closed shops and preference to unionists would cease. Unions would lose the protection from rivals afforded by the 'conveniently belong' criterion, and enterprise unions would be encouraged. Legal restraints on industrial misconduct by unions would be retained and strengthened.

The Coalition's industrial relations policy at the 1996 election was less radical. It did not propose the abolition of the award safety net. The greatest emphasis was on workplace agreements. The *Policy Launch Statement* promised 'labour market reforms that will give employees a genuine choice between award-based conditions (including safety-net wage increases for the lowest-paid) overseen by the Industrial Relations Commission and Workplace Agreements that will enable higher wages for higher productivity'. Take-home pay under a Workplace Agreement had to be no less than the amount required by the relevant award. The more expansive industrial relations program, *Better Pay for Better Work*, declared:

The most important industrial relations reform needed in Australia is one which will allow employers and employees to enter into direct arrangements with each other regarding pay and working conditions within a 'no disadvantage' framework of minimum conditions but without the uninvited intervention of trade unions, employer organisations or industrial tribunals and without the complexity of the existing system.

The 'fine print' made it clear that the 'no disadvantage' test would apply only at the time when an Australian Workplace Agreement (AWA) was made. That is, the validity of an AWA would not be affected by subsequent award alterations, even if the AWA then became inferior to the award. Closed shops and preference to unionists would be prohibited. Industrial action would be permissible during the negotiation of AWAs and certified agreements, but not during their period of operation.

Legislation to alter the industrial relations law was among the first measures brought forward by the Howard Government after its election in March 1996. Lacking a majority in the Senate, the government entered into negotiations with the Australian Democrats. These resulted in a signed agreement that entailed amendment of the original Bill and committed the Democrats to support its passage. Both the Minister (Peter Reith) and the leader of the Democrats (Cheryl Kernot) have since been criticized for giving too much ground to the other side.

The Workplace Relations and Other Legislation Amendment Act comprehensively amended the *Industrial Relations Act 1988*. (The 'old' Act was not repealed, though the convenience of users might have been better served by a fresh start.) One of the amendments changed the name of the statute to *Workplace Relations Act 1996*. That alteration, though semantic, announces the legislature's preference for employer–employee relations to be decided at the workplace with minimum third-party involvement. It is impossible here to set out in full the substantive changes in the law that the Act represents; the following are the most relevant:

1 There is a new 'stream' of agreements that displace award terms and, in some circumstances, collective agreements. 'Australian Workplace Agreements' are entered into by employers and individual employees and are lodged with an authority, the employment advocate, who must inquire whether an agreement satisfies a 'no disadvantage' test. The test entails an overall comparison between the agreement and a relevant award. If the advocate has any doubt about the outcome of the comparison, the matter must be referred to the Commission for decision. Unions have no right to be heard at any stage in the proceedings. The procedural requirements of the Act evince an expectation that the

employer will be the initiating party in the making of workplace agreements. An employer may decline to hire anyone who will not sign an agreement in terms specified by the employer.

2 The provisions for collective agreements are altered in various ways. The term 'certified' now applies to both agreements with unions and agreements with the employees at the workplace. In either case, agreements must be approved by majorities of the employees,[10] with the consequence that an agreement made by a union and supported by its members can be overturned by the votes of non-unionists.

3 The authority of the AIRC is reduced by restricting its arbitral powers to 'allowable matters'. The principal exclusions are work rules, amenities and union recognition (including preference). (One concession to the Democrats was a provision whereby the Commission can, in exceptional circumstances, go outside the list.)

4 The sanctions which employers may invoke against unions that engage in industrial action (other than that permitted in connection with the negotiation of agreements) are strengthened. Among the changes is the restoration of Sections 45D and 45E of the Trade Practices Act, which had been repealed in 1993.

Overall, the Coalition's legislation has effected an alteration in the bargaining strengths of employers and employees, favourable to the former. It has reduced the collective element in industrial relations law. Although there is a further weakening of the position of the AIRC, this is minor relative to the changes wrought by the pressures of the Accord partners in 1991 and the amending legislation of 1992 and 1993. The Commission retains the important responsibility of setting and maintaining 'a safety net of fair minimum wages and conditions of employment' (section 88B(2) of the Act). The present position of the government is that it will bring forward further reforms.

Regulate or Deregulate?

The history of labour market regulation points to a number of objectives: altering incomes and conditions of work; countering the perceived powerlessness of individual employees (both as to the terms of engagement and in the workplace); giving workers a measure of 'ownership' of their jobs; and the resolution or management of conflict (for the benefit of disputants, third parties or both). The cogency of these grounds for subjecting employers to interferences and restraints is challenged by deregulationist arguments. My principal concern in this section is with the substance of that challenge.

The argument from economic theory

I first consider what is sometimes described as the 'economic' case for deregulation. Some proponents, indeed, depict it as something on which 'economists' agree, though others may not. (Dissidents are, by implication, *not* economists, even if they regard themselves as such, hold credentials such as senior academic appointments in the discipline and publish in journals dedicated to economists' opinions and research.) It is an argument derived, ultimately, from analysis of the characteristics of competitive markets.

The Hayekian paradigm

F. A. Hayek visited Australia once (in 1976) but, so far as I know, did not comment directly on Australia's labour market arrangements. He delivered a lecture, 'The Atavism of Social Justice', which has obvious implications adverse to labour market intervention in the service of egalitarian ends (Hayek 1979). It adds nothing specifically Australian to the debate. Nevertheless, the Hayekian paradigm of free, competitive markets has influenced the development in Australia of opposition to the regulated system. For example, the economist Michael Porter, addressing the H. R. Nicholls Society in 1989 in a paper entitled 'The Centrality of Labour Market Reform', said:

> This paper also sets out to undermine the analytical base of policies based on terminology such as *the real wage*. It is central to the analytical basis of the 'Nicholls Agenda' that a myriad of [de]centralised wages and conditions are generated as part of the information exchange within markets, exchanges which generate employment contracts, which in turn enhance productivity, profits *and* wages . . . This 'Hayekian' view of labour markets is in direct contrast to the mechanistic view of wages and labour markets portrayed by advocates of the Accord, and indeed, by the bulk of the economics profession, which continues to talk about *the* wage.[11]

Many 'deregulationists' would not have heard of Hayek – this is not stated in a critical spirit – but he is nevertheless part of their intellectual heritage. His is a view of the world with which their adversaries must contend.

The simple idea that underlies the Hayekian paradigm is, as Porter says, that markets have a unique capacity to assimilate information, which they convert into 'signals', that is, prices. Those signals are all that participants in the market need to know. The actions they take, on the basis of the signals, will be consistent with the actions of others. The

coordinating function of prices makes possible the division of labour
and the levels of productivity and income that go with it. Hayek said:

> The great advance which made possible the development of civilisation and
> ultimately of the Open Society was the gradual substitution of abstract rules
> of conduct for specific obligatory ends – and with it the game for acting in
> concert by following common indicators, by which a spontaneous order was
> self-generated. The great gain attained by this was that it made possible a
> procedure through which all relevant information widely dispersed was
> continually made available to ever-increasing numbers of men in the form of
> symbols which we call market prices. (Hayek 1979: 6)

This was as applicable to wages as to other prices. Indeed, the flexibility
of relative wages, *more* than the relation between wages and other prices
(real wages), determined the success of the labour market in matching
supply and demand:

> It is the continuous change of *relative* market prices and particularly wages
> which alone can bring about that steady adjustment of the proportions of the
> different efforts to the distribution of demand, and thus a steady flow of the
> stream of products. It is this incessant adaptation of relative wages to the ever-
> changing magnitudes, at which in each sector demand will equal supply,
> which the trade unions have set out to inhibit. Wages are no longer to be
> determined by demand and supply but by alleged considerations of justice,
> which means in effect not only simple custom and tradition but increasingly
> sheer power. The market is thereby deprived of the function of guiding
> labour to where it can be sold. (Hayek 1980: 18)

The form of regulation that most exercised Hayek's thinking was the
British. Legal immunities granted to unions by the Trade Disputes Act
of 1906 had enabled them to wield inordinate power. Their conduct
militated against the benign operation of market forces, with the effect
that 'the country no longer has an internal price structure to guide the
economic use of resources'. Unions were 'the chief cause of unemployment, for which the market economy is then blamed' (ibid.: 54, 55). The
first and most important step towards deregulation in Britain was to
deprive unions of the 'privileges' conferred by the law of 1906.

The basic Hayekian model assumes that both employers and employees are price-takers. Hayek accepted that, where market power existed,
outcomes might not be benign. Trade unions, indeed, were possessors
of market power, which they ought to lose. Employers may have
exercised market power in the era of one-factory towns and low worker
mobility, but that was a different age (ibid.: 51).

The question remains whether the *distributive* consequences of the
competitive market's operation may warrant intervention. Consider the
simple analysis represented in Figure 2.1. The market equilibrium

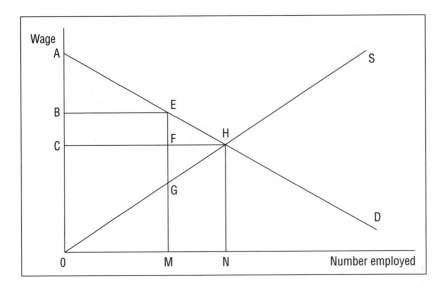

Figure 2.1 Intervention in a competitive labour market

entails a wage of OC and employment of ON. A regulator, thinking OC too low, imposes a minimum wage, OB. At that wage, workers enjoy a surplus of OBEG and employers a surplus of ABE. Now deregulate. The combined surplus rises by EGH. There is an unambiguous increase in the *employers'* surplus: it grows by BCHE. The change in the *workers'* surplus – the net result of adding FGH and deducting BCFE – *may be negative.* (The relative sizes of FGH and BCFE depend on the elasticities of supply and demand.) A full exploration of any specific choice between intervention and non-intervention would need to be in terms of general rather than partial equilibrium, but the simpler analysis serves to show the issues involved. On what ground may it be asserted that only the difference in the *aggregate* surplus (EGH) matters?

One answer, to be found in the literature, is that employers have the *ability* to compensate workers for loss. Unless they do so, however, this answer does not come to terms with the *purpose* of the intervention – to alter the distribution of income in the workers' favour. Another answer, which challenges that purpose, is that distribution is irrelevant or unimportant. To Hayek, it is an unimportant by-product of an arrangement which, over time if not immediately, benefits all (though some more than others):

> The term 'social justice' is today generally used as a synonym for what used to be called 'distributive justice'. The latter term perhaps gives a somewhat better idea of what is intended to be meant by it, and at the same time shows

why it can have no application to the results of a market order. There can be
no distributive justice where no one distributes. Justice has meaning only as a
rule of human conduct, and no conceivable rules for the conduct of
individual persons supplying each other with goods and services in a market
order would produce a distribution which could be meaningfully described as
just or unjust . . . I feel that in any game that is played because it improves the
prospects of all beyond those which we know how to provide by any other
arrangements, the results must be accepted as fair, so long as all obey the
same rules, and no one cheats. . . . It is not a valid objection to such a game,
the outcome of which depends on skill and particular individual circumstances and partly on pure chance, that the initial prospects for all individuals, although they are all improved by playing the game, are very far from
being the same. The answer to such an objection is precisely that one of
the purposes of the game is to make the full possible use of the inevitably
different skills, knowledge and environment of different persons. (Hayek
1979: 3)

For most people, the 'game' is the only one in town. They *must* play. Is it
unreasonable if they seek rule changes to improve their chances?
Hayek's implication that there is but one set of rules presents us with a
false choice: the game of cricket does not cease to exist if the LBW rule
is altered. Intervention to *modify* the consequences of the market does
not logically imply a preference for a non-market system. The American
minimum wage of around $US5 per hour does not render the United
States a non-capitalist economy (whether or not it achieves its intended
effect of raising the living standards of poorer Americans). That capital-
ism generates higher productivity than feudalism and socialism is true
but irrelevant.

An alternative reason for disregarding the distributional goals of
intervention is a judgement that they do *not* imply any improvement.
Employers' dollars are as good as (or better than) workers' dollars. If this
is conceded, it is unnecessary to look beyond the growth in aggregate
surplus represented by EGH in Figure 2.1. That position is advocated by
Gerald Garvey:

> Allowing wages to 'equilibrate', that is, to be determined by market forces,
> increases gains to trade and improves the lot of all concerned. It is thus a
> desirable policy *whatever* the effect on aggregate employment. The concern
> that the wages of those currently in employment may well fall is true, but
> such a fall increases the profitability of their hard-pressed employers! Put
> another way, the focus on wages and employment implicitly assumes that
> employers are 'less deserving' and their gains should be ignored. The
> pensioner whose super fund holds shares in such a company would not agree.
> (Garvey 1993: 259)

In the 'economic model of employment', says Garvey, labour services are
not different from other commodities:

This abstract, disembodied treatment evokes the common objection that labour is carried out by human beings whose feelings, goals, aspirations, self-esteem, and so forth are at stake. Labour, it is argued, cannot or should not be analysed like other inputs such as land or financial capital . . . [But if we adopt this position], we are effectively denying the humanity of the investor, the supplier, and often the consumer. The economic model surely abstracts from many details of human nature, but it does not do so in a way that is biased against labour. (Garvey, 1993: 247–8)

The losses that businesses incur from pro-employee intervention are borne by *people*, 'who paid their *own* past wages or profits for the rights to some of the returns to a company' (Garvey 1993: 339).

The ultimate recipients of investment income are, indeed, people, and some of them are workers or ex-workers (whose numbers and 'capitalistic' interests expand with the growth of funded super-annuation). These truths tell against a 'class struggle' approach to issues of distribution. They do not, however, mean that the inter-personal distribution of income is impervious to its functional division between wages and profits, or that we should be indifferent to *how* different people get their incomes. Even when due allowance is made for composition of the group that benefits from profits, we may still prefer to advance the welfare of those who gain from raising wages. The reminder that profits go to people does not, therefore, conclude the discussion about wage and profit shares. Moreover, interventions in the labour market such as the imposition of minimum wages are not necessarily undertaken with the purpose of converting profits to wages. The goal may be to alter *relative* wages, for example to benefit the low-paid.

This discussion is about a world in which labour is a commodity bought and sold under competitive conditions and has no attributes to distinguish it from other traded commodities. Even in this simple world, we find a category of reasons – distributional concerns – why people may, without logical error, advocate 'regulation'. Distributional judge-ments invoke values, which are outside the domain of objective eco-nomics. To claim that the 'economic model of employment' is hostile to regulation is to impose on it a burden which it cannot bear.

Is labour different?

There is little or no disagreement that the labour market has features which are 'special'. There *is* disagreement, however, about the conse-quences of those attributes. To some, they challenge the relevance of the Hayekian view of the world; others see it as unimpaired or even strength-ened.[12] The following paragraphs are about this issue.

The employment nexus

The commodity that is traded when an employer hires a worker is a strange one. The employer promises to pay for the employee's commitment of time and effort to the employer's benefit. Generally, the intensity of the effort is unspecified and the skill that the employee brings to the task may be known by the employer only within broad limits. There are bounds to the range of activities to be undertaken by the employee – someone hired as an engineer will not usually work as a pastrycook – but they may be ill defined. The employer also buys the right, within vague limits, to direct the employee. Thus both sides to the transaction are, to a degree, in the dark about it. Either or both may find a disparity between expectation and actuality. This may not be serious if a disappointed party can withdraw from the arrangement without placing itself or the other party in a worse situation than would have existed had the transaction not occurred. Obviously, however, that solution may be unavailable, especially after the relationship has run for a time. There is, then, a potential for disputation and for conduct towards the other party which some may regard as unfair or harsh. Workers may shirk because the cost to the employer of getting rid of them is too high, and employers may bully their workers because they know that the workers have little option but to put up with it. The market seems not to provide a solution to this problem.[13]

There is another aspect to the matter, related to the exercise of workplace power. Modern societies will not permit people to sell themselves into slavery, even if they understand what they are doing. This, presumably, is because the power wielded by the slave-owner over the slave offends widely held notions about the nature of humanity. In other contexts where people wield power over others (for example, the armed forces), restraints are applied. People who voluntarily join the army know that they must obey their superiors, but the officer who is seen to have misused the power to command may face a court martial. The ordinary employer has a power to direct. Even if its use accords with the employee's understanding of the relationship, this may not be acceptable to third parties, such as government. In nineteenth-century Britain, the state intervened, belatedly, to restrain employers from commanding employees (especially children and women) to behave in ways injurious to their health or morals. Today government prevents employers from requiring employees to act in ways likely to inflict injury or death on themselves or other employees, whether or not the employees themselves object. Plainly, there can be differences of opinion about interference with consensual behaviour. As to that, economics is silent.

On-the-job training

The skills of employees may grow while they are in the service of particular employers. This process may involve explicit training, 'learning by doing' or both. 'On-the-job training' includes all training that is bound up with the job, including not only training at the workplace but other training that forms part of the employment, such as attending on pay at a school to get skills that the employer needs. The current value of the employee to the employer is *net* of any training costs which the employer incurs. Other things being equal, it rises as the worker becomes more skilled and training costs diminish. How is this increment shared between the employer and the employee? Where the skills acquired by the employee are of the same value to other potential employers, there is a 'market' solution. The employee 'pays' for the training by receiving a lower wage. (Conceivably, the wage may be negative: the employer receives a fee for the training provided.) As the employee's net value rises, the wage increases commensurately, otherwise the worker will go elsewhere.

If the skills acquired are firm-specific, that is, they have more value to the present employer than to other potential employers, this 'market' solution does not apply. The employee who receives only his or her net value at any time 'pays' for skills that are potentially valuable to the employer but of a lesser (if any) value in the market. The employee's investment in human capital will be partially or wholly wasted if the employment relationship comes to an end earlier than expected. It will also be wasted, from the employee's viewpoint, if the employer reneges on an implicit undertaking to pay a wage that recognizes the employee's enhanced skill. Alternatively, if the employer pays for the training – by paying a wage that is, for a time, above the employee's current net value in anticipation of a later return on the investment – the employer incurs risks. The employee may leave, or, knowing that the employer's investment is a sunk cost, force the employer to pay a wage that deprives the employer of part or all of the expected return. A consequence may well be a reluctance on the employer's part to provide on-the-job training and, on the employee's, a reluctance to undertake it. Inasmuch as the training is inseparable from the job – the employee learns by just doing the work – there is a potential for disputation about the division of the costs and benefits. The outcome is indeterminate.

This is the basis of the idea of implicit contracts. An implicit contract entails an understanding between the employer and the employee that they will share both the costs and the benefits of firm-specific on-the-job

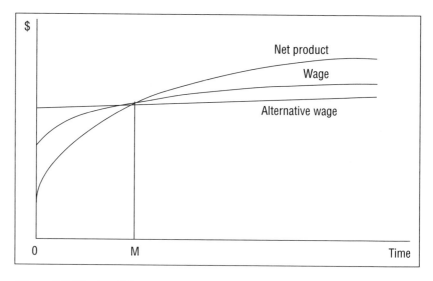

Figure 2.2 The implicit contract

training. It is likely that the employer initially pays the employee more than the employee's current net value but later pays less than the then increased net value. The employee initially accepts a wage that may be less than he or she could otherwise earn, but eventually gets a wage sufficiently above the alternative to compensate for the initial 'cost'. Each side becomes captive to the other. Such an arrangement is illustrated in Figure 2.2. For the period OM the worker is paid more than the value of the net product; thereafter the wage is less than the net product. The worker at first receives less than the available alternative wage but later gets more than he or she could earn elsewhere. (The alternative wage is shown as rising because the training may have *some* value to other employers.) There is no necessary reason why the period over which the worker is subsidized should coincide with the period over which the worker receives less than the alternative wage. Nothing turns on this. What is important is that the difference between the net product and the alternative wage creates scope for bargaining. Once the employment period has begun, both sides have made irretrievable investments – the employer by paying more than the net product and the worker by receiving less than the alternative wage. They later earn returns on their investments, but employers and employees can contest their relative dividends.

If there were contracts that fully defined the parties' obligations to each other and their observance were certain, a competitive market in contracts could exist. Their present values would reflect the state of demand and supply.[14] But the assumptions are unlikely ever to hold good. As we have already noted, the employment relation does not lend itself to a precise definition of rights and obligations. Moreover, the period within which the implicit contract operates may produce unpredictable alterations in the 'environment' (technology, prices, consumer tastes, etc.). There is arguable scope, in equity, for regulation to resolve issues associated with the indeterminacy and uncertainty of implicit contracts and unexpected outcomes. Moreover, without protection of implicit claims, employers may be discouraged from providing on-the-job training and employees from undergoing it.

Efficiency wages

The employee's usefulness is, to a degree, within the employer's control. One technique for extracting value, of course, is to tell the employee what to do. That may be an effective technique, but it has limitations. The mere devising of directions is costly, and the greater the reliance on command, the more likely it is that the employer will need to supervise the employee and to impose penalties for non-performance. For these and other reasons, there may be benefit in leaving the employee to exercise discretion.

Once the employee is seen as a person exercising discretion and able to perform at different levels, wages and conditions of employment may have a motivational role. The term 'efficiency wages' recognizes this. An employer may establish an explicit link between pay and performance (as in performance bonuses). But the connection may be more subtle. Employees who think that their terms of employment are fair may apply themselves more assiduously in the employer's interests than those who feel that their treatment is unjust. Employers have reason, therefore, to take into account considerations of fairness.[15] Granting and withholding promotion are common devices for inducing performance but may be counter-productive if employees do not recognize as fair both the process and the outcomes.

Wages and other terms of employment that are, in this sense, 'efficient' may not correspond with those that equilibrate supply and demand. For example, the employer who reduces wages because there is excess supply of workers risks a perception among the employees that the wages are unfair and a consequent loss of performance. 'Efficient' wages are likely to reflect a long-term view, on both sides, of the employment relationship and entail a reduced responsiveness to supply and demand.

Insiders and outsiders

Implicit contracts and efficiency wages both imply durable relations between employers and employees. Not all jobs are like this. Some require little on-the-job training, and for these the basic motivational devices of supervision and penalty are adequate. Typically they are routine tasks; performance may be controlled by machines. Employees who perform such work are likely, in an unregulated market, to be hired and fired as the demand for the product varies, and employers may see no reason to pay more than is necessary to get the required number of workers.

This distinction underlies the idea of dual labour markets. The 'primary' labour markets are those of the long-term employees, typically enjoying 'efficiency wage' benefits and having limited (though not zero) risk of being fired – the 'insiders'. The 'secondary' markets are those of the dispensable employees – the 'outsiders'. These categories may coincide with and be reinforced by distinctions such as those between 'staff' and others, between salaried and wages employees and between white-collar and blue-collar workers. Regulation that alters the lot of the 'outsiders' relative to that of the 'insiders' may cause little substitution between the two groups.

Market power

Market power is not to be confused with the employer's power to direct employees in the performance of their work. Highly competitive employers, possessing no market power, must pay what the market requires to *acquire* the right to command. In the same way, a slave-owner may have no market power: if there is a competitive market for slaves, the buyer must pay the going prices for slaves of different descriptions. Market power exists only when the employer (or slave-owner) can influence the price.

Market power is associated with lack of competition. A monopsony employer, facing a rising supply curve for labour, will find it profitable to pay a wage below the equilibrium level of a competitive market. Employment will be less than the quantity associated with competitive equilibrium, and a regulator who raises the wage toward the equilibrium level will also raise employment. As I have noted, Hayek recognized the theoretical possibility of such a situation but denied its contemporary realism. An employer's cartel, of course, may possess market power equivalent to that of the monopsony and exercise it in the collective interest of its members. Employers' associations may or may not operate as cartels. It is difficult to infer from experience whether they would do so in deregulated labour markets, precisely *because* regulators and unions have imposed minimum wages and conditions.

With rare exceptions – perhaps a small minority of professionals – individual employees lack market power. Trade unions, however, possess and exercise it. Union power can take one or more of several forms. If the union can control the quantity of labour supplied (for example, by combining closed shops and restricted membership), employer competition for a limited supply of workers will raise the wage above the competitive equilibrium. Alternatively, the union may impose a 'price' by persuading workers not to accept employment at less than the union rate. The number employed adjusts to that wage. In practice, the most usual way of imposing a price is the threat and actuality of collective industrial action. The greater the 'damage' the union is able to inflict on employers, the greater is its power to define wages and conditions that employers must accept. In whatever way the union affects the terms of employment, it is a regulator. The regulations of unions and law-makers differ in the means by which they are imposed and the sanctions by which they are sustained.

Unions *may* exist to counter employer power, just as employers may cohere to offset the power of unions. But union power is not *necessarily* countervailing power. Its *raison d'être* may be to alter wages (and other conditions) *relative* to those of competitive markets or to improve the outcomes for employees when actual employment terms are to any degree detached from the market – for example, when implicit contracts and efficiency wages prevail.

Regulation by unions (and employer counterparts) may not be a preferred (or tolerable) kind of regulation. First, we may disapprove of the exercise of power by 'regulators' who are not selected by an acceptable process, such as popular election or appointment according to law. Second, the *outcomes* of the exercise of private power – wages and conditions – may not commend themselves: we may think that the terms on which people are employed should be correlated with variables that have greater ethical appeal than collective bargaining power. Third, the 'enforcement' process – industrial action – carries adverse consequences to third parties. The disadvantages of private regulation were the mischief that H. B. Higgins' new province for law and order was meant to avert.

The scope for regulation

We have identified factors that attenuate the link between real-world employment and the competitive model. The implication is not that market realities have nothing to do with supply and demand, merely that supply and demand are less constraining than they would otherwise be.

There is, as a result, scope for non-market influences to have a larger role than the Hayekian model recognizes. These influences include, but are not confined to, legal intervention and the exercise of bargaining strength. They also include conceptions of fairness. We have seen, in the context of efficiency wages, why such conceptions may affect outcomes, but we need not exclude a more direct connection: that employers pay 'fair' wages, not only because it is expedient to do so but because they *want* to be fair. We can, if we wish, characterize ethical behaviour as voluntary 'rent-sharing', but whether that description illuminates is doubtful. The important point is that a quest for fairness in the labour market, however grounded, may found an agenda for dispute.

The essential issue as to the dominance of markets is posed by the simple comparison in Figure 2.3. Sub-figures A and B both contain conventional downward-sloping demand curves and upward-sloping supply curves. In each case a departure from the equilibrium wage generates a quantity disequilibrium (excess supply of labour), but the amounts differ. Whereas the excess supply in A might impose a strong downward pressure on wages, that of B might have little effect. Small quantity disequilibria – whether excess demand or excess supply – may be obscured by limitations of information, the willingness of people to wait for available jobs and available workers, and their capacity to 'make do' with arrangements that are workable but not ideal. Even when the wage is at the equilibrium level, these realities of the labour market will obstruct a perfect matching of the quantities demanded and supplied. Subfigure B, compared with Subfigure A, says that there is more scope for the intrusion of non-market forces. The comparison focuses attention on elasticities, whose magnitudes cannot be ascertained deductively.

Those imbued with the Hayekian perception of markets will ask how it is that resources are allocated between alternative uses *if* relative prices do not constitute effective signals. Why, for example, will wages set by regulators or wages constrained by conceptions of fairness not cause unemployment among some kinds of workers and excess demand for others? It must be fortuitous if wage relativities affected by these 'non-economic' intrusions are also 'economically' correct.

As suggested above, the matching or non-matching of supply and demand is a concept more precise in theory than in reality. Within a range, the 'misfit' occasioned by a non-equilibrium wage may be absorbed in ways that are not readily apparent and may broadly be described as 'making do'; and since it always occurs – even at the equilibrium wage – the 'making-do' that actually takes place is not necessarily to be attributed wholly to 'false' price signals. Prices, moreover, are not the *only* allocative device in the labour market. The worker choosing an occupation, an industry, a location or simply an employer may well take

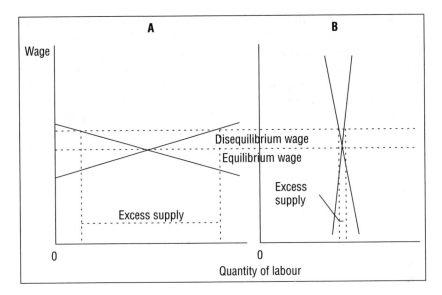

Figure 2.3 Alternative views of labour markets

into account the wages (and other terms of employment) that go with the alternatives; but it will be surprising if he or she does not *also* factor into the choice the availability and stability of employment. This applies both to new entrants to the labour force and to existing workers who contemplate change. Employers, too, may condition their decisions on the availability and quality of labour, as well as its price. Thus the burden of allocating labour which Hayekians impose *wholly* on the price mechanism is actually *shared* between prices and responsiveness to job opportunities and labour availability. Quantity adjustments imply that demand and supply curves are not independent of each other: the quantity of labour supplied depends on the wage *and* the quantity demanded, and the quantity demanded on the wage *and* the quantity supplied. It is possible but unnecessary to formalize the resulting association between excess demand or supply and the wage. What is important here is that quantitative adjustments *reduce* the economy's dependence on the allocative function of wages. To assert that the world would be *better* if wage relativities reigned supreme is beside the point (as well as disputable). They do not and cannot.

Summary

Even in its purest form, the market equilibrium model cannot exclude arguments for regulation to achieve distributional goals. Acceptance or non-acceptance of those arguments is not an 'economic' question. When allowance is made for on-the-job training and for the use of wages and conditions to motivate ('efficiency wages'), it becomes necessary to recognize that factors other than simple supply and demand do affect wages and conditions, even in non-regulated markets. The specific effects of these 'non-market' forces may or may not be welcome; this, too, is not an 'economic' issue. Market power possessed by employers (individually or as members of cartels) or employees (through unions) also alters the terms of employment in ways that are not necessarily to be approved.

Wages and related terms of employment have an allocative role, but the consequences of interfering with them are not simple. There may be a significant range over which allocative 'failure' is not discernible (perhaps meaningless). Even if failure can be discerned, the distributional consequences of relying on the adjustment of wages and conditions to 'correct' matters may be unacceptable.

The case for or against labour market regulation, involving as it does both empirical questions and issues of values, cannot be reduced to theory. Theory poses questions; it does not provide answers. A proper recognition of its limitations necessitates a more prosaic approach, reflective of the diversity of 'regulation' in both its form and its effects.

The 'Enterprise Focus'

Inasmuch as the foregoing discussion was about the efficiency of the labour market, it was about allocative efficiency. An alternative notion of 'efficiency' invoked by proponents of labour market reform in Australia is equivalent to what economists have called 'x-efficiency'. This relates to the success with which allocated resources are used in production and embraces such determinants of performance as managerial effectiveness and workforce cooperation. It has been argued, with that kind of 'efficiency' in view, that labour market reform must promote an 'enterprise focus'. That is, the locus of decisions about wages and conditions should be the enterprise, and decision-making at that level must take the place of more centralized processes. I have decided to deal with this argument by discussing the most fully developed Australian exposition of it, namely, that of the Study Commission appointed by the Business Council of Australia. I apologize to others who feel that their contributions deserve notice.

The BCA in March 1987 adopted a policy statement, 'Towards an Enterprise based Industrial Relations System'. The Study Commission was appointed in the following October. In its terms of reference for the Study Commission, the BCA said:

The Australian economy is irrevocably being more fully exposed to international competition. It is also grappling with chronic balance of payments and external debt problems. In those circumstances, all aspects of our economic and industrial life need to be examined to ensure that we maximise our creativity and comparative advantage and that unnecessary impediments to international competitiveness are eliminated. As one contribution to these objectives, the Business Council of Australia has decided to undertake a review of Australia's industrial relations. (Hilmer et al. 1989: ix)

Such a linkage of industrial relations reform to perceived problems in Australia's external accounts was common in the late 1980s and early 1990s. It was, indeed, a consideration underlying the shift in wage policy described above (page 40 ff.). Less has been heard of it recently. It is convenient here to point out that it was (and remains) fallacious. The claim that reform of industrial relations will raise *productivity* through better workplace performance is intelligible. It may or may not be factually correct, and if it is correct, the gain may or may not be quantitatively important. But there is *no* reason why such an outcome will reduce the prices of Australian products relative to those of the products of other countries (relative prices being mediated by exchange rates), increase exports more than imports, or reduce foreign debt. It is possible, indeed, that better productive performance will cause foreigners to invest more in Australia. More foreign investment will tend to raise the external value of the Australian dollar, thus *decreasing* competitiveness. This is not a reason for keeping productivity low. But it reinforces the lesson that those who see solutions to balance of payments and foreign debt problems in 'better' industrial relations are mistaken.[16]

The terms of reference recorded the BCA's wish 'to create an industrial relations environment where people can work together most effectively and with greatest satisfaction; where the highest possible productivity becomes the common goal for all, and where healthy enterprise performance provides the best outcomes for employers and employees alike'. There was evidence that Australia's enterprises were not as productive as those of competitor countries, and 'strong grounds for believing that this is due in part to the way we have organised our industrial relations system'. It was the Council's view that 'past reviews of the industrial relations system'[17] had been preoccupied with legal and institutional aspects of the system; they had concentrated on 'the system's role in the distribution of our national product and its role in overall economic management'. What was needed now was an approach 'that shifts the balance towards the size of the national cake'. The BCA envisaged 'a fundamental reorientation of the system away from one largely focused outside the enterprise and adversarial in nature and towards one which is centred on the enterprise, develops a high degree of mutual trust and interest, and strengthens the direct relationships between employers and employees'.

Thus the Study Commission hardly began with a *tabula rasa*. There is no sign that the pre-judgement of issues caused it any discomfort.

In the first of its three reports, *Enterprise-based Bargaining Units: A Better Way of Working*, the Study Commission estimated, 'conservatively', that 'across much of Australian industry' productivity was '25 per cent below that of comparable countries with which we are trying to compete and at least that much below potential' (Hilmer et al. 1989: 26). To what extent was this productivity deficit due to the industrial relations system? Existing arrangements were hostile to workplace cooperation:

> The central premise of the current approach is that relations at work are inherently adversarial. On that assumption, the regulatory framework has been directed at 'protecting' the public interest from the consequences of unconstrained conflict. If that starting point was ever valid, it is not today. Technological innovation, modern management techniques, higher education levels, rising living standards and changing community attitudes have already led to the breakdown of dehumanised industrial environments and class-based antagonisms. It has been increasingly recognised worldwide that managers and employees in individual workplaces have more common interests than inherent conflicts. The level of conflict in Australia is much higher than it would be if Australian bargaining structures were less remote from enterprises that are the natural unit around which common interests develop. (Hilmer et al. 1993: 7)

Aspects of the industrial relations system that, taken together, were a major cause of low productivity were: award provisions that enforced over-manning; the necessity of involving external union officials in discussions of proposed changes to working arrangements; job and union demarcations that caused wasteful practices, needless downtime and disputes, and dysfunctional relations between the skills possessed by employees and job requirements; under-utilization of capital due to restrictions of working time and excessive penalty rates for non-standard hours; and an undue emphasis on uniformity as between enterprises (Hilmer et al. 1989: esp. Ch. 4). Moreover, the system induced management to leave industrial relations to experts. Employee relations were not seen as 'a mainstream management activity central to competitive success'. The specialist's task was to ensure that employment terms did not disadvantage the firm relative to its competitors. As a result, line managers lacked skills in employee relations (ibid.: 74).

The concrete reforms proposed in *Enterprise-based Bargaining Units* were directed to two areas: union coverage and agreements. The Study Commission favoured enterprise or industry unions:

The concern has been to find a uniquely Australian solution that will speed up the reduction of the number of trade unions *in each workplace*, the ultimate goal being one per workplace with a workplace focus. Whether that one union were an enterprise union or a reasonably autonomous branch of a larger union is not something that, it is believed, is necessary or sensible to prescribe in advance. (ibid.: 84)

Although the union rationalization provisions of the *Industrial Relations Act 1988* were 'a welcome recognition of the bargaining unit problem', the response was inadequate (ibid.: 87). The Study Commission proposed further alterations to the Act to facilitate unions attuned to enterprise-level bargaining. There should be a 'two-stream' system of legal prescription, comprising awards and agreements, with encouragement to the parties to move to the latter. The 1988 Act, 'by providing the new option of certified agreements', had already gone some way to recognizing the 'lack of flexibility under the award system'[18] (ibid.: 114). The relevant provisions should be altered so that, among other requirements, agreements would have a minimum term of twelve months and ordinarily could not be altered during their currency; they would be confined to single employers and their unions or employees; they must cover the entire employment relationship, to the exclusion of awards; the Commission would no longer be empowered to refuse certification because the terms of an agreement were contrary to the public interest (the only grounds for refusal of certification would be lack of grievance-settling procedures and failure of the parties to satisfy the Commission that the agreement had been freely entered into); the Commission would be prevented from taking account of the contents of agreements when making awards; and there would be no public right of access to agreements (ibid.: 123–4).

Many non-union firms were brought within award coverage by common rules or roping in. Consideration should be given, in the longer term, to limiting awards to enterprises where employers or employees were represented by registered organizations (ibid.: 124–5). In many workplaces employers and employees would prefer to be union-free. The system 'ultimately' should allow this preference to be recognized, and there should be 'an avenue for such enterprises to develop working arrangements that override awards through registering enterprise agreements with their employees' (ibid.: 102–3). The report was silent on the question whether non-union agreements would be individual, collective or both.

Enterprise-based Bargaining Units generated a debate in the pages of the *Journal of Industrial Relations*. (Frenkel & Peetz 1990 a, b; Hilmer & McLaughlin 1990; Drago & Wooden 1990). I do not describe in detail or depth the criticisms and responses. The important issues, as I see them, were these. First the critics made a good deal of the pre-judgement of issues inherent in the terms of reference and the Study Commission's acceptance of them. Second, there was a question about the adequacy of the empirical support for the Study Commission's assertions. In this respect, the attack was wide-ranging, but the attribution of a 25 per cent productivity deficit to the industrial relations system was subject to especially trenchant criticism. Third, it was said that the report had failed to consider the possibilities for change or adequately to appreciate the changes occurring within the existing institutional setting, a failure linked to the Study Commission's approach to its task (encouraged by its terms of reference).

The Study Commission's second report, *Avoiding Industrial Action: A Better Way of Working*, appeared in 1991. Its subject was industrial disputation, which the Study Commission duly linked to external economic problems: 'With competition getting tougher by the day and with Australia's foreign debt service obligations already at levels not seen for more than fifty years, it hardly needs saying that a relatively high level of industrial disputation is something that Australia cannot afford' (Hilmer et al. 1991: 3). The Study Commission adopted the view of Deery and Plowman that the system of awards and provisions for their enforcement were 'predicated on contradictory premises'.[19] The 'contradiction', whose history was traced in some detail, resided in the fact that the conciliation and arbitration system was intended to prevent strikes and lockouts, but left employees and their unions free to demand terms of employment superior to those awarded by the arbitrators. It was exacerbated by the long-standing arbitral tradition that awards should be 'fair'. That tradition led to the making of awards that prescribed uniform minimum terms, leaving to informal processes the achievement of additional benefits (such as over-award payments) that unions might wish to extract and employers might be willing or persuaded to concede (Hilmer et al. 1991: Ch. 2). This may, indeed, have been a deep-seated problem, militating against the tribunals' capacity to control the growth of aggregate wage levels and to enforce fair relativities. Another view is that the ability of unions to bargain for additional benefits was a useful element of flexibility at the margin of the system. But the relevance of the 'contradiction' to the extent of industrial action becomes unclear when account is taken of the evidence – much of it cited by the Study Commission (ibid.: Ch. 3) – that, predominantly, strikes in Australia are short-term, are not about wages or hours, and end without negotiation.

Adoption of the proposals of the first report, in the Study Commission's judgement, would assist the avoidance and resolution of disputes between managers and workers and hence reduce industrial action. There were various ways in which management itself could create better workplace relations (ibid.: Ch. 4). But systemic changes, additional to those of the first report, were also necessary. In relation to agreements, the additions were minor. For the award stream, the Study Commission proposed that the law require all awards to have specified periods (at least twelve months) and preclude their variation within them; that industrial action during the term of an award be prohibited; and that at the end of the specified period, an award be renewed, extended or renegotiated, or otherwise expire – that is, an expired award would not remain automatically in force (ibid.: 87). These proposals, which treat awards as pseudo-agreements, rather than as instruments of ongoing regulation, did not preclude over-award bargaining; but 'resort to industrial action in pursuit of over-award benefits would be a contravention of the Act and potentially open to common law . . .' (ibid.: 90). The ability of employers to *grant* over-award wages would 'ensure the wage structure does not lose its capacity to respond to market conditions'. For a time, the expiry of an award would bring no relief from statutory and common-law sanctions against industrial action. This was appropriate 'while the present union and award structures remain and while the enterprise focus remains low' (ibid.: 96). In the longer term, the service of a log of claims would attract some legal immunities (ibid.: 95–6).

The Study Commission raised the question whether the fixed-term character of awards should prevent their adjustment in response to national wage and other test case decisions of the tribunals. It was equivocal on the point, but saw a long-term solution in the demise of such cases:

> Obviously, the continuation of National Wage Cases and other test cases setting nationally applicable decisions complicates the return to explicit fixed-term awards, but the benefits of consciously and explicitly developing the concept still outweighs those complications. Over time, too, with the growth of fixed-term awards and changes to union structures, away from craft unionism to one union per workplace, away from multi-industry awards to agreements based on the enterprise, the rationale for National Wage Cases would decline. (ibid.: 91–2)

Should compulsory arbitration itself have a future? Its early disappearance 'would not seem feasible without the emergence of some national consensus' (ibid.: 98). But it 'need not always be at the core of Australia's industrial relations'. Two reasons were usually given to justify the system: 'the social goal of providing an equitable minimum wage' and the consequences for the public generally of industrial action and economically damaging outcomes to disputes. The social goal was increasingly an anachronism, derived from a time when there was little of a welfare system and Australia could function as an 'island' economy:

Despite the great changes that have taken place in the last ninety years – the gradual winding back of protection and the opening up of the Australian economy to world competition and the growth of the welfare state – our industrial relations system continues to emphasise these social objectives and their attainment through compulsory arbitration. There is a growing need to reassess the future of compulsory arbitration and its social objectives in the light of these great changes. Increasingly, the economic costs of pursuing social objectives through the industrial relations system are going to impair Australia's economic performance. (ibid.: 108)

The public interest arguments were rebutted by the system's failures. There was too much industrial action. And the economic consequences of dispute settlement, which the system sought to alleviate, were themselves due to 'the craft and occupational nature of awards, bargaining structures and unions'. The view that reduced state intervention in employer–employee relations would be 'a net benefit for the country in the longer term' would gather strength; 'in the context of debate about future constitutional reforms and change to Commonwealth/State relations, a debate likely to occupy policy-makers throughout the nineties, the Business Council and the business community generally should put the issue of compulsory arbitration firmly on the agenda' (ibid.: 109).

The final report, *Working Relations: a Fresh Start for Australian Enterprises*, was published in 1993.[20] A 'fresh start' was needed because changes that were acknowledged to be under way were 'not delivering the pace and magnitude of improvement required to lift the performance of Australian firms to levels needed for international competitiveness' (F. Hilmer et al. 1993: foreword). Competitive workplaces were 'imperative to help overcome the problem of rising foreign debt' (ibid.: 10).

In commissioned research, businesses were asked to assess their own competitiveness. Respondents identified the four most important determinants of competitive performance as cost/price, quality, reliable delivery, and service. Each was asked to rate itself in these respects against its best competitor. In relation to cost/price, 11 per cent described themselves as 'extremely good', 44 per cent as 'good', 35 per cent as 'average' and 10 per cent as 'poor'. On the other criteria, about a quarter of the sample rated themselves as 'extremely good', with fewer calling themselves 'average' or 'poor'. The Study Commission offered the following interpretation:

> The data show that:
> - the workplaces in the survey tend to rate themselves toward the 'good' end of the scale . . .
> - only about a quarter of respondents rate themselves as extremely good compared to their best competitor on quality, reliable delivery and service

- on the most important factor – cost or price – only 11% of Australian enterprises rank themselves as extremely good.

In short, in the main areas where workplaces believe their performance counts most, comparatively few rate themselves on a par with their best competitors. There is still a considerable way to go before Australian businesses match the best in the world. This is despite the fact that nearly three quarters of respondents reported improvements in labour productivity in the two years before the survey and that more than half of those reported labour productivity increases of over 10%. (ibid.: 81)

This analysis exemplifies the hazards of the 'competitiveness' criterion. If, indeed, the respondent businesses did rate themselves against their best competitors, it would be reasonable to think that those who were 'extremely good' or 'good' saw themselves as outperforming those competitors, those describing themselves as 'average' thought that they were about on a par, and those calling themselves 'poor' regarded themselves as inferior. The proportions seeing themselves as ahead of their best competitors (extremely good plus good) ranged from 55 per cent (cost/price) to 78 per cent (service), while those that were inferior ranged from 3 per cent (service) to 10 per cent (cost/price). Rated against *representative*, rather than *best*, competitors, the respondent businesses would be even further ahead. If the best competitors were all foreign, and the respondents accurately assessed their own performances, the survey would suggest a remarkable level of international 'competitiveness'. There is no information, however, on how many of the best competitors were foreign. If, to take the other extreme, we assume that they were all Australian, then either the sample was biased or the respondents deceived themselves, for it is not credible that there would be 55–78 per cent above-average performers and only 3–10 per cent below average. (If 'average' means 'equal to the best', such an outcome is even more fanciful.) *Either* the 'evidence' pointed to a conclusion opposite to the Study Commission's *or* it was worthless.

Reaffirming (without evidence) its conviction that the average Australian enterprise was 'about 25 per cent below best practice in terms of productivity broadly defined, that is, including value and timeliness effects as well as cost per unit', the Study Commission 'assumed' the enterprise's best competitors to be continuously improving their performance by 6 per cent a year, a rate 'consistent with the performance achieved in the best Asian countries, though it may well be less than the performance of the best enterprises'. To eliminate the 25 per cent 'gap' by 2000 would require the Australian enterprise to reach productivity growth of 11 per cent a year. Few firms were achieving this. 'In short', the Study Commission concluded, 'we are facing a challenge which reform to date has been unable to meet' (ibid.: 92–3). I refrain from comment on the reasoning which underlies the 11 per cent target, but point out that it is a rather stringent test to apply to any system of industrial relations. One might think that a system could miss the target by a substantial margin but still perform creditably.

Whether the alleged productivity shortfall was necessarily due to work practices was not discussed. The Study Commission did, however, consider whether defective working arrangements were the fault of management:

> It has become commonplace for management to be criticised for a lack of skills in award restructuring and workplace reform ... However, even if one accepts that employee relations management is an under-developed skill among Australian managers, one cannot leap from this fact to the conclusion that Australian management is poor and that managerial reform alone, without fundamental reform of the industrial relations system, will lead to the required rate of improvement. (ibid.: 93)

The system gave management little incentive to develop skills in employee relations. It could be argued, indeed, that 'the centralised system of conciliation and arbitration went a good way to disenfranchising line managers in the area of employee relations' (ibid.: 95). If the implication is that tribunals replace line managers in making decisions about the myriad issues that arise on the job, tribunal members would be greatly surprised. Not only is it at odds with their experience: it is not even credible that they would have the time for such an involvement. It *is* true that awards and agreements limit managerial discretion: if employers want people to work on Sundays, they must pay penalty rates. But why would management not develop the 'employee relations skills' to get the best from their workers *within* such constraints? Of course, the terms of awards, like any other rules governing behaviour, may be revisited to ensure that they have not become outdated or needlessly restrictive. That, precisely, was the purpose of award restructuring.

There was another way in which the system inhibited workplace performance. This was the support given to unions:

> The main factor shaping union behaviour within the industrial relations system is the guarantee of representation rights, supported by the ease with which the award system produces across the board changes in employment conditions. These features will maximise the incentive (and opportunity) unions have to think in terms of factors quite divorced from the concerns of particular enterprises ... This is likely to mean that where there is a conflict between union goals and aspirations and those of members in specific enterprises, the union will have an incentive to give precedence to the union's goals ... The frequency with which many unions still have difficulty accepting agreements their members make in enterprises – at times to the point of seeking to exercise a veto – is a reflection of this. (ibid.: 102)

The serious question thus raised is not whether union leaders sometimes adopt stances that reflect considerations wider than those of
particular enterprises – undoubtedly they do – but how important this is
as a constraint on workplace performance. On that question, the report
has little to offer. Likewise, there is no evidence provided of the
prevalence of unions' 'vetoing' agreements with which their members are
content. In instances where this does occur, the process by which management and employees have reached agreement may bear examination. The union's view is not necessarily without merit. Multiple
unionism, where it exists, *may* breed conduct conducive to the maintenance of the roles of particular unions, but the source of the pressure
to preserve demarcations may be the shop floor itself (with union
membership reflecting the employees' perceptions of their separate
interests). There are complex interactions between unions and members, and an assumption that the union is an autonomous actor is too
simple.

The Study Commission propounded 'a new framework of employee
relations for Australia'. Implementing it might take time, but it was
important 'to define the parameters of such a system so that we can
design towards an accepted goal' (ibid.: 105). There would be no
compulsory arbitration and awards would be phased out (ibid.: 108).
The law would provide for three kinds of agreements:

1 *Individual Employment Agreements,* ordinarily 'made by a potential
employee seeking employment, at the terms offered by the employer,
subject to any negotiations they undertake';
2 *Open Collective Employment Agreements,* made between individual
employers and their employees. An agreement would continue indefinitely, but some of its terms might be periodically renegotiated; and
3 *Fixed-Term Collective Employment Agreements.* The parties would agree on
an expiry date. There might be an agreed procedure for renegotiating
an agreement; if not, industrial action would not give rise to suits for
damages, 'because the parties' clear intention would have been to end
the agreement on its expiry' (ibid.: 116–18).

Representation by a union would be at each employee's choice: the
employees 'should be free to choose any agent, including a union of
their choice, without limitation by law of the union's capacity to
represent them'. Good management, however, was 'likely to see employee representation reflecting a high degree of common purpose and, as
a result, fewer rather than more unions in enterprises' (ibid.: 108–11).
Whether unions had any part in agreements would itself be a subject of
negotiation: 'depending on the recognition they are given in the
agreements their members make, unions may or may not be parties and

may or may not have responsibilities' (ibid.: 116). Negotiators would not
be allowed to agree to compulsory unionism (ibid.: 113).

The Industrial Relations Commission would have a much reduced
role. It might function as a small claims tribunal to conciliate and make
recommendations to employers and employees, who could agree in
advance to accept the recommendations. Employers and employees
could use its good offices in resolving collective and individual problems, but 'the Commission would lose its main "policy" functions, that
is, those to do with the management of wages policy'. It would also lose
its traditional structure and organization. It would be 'headed by a
senior official with, say, departmental head status' and would function
on a regional basis. The Advisory Conciliation and Arbitration Service
in the United Kingdom was 'one model of such a system' (ibid.: 120–2).

There would be 'legislated safety net minima' fixed by governments
'in the light of economic conditions, prevailing standards of living and
social security arrangements, following consultations with peak councils
of employers and employees and other interested parties' (ibid.: 122).
The Study Commission seems to have reached this position with some
difficulty. It saw 'a case for allowing employers and employees to make
whatever arrangements they wish on employment conditions' (ibid.:
131). Why did that case not prevail? One reason was 'a genuine concern
in the community that reform of employment relations, particularly
reform that downgrades the role of compulsory arbitration and the
award system, will lead to reductions in employment standards'. This was
a concern based on a belief that there would be a shift in the 'balance of
power' to employers, especially in times of unemployment, and that
employers would use the opportunity – and be compelled by competition – to drive down wages and working conditions so as to reduce costs
(ibid.: 129). Though acknowledging the concern, the Study Commission
was reluctant to concede its justification, for it implied an excessive
emphasis on cost and price relative to reliability, quality and service:

> In order to be competitive on those factors, enterprises must win the trust
> and confidence of their employees: reliability, service and quality only follow
> from commitments given freely. Those commitments are hardly likely to be
> forthcoming from employees whose wages and working conditions are a
> disincentive to better performance, as they would be in the case of an
> exploitative employer. (ibid.: 130)

But managers might not always act rationally. Hence the Study
Commission accepted the argument as a reason for legal prescription of
a safety net. Another reason, seemingly not very different, was that
employers sometimes make wrong decisions and employees may be
worse off as a result. That potential for error had 'provided a case for

Government intervention in employment relations and should continue to do so in future' (ibid.: 131–2). The Study Commission made clear its misgivings about the concession it had made: 'In supporting such intervention we are conscious that it has costs, for example, a potential discrimination against the unemployed who might be prepared to accept employment at less than mandated pay rates; but our judgment is that the community, and business, is prepared to pay those costs' (ibid.: 132). There was no discussion of the *level* of government-determined safety-net wages and conditions.

An objective of reform was 'to take the politics out of employment relations': 'The intrusion of politics into employment relations has been a major barrier to greater common purpose and commitment in Australian enterprises. All our discussions with business people tell us that the sooner employment relations is off the political agenda the easier it will be for Australian enterprises to meet their competitiveness goals' (ibid.: 124). The notion of government and parliament prescribing minimum wages and conditions sits awkwardly with this objective, which invites the question whether it might not be better to rely on institutions – the arbitration tribunals – which are somewhat distanced from current politics. The answer of the Study Commission is precisely that the tribunals *are* so distanced:

> The belief that the compulsory arbitration system represents the most desirable mechanism to pursue economic and social objectives is a curious one. In particular, the achievement of those aims through the decisions of a tribunal whose views may differ from those of the Government of the day seems especially problematic . . . Greater certainty would be brought to this area if Governments took the necessary action to implement their economic and social policies, including protecting and enhancing the position of the lowest paid, directly rather than relying on an administrative tribunal. (ibid.: 134)

The Study Commission's self-contradiction exposes an important choice. *If* a measure of labour market regulation, including regulation of minimum wages, is desirable, is the cost of incorporating it in political disputation to be preferred to that of excluding it (or attempting to do so)? In the case of monetary policy, there appears to be a widespread and growing acceptance that central bank independence has merit. There was in Australia a long presumption (apparently ending in the 1990s) of the virtue of independence in the prescription of wage policy and dispute resolution – that it was better for wages and conditions *not* to be the subject of competition between political parties. Was the presumption necessarily misguided?

Save for the proposed safety net, whose content is uncertain, the Study Commission's agenda is one for removing institutional involvements in the labour market and allowing a wide scope for employers to determine the wages and conditions on which people are employed. The 'enterprise focus' is both anti-union and anti-arbitration. There is a hope that employers, freed from these unwelcome intrusions, will see advantage in methods of management that induce cooperative attitudes among their employees. The opposite scenario – that employers rely on authority and discipline, reinforced by competition for employment, to minimize labour costs – receives little credence. Issues of distributive fairness are (except for the safety net) accorded no importance, in the belief that increasing the size of the 'cake' is ultimately to the benefit of all. Moving towards a labour market with this degree of 'enterprise focus' – in fact, employer dominance – is justified by Australia's 'productivity gap'. The reality and extent of the gap are contentious. That it is due to phenomena of the labour market, and that the recommended reforms will remove or substantially reduce it are, in the main, assumptions, based on a judgement that the institutions of the labour market inhibit both managerial flexibility and employee loyalty to the enterprise. The Study Commission does not entertain the possibility that allowing enterprises to compete in product markets by using cheap labour will discourage innovation and efficiency; nor does it seriously consider the scope for improved managerial performance *within* the constraints that the institutions impose on managers. The inference that the outcome of the project was tainted by the pre-judgements spelt out in the terms of reference, and shared by the Study Commission itself, is difficult to resist. In all, there are grounds for equating the Study Commission's 'enterprise focus' with a labour market that would be harsher to many workers and would deliver little in the way of benefit that could not otherwise be achieved.

The limitations on management that flow from the industrial relations system have, in fact, been investigated empirically. Results of the initial Australian Workplace Industrial Relations Survey (AWIRS I), which was undertaken in 1990, were available by the time that the Study Commission completed its work. Managers who participated in the survey were asked about impediments to the making of significant efficiency changes. Fifty-seven per cent reported no barriers. Of those who had encountered barriers, 29 per cent mentioned lack of money or resources, 20 per cent management or organization policy, 14 per cent unions, 12 per cent government rules and regulations, 7 per cent awards and 24 per cent other obstacles (Callus et al., 1991: 204). A supplementary inquiry, to give a fuller coverage of small employers, was undertaken by J. E. Isaac, the Australian Chamber of Commerce and Industry and the Department of Industrial Relations (Department of Industrial Relations 1993b). Isaac wrote a monograph based on the results of AWIRS I and the further survey. In the light of that evidence, he found it 'reasonable to suppose that economic performance is driven essentially by management will, initiative and competence; and that, given such qualities, the existing award system would not stand in the way of improved economic performance' (Department of Industrial Relations 1993a: 46).

The surveys, overall, provided 'no support for the view that the present institutional arrangements need to be changed in order to promote better industrial relations or improved productivity performance' (ibid.: 48). In AWIRS II (carried out in 1995), 59 per cent of managers surveyed had wanted to make significant efficiency changes but could not. Of these, 31 per cent referred to financial/economic factors, 26 per cent to management, head office or government policy, 15 per cent to employee/delegate or trade union resistance, 10 per cent to awards/agreements and 38 per cent to other impediments (Moorehead et al. 1997: 255–6). Multiple reasons were accepted in the three surveys, so there are likely to have been overlaps between the union-related barriers and the award-related barriers. None of the surveys allows any judgement to be formed as to whether the restraints reported by managers were justified. Even so, the data make it difficult to accept the emphasis of the BCA and its Study Commission on industrial relations as the impediment to more productive performance.

The Sins of Unions

In addition to the general and conceptual objections to unionism that form part of the cases for deregulation derived from the 'economic' model and the 'enterprise focus', there are criticisms that pertain more to specific union behaviour. The two sets of criticisms would be seen by their authors as related and complementary. They nevertheless merit separate notice. An attack on union misconduct has been a conspicuous part of the agenda of the H. R. Nicholls Society. More recently, in the context of the dispute about waterfront unionism, it has been at the forefront of political debate.

The productive activities said to have been especially afflicted with union malpractice include coal and metalliferous mining, commercial building, paper manufacture, meat (wholesale only), electricity production, shearing, live sheep exports and the waterfront. Coming behind these would be shipping, the oil industry and even schoolteaching and nursing. In addition, there have been isolated instances of alleged misbehaviour in what are not normally seen as 'bad' areas. Confectionery and fruit canning are examples. The 'offences' include (not necessarily in order of importance) the following: enforcement of over-manning and wasteful work practices; resistance to technical and managerial progress; unreasonable requirements for amenities; imposing union requirements contrary to the wishes of both employers and employees; corruption; condoning and even abetting workplace misconduct; arrogation of workplace power by union delegates; maintenance of closed shops and victimization of non-unionists; resort to industrial action as the first rather than the last response to grievances; and contempt for legal obligations (including court orders).

Detailed discussion of the specific complaints would require more space than is available here. This is not to trivialize them. On the contrary, there has been a significant incidence of union misconduct that has contributed both to employer antipathy to the industrial relations system and to public cynicism about unions and their leaders. It is easy to cite instances of union misbehaviour that most people would think outrageous. A satisfying analysis, however, requires more than disapproval. The questions to be considered vary from instance to instance, as must the answers. One is the extent to which current behaviour is explicable by the history of industrial relations in the firm or the industry or by the nature of the work performed. It is obvious that those factors have much to do with the state of affairs in coalmining, in the meat industry and on the waterfront. Treating the union as a *deus ex machina* is a mistake. Related to this question is a second: could unions that misconduct themselves do otherwise without forfeiting membership support? Bound up with that question is the issue of whether union behaviour is member-driven or leader-driven. Third, what are the responses of employers and managers to perceived union misconduct, and are those responses the most likely to alleviate the problem? There are instances where the pattern of misconduct has evolved over long periods and management has contributed by tolerating or even being complicit in it. In such instances, 'drawing a line in the sand' has sometimes been effective. Distinguishing between situations where it is likely to succeed and where it is not is by no means easy. A further question relates to the efficacy, in both the short and long terms, of legal remedies: which are the most likely to produce desired outcomes?

None of this is to deny that deunionizing the labour force and disempowering unions will reduce the amount of 'anti-social' conduct for which unions can be blamed. But is the cure worse than the disease?

The Legal Regime

The employment relationship raises legal issues that go far beyond those associated with a sale of apples across the counter. They arise largely from factors previously noted: the time dimension of employment, the ill-defined character of the traded commodity, the employer's entitlement to command and the exposure of either side to loss if the relationship comes to an end. Moreover, issues of distributive fairness arise in connection with employment as they rarely do in across-the-counter transactions. What legal arrangements are suited to such a market?

Hayek was concerned that the legal framework facilitate the market 'game':

> If there is to be an efficient adjustment of the different activities in the market, certain minimum requirements must be met; the more important of these are . . . the prevention of violence and fraud, the protection of property and the enforcement of contracts, and the recognition of equal rights of all individuals to produce in whatever quantities and sell at whatever prices they choose . . . The decision to rely on voluntary contracts as the main instrument for organizing the relations between individuals does not determine what the specific content of the law of contract ought to be; and the recognition of the right of private property does not determine what exactly should be the content of this right in order that the market mechanism will work as effectively and beneficially as possible. (1960: 229)

Trade unions ought to be subject to 'the general principles of law applicable to all other citizens'. They should not enjoy the immunities from actions in tort conferred on them by the Trade Disputes Act of 1906.[21] The implication, roughly stated, is that labour relations should be regulated by the common law. (This is only roughly correct, because by 1906 unions had statutory protection against common-law doctrine challenging their very right to exist.)

The common law is law made by judges. A labour market that is subject to the common law *is* regulated. Acts of parliament and awards are other types of regulation. The superiority of one type of regulation or the other (or, to be more realistic, of one combination over another) is a matter for judgement, informed by a knowledge of the alternatives. Some advocates of reliance on the common law seek to clothe it with intrinsic merit – as in Hayek's phrase 'the general principles of law applicable to all other citizens'. Lord Wedderburn (an advocate of collective labour law) asks how far labour law is to be 'free from the constraints of a common law philosophy . . . which emphasises the employee's subordination and the supremacy of managerial prerogative despite the camouflage of contractual equality'. He complains that the question 'receives peculiarly little attention in England because of the prejudice which has long been held that the common law by virtue of being "the ordinary law of the land" must be correct in its appreciations of all types of social issue' (Wedderburn, 1991: 26).

The common law conceives of the employment relationship as a contract freely entered into by an employer and an employee, each acting as an independent party. It discourages interference by others (including unions). With some exceptions (a contract to commit murder will not be enforced), the common law gives effect to what the contract provides. Thus if the employee, in negotiating the contract, demands a wage higher than that generally paid to similar employees and the employer agrees to the demand, the employer must pay the higher wage; if the employee agrees to work for less than the prevailing rate, he or she cannot subsequently require the employer to make good the shortfall. On many of the incidents of employment, however, the contract will be silent. Disputes about these will, if necessary, be resolved by the courts, which have developed principles that are applied to typical situations. An employee is assumed to be competent to perform work for which he or she is engaged unless the employee informs the employer of limitations to his or her competence. The common law recognizes the employer's right (within ill-defined limits) to direct the employee in the performance of his or her work. The employee has a duty to promote the employer's interests. Until recently, at least, the employer was under no obligation to protect or promote the employee's future interests.[22] Either side may bring the contract to an end by giving notice and need not give reasons for doing so.[23] Where one side, by its conduct, 'repudiates' the contract, the other may accept the repudiation and withdraw from the contract. This is the basis on which employees are 'sacked' without notice for misconduct. (Employers often choose not to rely on this right, with its risk of dispute, and either give the normal notice or make payment in lieu thereof.) There is, of course, much more than this to the common law of employment, but the summary is enough for our purposes.

Friends of the common-law regime typically make three points. First, its emphasis on individual contracting and the discouragement of collective intervention allow the labour market to operate in something like the Hayekian manner. For example, N. R. Evans, in a paper, 'The Right to Strike and the Law of Contract', delivered to the H. R. Nicholls Society in 1991, asserts that the law of contract underpinned British economic growth in the nineteenth century. The reason is 'simple enough':

> A contracting society, in contrast to a regulated society, can use all of the widely dispersed information throughout that society in order to satisfy, as efficiently as possible, the provision of goods and services, the formation of new capital, and the investment of time and money in new ventures . . . A regulated society, a regulated labour market, can only use an infinitesimally small proportion of the knowledge base within any society. To put it kindly, our labour market regulators are not intellectual giants. Even when they are

advised by the learned Treasurer of the H. R. Nicholls Society, Mr Purvis, their capacity to comprehend, let alone foresee, the infinitely variable detail of many thousands of different workplaces, is inevitably subject to very great constraint.

Second, the objection that the employment contract will reflect the employer's superior bargaining power is countered by the response that no superiority exists where markets are competitive. Third, it is said that the dangers that may at first seem implicit in the undefined terms of the contract – especially the employer's power to direct the worker – are adequately limited by the sanction, available to either side, of ending the contract. The sanction has force because each side stands to lose something if the relationship comes to an end. Neither can be pushed too far, however, because competition in the external market ensures that each has an escape from the excessive demands of its present partner (Epstein 1985).

I have discussed these contentions in the context of my consideration of the 'economic' argument for labour market deregulation and do not repeat what I said there. Suffice it to say that labour market outcomes are not nice merely because they are contractual.

Foremost among the critics of contractual regulation of the labour market was Sir Otto Kahn-Freund, the British scholar of labour law. Kahn-Freund emphasized the reality (as he saw it) of employer power:

> But the relation between an employer and an isolated employee or worker is typically a relation between a bearer of power and one who is not a bearer of power. In its inception it is an act of submission, in its operation it is a condition of subordination, however much the submission and the subordination may be concealed by that indispensable figment of the legal mind known as the 'contract of employment.' The main object of labour law has always been, and we venture to say will always be, to be a countervailing force to counteract the inequality of bargaining power which is inherent and must be inherent in the employment relationship. Most of what we call protective legislation – legislation on the employment of women, children and young persons, on safety in mines, factories, and offices, on payment of wages in cash, on guarantee payments, on race or sex discrimination, on unfair dismissal, and indeed most labour legislation altogether – must be seen in this context. It is an attempt to infuse law into a relation of command and subordination. (Cited in Davies & Freedland 1983: 18)

Kahn-Freund warned of the semantic hazards in interpreting the employment relationship:

> Nothing is more misleading than the ambiguity of the word 'freedom' in labour relations. By restraining the power of management over the individual worker the law limits the range of the worker's duty to obey rules made by

management. Protective legislation thus enlarges the worker's freedom, his freedom from the employer's power to command, or, if you like, his freedom to give priority to his own and his family's interests over those of his employer. Yet paradoxically, such liberating legislation must appear to the lawyer as a restraint on freedom, on the 'freedom of contract' which in this context is the term the law uses for the subjection of the worker to the power of management, or as 'statutory restrictions', the name given in older textbooks to legislation passed for the protection of the workers. This paradox cannot be condemned. It is necessary for the law to see relations of subordination in terms of co-ordination, that is, an act of submission in the mask of a 'contract', because this is the fiction through which it exorcises the incubus of 'compulsory labour.' One should not underestimate the real significance of verbal magic. (ibid.: 24)

The case against the common law as seen by Kahn-Freund is, then, that it sustains the powerlessness of the worker as an individual operating unaided in the market and constrains him or her to submit to (possibly oppressive) managerial direction.

The obvious alternatives are direct legal prescription and 'regulation' that enables workers to transcend their individual impotence by acting collectively. These are not exclusive, but, in the mixture of them, Kahn-Freund supported a strong component of the latter. Such was the choice made by the British parliament in 1906. Kahn-Freund described the system that grew out of the 1906 Act as 'collective *laissez-faire*': having removed the common-law restraints on collective action, the Act left employers and employees, and their associations, to their own devices. The chief objection to reliance on prescription was its limited effectiveness:

> The law has important functions in labour relations but they are secondary if compared with the impact of the labour market (supply and demand) and . . . with the spontaneous creation of social power on the workers' side to balance that of management. Even the most efficient inspectors can do but little if the workers dare not complain to them about infringements of the legislation they are seeking to enforce. The Truck Acts and other protective legislation began to be effectively enforced when membership in trade unions gave workers the strength to insist on the maintenance of the legal standards . . . The law does, of course, provide its own sanctions . . . but in labour relations legal norms cannot often be effective unless they are backed by social sanctions as well, that is by the countervailing power of trade unions and of the organised workers asserted through consultation and negotiation and ultimately, if this fails, through withholding their labour. (ibid.: 19–20)

The advantages of 'regulating' the labour market by empowering trade unionism include the built-in enforcement capacity noted by Kahn-Freund. Another is the ability of unions to articulate the goals and problems that are most important to workers. Legislators, by contrast,

are likely to be further from the workers and may adopt priorities different from theirs. Democracies do not operate simply by having elected
representatives hand down edicts from on high. Rather, they preserve
scope for people individually *and* collectively to pursue their interests
through means other than legislation. Unions are part of the network
of pressure groups that is intrinsic to democratic society. Union
members, further, may have a sense of 'owning' the outcomes of union
endeavours and be disposed to make them work, to the possible benefit
of employers as well as themselves.

There are, however, problems in relying on union empowerment,
some of them exemplified by the British experience under collective
laissez-faire. The exact *amount* of power that unions acquire and the
particular *uses* they make of it may not be supported, even by people who
believe that labour market regulation is necessary. Britain's largely
unsuccessful essays into incomes policy (described by a general secretary
of the Trades Union Congress as an 'impertinence') reflected a concern
about the macro-economic effects of the exercise of union power. In
Australia, some have found distasteful the spectacle of elected governments, via the Accord, co-opting the ACTU into their decision-making
processes. The effect on workers of the unions' pressing the interests of
their members is uneven. Some unions have achieved high wages and
good conditions, but their successes may have harmed workers in non-
unionized employment or those represented by ineffectual unions. Such
disparities do not necessarily commend themselves. The efforts of
unions to promote or preserve their institutional interests relative to
those of other unions may cause or exacerbate demarcation disputes
and unproductive work practices. And the internal politics of unions are
not always attractive. Again, the *degree* of infringement of managerial
autonomy by the requirement to share workplace power with union
officials and delegates is not necessarily what is advocated by those who
think that *some* limitation is desirable. Finally, the unions' weapons for
enforcing their demands – strikes and related forms of industrial action
– inflict damage, not only on the immediate employers, but also on third
parties (including powerless citizens). All this is to say that collective
laissez-faire is a coarse regulatory instrument.

The dilemma that these reflections manifest became a concern to
Kahn-Freund. The editors of the third edition of his *Labour and the Law*
comment:

Kahn-Freund himself in his last published work . . . stressed the dangers
inherent in the British tradition of direct trade union democracy, and in the
linked tradition of union control of access to jobs. He continues by indicating
doubts about the capacity of the existing collective bargaining system to

respond to the great social demands which had come to be made of it, and
concludes, 'That which . . . I have called "collective *laissez-faire*" may be
in need of adjustment more than any other part of the British heritage'.
(ibid.: 2–3)

The 'adjustment' of collective *laissez-faire* can cover a vast range of policy
options, including the partial disempowerment of unions effected by the
Thatcher and Major governments in the UK. Kahn-Freund had in mind
nothing so draconian, but the principle is plain: there is no natural
order of things in relation to the degree and the exercise of union
power. What is right will vary with time, place and personal judgement.

The traditional Australian system was an attempt to combine union
empowerment, restraint on the unions' exercise of their power, and direct
prescription of the terms of employment. It recognized and strengthened
the unions' role in representing collectively the interests of their members
and, indirectly, the interests of other employees, but it sought to avert
some of the less attractive features of collective *laissez-faire*. That the
interests of employers and employees were often not in harmony was a
fundamental presumption, but it was a goal of the system to minimize the
disruptive effects of the differences. Kahn-Freund could not think 'of any
person who in our century has done more to substitute a legally organised
dialogue for ordeal by battle than the late Mr. Justice Higgins, the
principal Founding Father of the Australian system of arbitration and
conciliation' (ibid.: 27). Few would argue that the 'new province for law
and order', judged against a criterion of preventing industrial action, was
a resounding success. Conciliation and arbitration may, however, have
altered to a significant degree the nature of industrial action – away from
long-term to short-term action, and away from disputation about wages
and hours towards resistance to and protest against exercises of
managerial discretion. Indeed, it may have been a fault of the system that,
constrained by a succession of High Court decisions limiting interference
with 'managerial prerogative', the arbitrators misdiagnosed the sources
of industrial conflict, giving undue weight to wages and hours of work and
not enough to the incidents of the workplace.

But the system was not only about managing industrial conflict. It was
also concerned with the establishment and maintenance of a regime of
wages and conditions that was fair to workers at large, and as between
groups of workers, and into which were factored considerations of
public interest. The public interest consisted, to a large degree, of the
avoidance of adverse macro-economic outcomes, especially unemployment and inflation. An investigation of the system's macro-economic
successes and failures, of its impact on relative wages and conditions, and
of the extent to which the tribunals, over the long term, actually altered

outcomes relative to those that would have obtained in a world of collective *laissez-faire*, is a complex task.[24] Conclusions capable of winning general assent have been elusive. It is a reasonable conjecture, however, that the tribunals defined minimum standards which softened disparities that would have arisen if every group of workers depended on its own bargaining power or if individual workers, acting separately, were forced to accept or reject such offers as employers chose to make. *Some* indication that the system countered disparities is afforded by experience in the partially deregulated labour market of the 1990s: wages under enterprise bargains have risen significantly faster than both award wages and average earnings. Chapter 3 in this volume provides the first comprehensive review of these three issues, and concludes that the tribunals have made a difference.

Conclusion

Australian industrial relations always were a hybrid of conciliation and arbitration, collective bargaining and employer power. Since the 1980s, the influence of conciliation and arbitration has diminished, but a significant residual survives. Its main current role in the labour market is the prescription of safety-net terms that afford a degree of protection to vulnerable employees.

Collective bargaining applies to a minority – by no means a trivial one – of the labour force. The Department of Workplace Relations estimates that at 30 June 1998, 16 per cent of all employees worked under collective agreements certified by the AIRC.[25] Adding to these workers those who are covered by formal agreements under the state systems may well raise the total scope of enterprise bargains to about a quarter of all employees. The potential of collective enterprise bargaining to be the paradigm of Australian industrial relations is challenged, however, by the low and declining level of unionism, which cannot be ascribed to hostile legislation because it pre-dates the relevant changes in the law (which may, of course, exacerbate the unions' recruitment and retention problems). If the trend continues, both the legitimacy of the unions' claim to speak for employees and the relevance of labour law that assumes collectivism must come under question. Those who believe that regulation is necessary will, in that event, need to contemplate the *form* of regulation appropriate to a largely non-unionized labour force. Even the Labor Government thought it appropriate in 1993 to introduce a form of agreement devised for enterprises employing no or few union members. The Coalition has gone further in altering the law to accommodate and encourage deunionized industrial relations. Australian unionism is far from 'finished', but it is in a defensive position.

As of now, the changes that have occurred in Australian industrial relations are the cause of divergent experiences among workers. The minority of employees to whom collective agreements apply have fared well in the 1990s. For the bulk of the labour force, however, the combined effect of the deregulationist forces at work in Australia is a shift toward employer-determined wages and conditions, tempered by safety-net restraints. In such a context, the nature of the safety net is controversial. On the one hand, it is seen as little more than a safeguard against the exceptional, averting employer conduct that all but a few would regard as exploitative. On the other, there are endeavours to maintain it as a real force in the labour market, impinging significantly on the offers actually made by employers and not confined to the lower end of the pay distribution. The boundary between these options may be blurred, but the difference is part of current debate.[26]

Notes

1 For a comprehensive review of British legislation restricting unions, see Undy et al. 1996.
2 For example, the Minister of Industrial Relations, Peter Cook, (1991) said that there had been a lack of appreciation of the significant reality that 'the fundamental source' of wage outcomes since 1983 'lies with the Government's Accord with the trade union movement, not with the delivery mechanism facilitated, until recently, through National Wage Decisions of the Commission'.
3 The quotations from Geoff Allen's paper are taken from Committee of Review of Australian Industrial Relations Law and Systems 1985: 221–3. An edited version is in Blandy & Niland 1986: 334–50.
4 John Stone (formerly Secretary of the Commonwealth Treasury, later a senator for the National Party), Barrie Purvis (director of the Australian Wool Selling Brokers' Employers' Federation), Ray Evans (executive officer at Western Mining Corporation Ltd) and Peter Costello (then a barrister, now Treasurer of the Commonwealth).
5 From the Society's home page.
6 Papers presented to the inaugural seminar in February–March 1986.
7 In 1997, however, the Society expressed bitter disappointment with the measure of industrial relations reform achieved by the Howard Government in 1996 (H. R. Nicholls Society, 1997).
8 'The Industrial Relations Future: the CAI Perspective', from the H. R. Nicholls Society's home page.
9 'Guest of Honour's Address', from ibid.
10 'Greenfield' sites are an exception.
11 From the H. R. Nicholls Society's home page.
12 An example of the former is Solow 1990; of the latter, Garvey 1993.
13 Garvey (1993: 329) describes 'the economics of managerial prerogative' as 'a topic from the too-hard basket'. Although I agree with Garvey that further

theoretical analysis and empirical research may elucidate the *reasons* why the power to direct typically rests with the owners of capital and the managers who represent them, I doubt that it will show that the *exercise* of the power to direct is unproblematic.

14 Garvey (1993: 297), drawing on arguments of Lazear, advances this contention.

15 Treating employees too well may induce cynicism and search for further opportunities to exploit the employer. An explanation of wage relativities in terms of psychological imperatives may be found in Jacques 1967.

16 See Krugman 1997: Chapter 1 (I thank Colin Rogers for this reference). Those who believe that deregulationist labour market policies, especially when embedded in a broader commitment to free markets, will rectify foreign-account problems, should ponder the present balance-of-payments problem of New Zealand.

17 A likely allusion to the Committee of Review of Industrial Relations Law and Systems (the Hancock Committee), which had reported in 1985.

18 This was a puzzling observation, because the then-existing provisions of the Act for certification of agreements (in section 115) were not materially different from those of section 28 of the former Conciliation and Arbitration Act, of which the Study Commission was well aware.

19 Deery & Plowman 1991:115–16, quoted in *Avoiding Industrial Action*: 27.

20 Garvey's study, noted in the previous section, was attached to this report. Although his area of discourse was somewhat different from the Study Commission's, Garvey fortified the Commission's confidence in the correctness of its prescriptions.

21 Hayek 1980: 51.

22 The House of Lords decided in 1996 that an employer was liable in damages for the detriment suffered by innocent employees of a fraudulent business whose future employment opportunities were likely to be impaired by their association with the business. *Malik v Bank of Credit and Commerce International SA (in liq)* [1997] 3 WLR 95.

23 The required notice is commonly the length of the pay period, i.e. one week for persons paid weekly, one month for persons paid monthly, etc. Under US common law, contracts are terminable 'at will'. That is, either the employer or the employee may end the relation without assigning any reason and, unless the contract otherwise specifies, without notice.

24 I offered some views about the arbitration tribunals' ability to influence outcomes, and the degree to which they had made use of their ability, in 'The Arbitration Tribunals and the labour market', in Blandy & Covick 1984.

25 Department of Workplace Relations and Small Business, *Wage Trends under Enterprise Bargaining*, June Quarter 1998.

26 It is evident, for example, in the contrast between the 'safety net' maintained by the AIRC and the single minimum wage – well below the AIRC's federal minimum wage – prescribed by the Minister for Labour Relations in Western Australia.

(Aust/alia)

CHAPTER 3

Wage Regulation, Low-wage Workers, and Employment

Jeff Borland and Graeme Woodbridge

J31

J53 J58

There may be many good ends that regulation of the labour market can serve, and the potential damage done by such regulation may be greatly exaggerated, as argued in the previous two chapters. But does regulation do any good? Does the Australian labour market and wage structure look different as a result of 90 years of active regulation by the industrial tribunals? Chapter 3 answers these questions. It concludes that the Australian wage structure does look different in an egalitarian way. Any move to obtain major employment growth through deregulation would require dismantling not only of the system of industrial tribunals but also of unions and a major reshaping of the social welfare system.

Argument about the appropriate degree of wage regulation has been one of the few constants in political debate in Australia throughout the twentieth century. Most recently, controversy over wage regulation has been manifested in debates over the role of the Australian Industrial Relations Commission in making safety-net wage adjustments. On the basis of arguments that wage regulation has adverse employment consequences for low-skill workers, one group of commentators has proposed that the role of the AIRC in wage-setting should be reduced. For example, Dawkins and Freebairn (1997: 415) state that 'employment prospects would be greatly enhanced if wages growth especially of low skilled employees could be restrained', and suggest that this might be achieved by 'freezing' safety-net wage adjustments for four years. Other commentators have argued that it is in society's interests that the role of the AIRC in wage-setting be maintained. Hancock, for example, has written: 'Protection of the low-paid in a labour market characterised by disparities of bargaining power has, since the inception of industrial arbitration, been among the major functions of the tribunals ... Although their performance can be criticised on various counts, they

86

have, on the whole, been a civilising influence on the labour market'
(1998: 62).

One main theme that can be drawn from discussions of wage regulation in Australia is that an appropriate assessment of the overall social
welfare consequences of wage regulation must take into account both
efficiency and equity. A common perception is that there is in fact a
trade-off whereby regulation improves equity in society but at the cost of
reductions in efficiency. The same perception is evident in international
debates over the role of the minimum wage. An example is Freeman's
statement:

> At best, an effective minimum wage will shift the earnings distribution in
> favour of the low-paid and buttress the bottom tiers of the distribution from
> erosion. At worst, minimum wages reduce the share of earnings going to the
> low-paid by displacing many from employment. Neither outcome is certain,
> so that enacting a minimum is a risky but potentially 'profitable' investment
> in redistribution. It is the balancing of risk against gain that makes a mini-
> mum so controversial. (1996: 639)

Of course, a proper balancing of the benefits and costs of wage
regulation would require taking into account a whole range of efficiency
and equity considerations. Aspects of efficiency include effects on
employment, wage inflation, worker training and output in the economy. Consequences for equity can be summarized in effects on the
distribution of lifetime income. Clearly, a full assessment of each of these
aspects is a large and difficult task.

The object of this chapter is more modest: to analyse one specific
aspect of the efficiency consequences of wage regulation – how wage
regulation affects employment of low-wage workers.[1] Although this is
only a small part of the overall effects of wage regulation, it is nevertheless an important one.

Changes to the system of wage regulation under the *Workplace Relations
Act 1996* have meant that the role of the AIRC has been restricted to
setting safety-net wage increases for workers who have not obtained wage
rises through enterprise bargaining, and to specifying changes to award
minimum wage rates (which provide a floor for wage-setting through
enterprise bargaining). In setting a safety net of fair minimum wages and
conditions, the AIRC is required by its Act to have regard to:

(b) economic factors, including levels of productivity and inflation, and the
     desirability of attaining a high level of employment;
(c) when adjusting the safety net, the needs of the low paid. (AIRC,
     1997: 17)

Hence one of the two main factors the AIRC has sought to take into account in its safety-net judgements has been the employment consequences of wage increases, in particular for low-wage workers. It is this issue that is addressed in this chapter. The other main factor that has been taken into account by the AIRC has been the distributional consequences of changes to wages for low-paid workers. This is examined in detail in Chapters 4 and 5 in this volume.

This chapter presents a simple framework for understanding how wage regulation might affect employment of low-wage workers, and reviews empirical evidence relevant to assessing the magnitude of this effect. The second section describes how the wage regulation system in Australia might affect earnings of low-wage workers. The third section summarizes basic theoretical ideas that are useful for predicting the employment consequences of increases in wages for low-wage workers. The fourth section reviews empirical evidence on the effect of the wage regulation system on earnings outcomes for low-wage workers in Australia, and the fifth section examines studies of the own-wage elasticity of demand for low-wage labour. An assessment of the overall benefits and costs of wage regulation for low-wage workers is presented in the final section.

Throughout this chapter the term 'system of wage regulation' will be used to represent the effects of government on wage-setting. In reality, there is no such thing as a *system* of wage regulation. Instead we choose, from the overall regulatory structure for labour markets in Australia, a set of features likely to affect wage determination, and identify those features as 'the system of wage regulation'. But these features may have effects on other labour market outcomes apart from wages. For example, the arbitration system in Australia, which we identify as one feature of the wage regulation system, has always been involved with setting conditions of employment as well as wage rates. Hence the analysis of the effects of wage regulation in this chapter should be seen to provide only a partial perspective on the labour market consequences of that regulatory system.

Wage Regulation and Earnings Outcomes

In what way might a system of wage regulation affect earnings for those on low-wages? To answer this question it is necessary to understand what is meant by wage regulation; it is then possible to think about how that system might affect earnings outcomes. To do this, we avoid the difficult task of identifying what the structure of wages would look like if there were no regulation. Instead, we assert that there are four main dimensions to the regulatory structure for wage-setting in Australia:[2]

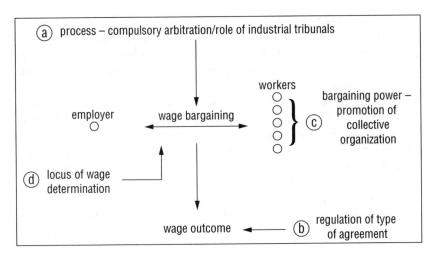

Figure 3.1 The system of wage regulation in Australia

1 Regulation of the process of wage bargaining and wage determination through compulsory arbitration;
2 Regulation of the form of agreement over wages that can be made between a worker and employer;
3 Regulation of bargaining power: Promotion of collective organization of workers in trade unions; and
4 Regulation of the 'locus' of wage determination.

Figure 3.1 provides a simple diagrammatic representation of these aspects of the system of wage regulation in Australia.[3]

Each of these aspects may have some effect on the absolute and relative earnings of low-wage workers. Generally this will be in the same direction for each aspect of wage regulation – to raise the earnings of low-wage workers relative to the non-regulated alternative – although the mechanism through which each effect occurs will differ. We look at each aspect separately below.

A more complete description of the current means of regulating the Australian labour market is found in Chapter 2. Here we highlight those aspects of the functioning of the industrial tribunals that are central to our enquiry. A party to an industrial dispute, over, for example, wages and conditions of employment, is able to refer the matter to the appropriate tribunal for conciliation and/or arbitration. Where arbitration occurs, the decision of the industrial tribunal is then binding on all parties to the dispute. Hancock has written that 'the history of Australian arbitration reveals a number of ideologies. [One is] ... the responsibility of the arbitrator is to set "fair" wages and conditions' (1983: 44). It is this concern with fairness, both in terms of absolute wage levels and relative wages between groups of workers, from which the potential effects of compulsory arbitration on earnings outcomes are generally held to derive (see also Isaac 1981, 1982; Plowman 1986).

An industrial tribunal's decision on terms and conditions of employment for a particular group of workers introduces regulation of the type of agreement that can be made between those workers and employers. The award system provides the instrument through which changes to the relative earnings of low-wage and high-wage workers can be enforced.

Fundamental to government regulation of trade unions is the act of registration. Registration with an industrial tribunal confers two important benefits on unions: it increases the extent of union coverage and it gives them a significant role in wage bargaining. Unions are expected to use this influence to raise the wages of their members above wages of similar non-union members. It is also argued (e.g. Freeman 1982) that they will seek to reduce earnings dispersion among members. The precise nature of any union effect on earnings dispersion is likely to depend on union structure – for example, where unions are organized on an industry basis they would be expected to reduce earnings dispersion between low-wage and high-wage workers within each industry.

The 'locus' of wage-setting is the level at which wage determination takes place, for example at the level of enterprise, industry or nation. The proportion and types of jobs covered by industrial tribunals and trade unions, and regulation of the types of agreements that can be made between employers and workers, will affect the locus of wage determination. For example, a government can regulate the conditions that need to be satisfied for a wage agreement to cover workers at multiple enterprises. If the requirements are hard to comply with, this will tilt the locus of wage bargaining away from multiple enterprises towards individual firms. The locus of wage determination is likely to affect the degree of uniformity in wage outcomes. Where the locus is at the national level, smaller variation in earnings between, for example, workers within particular occupations or skill groups might be expected than where wages are set at each firm.

Of course, it is important to be aware that the effect on earnings outcomes of each aspect of the system of wage regulation has varied greatly. At any particular time the scope for the wage regulation system to affect earnings outcomes will depend on the extent of coverage of wage decisions made by industrial tribunals, on the proportion of workers on minimum-award wage rates, on the role of unions in wage-setting, and on the locus of wage-setting. In the initial phases of the Accord during the mid-1980s, industrial tribunals' wage decisions had almost universal coverage so that there was considerable scope to affect overall earnings outcomes;[4] whereas after enactment of the *Workplace Relations Act 1996*, which has restricted the role of the AIRC to making decisions on safety-net wage adjustments, the scope for affecting overall earnings outcomes has been reduced.

There are also reasons why the system of wage regulation in Australia might be expected to have little effect on earnings outcomes. First, decisions on wages by industrial tribunals have generally specified minimum rates of pay, and employers and workers have been free to negotiate payments above the specified minima. Hence where the minimum rates are not a binding constraint, earnings outcomes may be unaffected by the process of arbitration and regulation of wage agreements.

Second, it can be argued that decisions of industrial tribunals will, through the influence of employers and trade unions, reflect market pressures. That is, supply and demand forces are likely to affect the relative bargaining power of employers and workers so that 'arbitrators who respond to bargaining realities are . . . recognising market relations' (Hancock 1983: 50). Of course, other factors apart from product and labour market competition are likely to affect bargaining power. Hence, decisions of industrial tribunals that reflect bargaining power of workers and firms will also reflect those other factors. For example, where mobility costs for workers who exit from an employment relation are high, this would be expected to lower the bargaining power of those workers.

Third, some apparent constraints imposed by the system of wage regulation may, when compared with outcomes that would prevail in the absence of regulation, not really be constraints. This argument is primarily about the role of equity and fairness in wage-setting under compulsory arbitration. Isaac, for example, claims that 'wage determination, whether by collective bargaining or arbitration, is an administrative process in which certain norms or criteria are used as a basis for settlement' (1982: 503). Thus equity concerns may play a part with or without wage regulation.

Wage Regulation and Employment of Low-skill Workers

How might wage regulation, and in particular an increase in the wage of low-skill workers relative to that of high-skill workers, affect employment outcomes for low-wage workers? This may seem a simple question, but in fact it is quite difficult to answer. As Dolado et al. (1996: 330) have noted of the effects of changes to minimum wages, 'economic theory has no unambiguous prediction about the employment effects of minimum wages'. Instead, any prediction of the employment consequences of a change in wages of low-wage workers must depend to a large degree on judgements made about how the labour market works. In this section, therefore, a range of alternative perspectives are presented on the employment effects of wage regulation for low-wage workers.

We examine employment outcomes for low-wage workers under the following scenario. Suppose there are just two types of labour: 'low-wage' and 'high-wage'. It is assumed that the direct effect of wage regulation is to impose a minimum wage rate for low-wage workers which is above the rate that would obtain in the absence of regulation. There is, however, no direct effect of regulation on wage rates of high-wage workers.

The overall effects on employment of low-wage workers can then be separated or 'decomposed' into two parts:

1 The size of increase in labour costs due to the regulated increase in wage rates for low-wage workers; and
2 How the increase in labour costs affects labour demand and employment.

Change in labour costs

Changes in the effective cost of labour due to an increase in minimum wage rates for low-wage workers can be characterized in two ways:

1 *Increase in the relative price of low-wage labour.* A regulated increase in wages of low-wage workers will make them more expensive compared to other workers and to capital.
2 *Change in the absolute cost of labour.* Increases in minimum wage rates for low-wage workers may raise the average cost of labour, or in a dynamic context, increase the aggregate rate of wage inflation.

The size of effect on labour costs from an increase in wage rates for low-wage workers will depend on factors outside the wage regulation system that may act to offset the regulatory wage increase, such as changes to wage rates of high-wage workers, and employers' actions to reduce the effect on labour costs of regulatory wage increases for low-wage workers. First, as a result of the wage increase obtained by low-wage workers, high-wage workers may also achieve some increase.[5] Second, employers may seek to reduce the impact on labour costs of changes in wage rates for low-wage workers implemented through the wage regulation system. They may absorb an increase in monetary compensation to low-wage workers by reducing some other aspect of compensation (for example, non-pecuniary fringe benefits), or by increasing the effective labour input from each hour of paid labour supplied by a worker (for example, increases in unpaid overtime).

Labour costs and employment: changes in the relative cost of low-wage labour

How a change in labour costs affects the employment of low-wage workers will, as has already been emphasized, depend crucially on the nature of the labour market in which that change occurs. Here, three main scenarios will be considered: where labour markets are perfectly competitive; where employers in labour markets have monopsony power; and equilibrium wage dispersion models. In order to focus on the employment consequences for low-wage workers it is assumed throughout that the increase in wage rates for low-wage workers is the only change in the cost of labour for a firm.

Perfect competition

In a perfectly competitive labour market the unambiguous prediction is that a rise in the wage of low-wage workers will cause a decrease in employment of that group of workers. Decreases in employment of low-wage workers will occur in two ways, generally referred to as substitution and scale effects. First, the increase in the relative cost of low-wage workers will cause employers to choose to substitute other factors of production for low-wage workers. Second, the increase in the marginal cost of production that occurs due to the higher cost of employing these workers may necessitate an increase in the price of output, and hence there will be a reduction in the level of employment due to a decline in demand.

The main factors that will determine the size of the substitution and scale effects are summarized in the 'Hicks-Marshall rules of derived demand' (see for example Elliott 1991: 243–5). These 'rules' state that the responsiveness of employment to changes in the cost of labour will be greater:

- the higher is the responsiveness of consumer demand to changes in the price of the good that low-wage workers produce;
- the more easily other factors of production can be substituted for low-wage workers;
- the larger is the share of total cost of production accounted for by low-wage workers; and
- the smaller is the effect of an increase in demand for other factors of production on the cost of those factors.

An important point is that the effect of each of these factors, which determine the responsiveness of employment to a change in labour costs, is likely to vary over time and across sectors of the economy. How employment is affected by an increase in labour costs will therefore also vary over time. For example, increases in international competition are likely to have increased the responsiveness of demand by consumers in Australia to changes in prices of domestically produced import-competing goods. Hence increased international competition will have the effect of magnifying the employment effects of an increase in wages for low-wage workers in those import-competing industries.

Monopsony

The important characteristic of a monopsonistic labour market – compared to perfect competition – is that a firm is no longer a 'price-taker' facing a constant wage rate. Instead it must pay a higher wage rate to attract each extra worker or unit of labour.

In monopsonistic labour markets it is possible that an increase in labour costs can actually increase employment (see, for example, Elliott 1991: 304–6; Manning 1994a, 1996). Where a monopsonistic firm has been able to set a wage below the 'competitive market equilibrium' wage, the level of employment will be determined on the supply side of the market. Thus an increase in wages for low-wage workers will increase labour supply and hence employment. It should be noted, however, that even with a monopsonistic labour market, a sufficiently large increase in wages will always cause a decrease in employment. Moreover, where the initial wage level is set above the 'competitive market equilibrium', employment at the firm is determined on the demand side. In this case any further increase in wages will have the effect of reducing the level of employment.

An important issue regarding monopsonistic labour markets is empirical relevance. In most textbooks such markets are treated as a theoretical curiosity; it is often argued, for example, that the only situation where this type of labour market would be expected to occur is the 'one company town'. But more recently some labour economists have argued that the concept of a monopsonistic labour market is of wider relevance. For example, Manning (1996: 197) suggests that females' choices of workplaces are often restricted by family considerations, and that for this reason firms may have some degree of monopsony power in hiring female employees. Alternatively, Card and Krueger (1995: 369–83) discuss how imperfect information and search costs may explain why a firm will not treat as a constant the wage rate it must pay to attract each extra unit of labour.

Equilibrium wage dispersion models

Equilibrium wage dispersion models extend the partial equilibrium monopsony model just presented. By examining a situation where workers have imperfect information about available job offers, and there are a large number of firms, each of which chooses a wage offer to make to potential workers conditional on the distribution of wages offered by other firms, the hiring and turnover rates become choice variables for individual firms.

Card and Krueger (1995: 381) suggest there are three main types of findings from equilibrium wage dispersion models. First, in equilibrium wages can differ systematically across firms. Second, one type of equilibrium may involve one set of firms choosing a low-wage/high-turnover policy, and another set of firms choosing a high-wage/low-turnover policy. In this equilibrium all firms earn equal profits: firms following the former strategy earn a higher profit per worker but have wage offers accepted relatively infrequently and workers who quit fairly rapidly, whereas firms following the latter strategy earn a lower profit per worker but have their wage offers accepted more regularly and have a lower quit rate among workers (see, for example, Burdett & Mortensen 1997). A third finding is that setting a minimum wage above the level set by a low-wage/high-turnover firm may increase employment. This can happen where an increase in the wage it must pay causes labour turnover in the firm to fall, and hence an expansion in its steady-state labour force (Manning 1994b). But it is important to note that such an increase in employment does not imply that economic efficiency is necessarily improved. To make an assessment of the consequences for efficiency it is also necessary to take account of the effects on the behaviour of workers as they are looking for jobs.

One general point, alluded to on page 93, but which merits further emphasis, is that the employment response to a change in labour costs is likely to vary with the time-horizon considered. Simply stated, the longer the period over which adjustment in a firm's input demands is examined, the greater the extent of adjustment that is likely to have occurred. The variety of factors that account for the potential difference between short-term and long-term adjustment include time-lags involved in recruiting and training substitute labour for low-wage workers, organizational costs in restructuring production processes, time taken to identify and instal new capital, and the cost of severance payments to low-wage workers who are laid off.

Labour cost and employment: changes in the aggregate cost of labour

Where an increase in wage rates for low-wage workers raises the aggregate rate of wage inflation, there may be further economy-wide factors that affect the employment of low-skill workers. The main determinant of such effects is likely to be the prevailing macro-economic

environment. Factors such as the existing rates of wage and price inflation would be expected to be particularly important here. For example,
where the existing rate of wage inflation is already such that the Reserve
Bank is seeking to reduce demand-pressure through increases in interest
rates, further increases in wage inflation from wage adjustments for low-
paid workers (and spillover effects) might cause a larger rise in interest
rates than would otherwise have occurred, and this in turn may cause a
decline in labour demand and employment.

Summary

The effect of the wage regulation system on employment outcomes for
low-wage workers will represent an amalgam of various responses.
Changes in the relative prices of different types of labour will cause firms
to adjust their demands for labour and for other factors of production.
Policy-makers may also affect employment through their response to
increases in the rate of wage inflation. The overall effect of these
changes in employment may be to alter both the aggregate level of
employment and the composition of employment between low- and
high-wage workers.

The theoretical analysis suggests a wide range of factors determining the
magnitude of each type of effect on employment: the size of changes to
award wages and their effect on labour costs; firms' objectives; the types
of labour markets in which firms operate; the nature of consumer
demand for the products which firms produce; and firms' production
technologies. Alternative assumptions about these factors can lead to
different predictions on employment outcomes for low-wage workers –
as, for example, in the case of whether it is assumed that the labour
market is perfectly competitive or monopsonistic. This implies that the
question of how employment of low-wage workers will be affected by an
increase in wages must be resolved empirically. The next two sections
therefore review some empirical evidence on the key issues: whether
wage regulation affects earnings outcomes for low-wage workers, and the
effect of a change in labour costs on labour demand for low-wage
workers.

Does Regulation Affect the Earnings of Low-wage Workers?

In this section a range of empirical evidence on the effects of the system
of wage regulation in Australia on earnings outcomes will be presented.
Findings from previous empirical studies are reviewed, and results from
original empirical analysis comparing earnings outcomes in Australia
and the United States are described.

Previous empirical studies

Several studies have examined the effects of wage regulation on earnings outcomes for low-wage workers in Australia. Here three main types of studies are described: cross-country studies, time-series analyses for Australia, and studies which analyse how actual wage rates differ from the structure of minimum wage rates established through the system of wage regulation. Summaries of studies using the first approach are presented in Table 3.1, and summaries of studies which use the latter two approaches in Table 3.2 (Panels A and B respectively).

In a review of evidence on the effects of wage regulation on earnings outcomes in Australia written in the mid-1980s, Norris concluded:

> I fully expected to reach the earlier conclusion . . . that the wage structure in Australia was 'very similar' to that in Britain and that there was little evidence that the arbitration system yields a more compressed earnings structure . . . I now doubt whether that conclusion is appropriate. To be sure the two sets of wage relativities are not greatly different . . . However, virtually every difference identified pointed in the same direction, that relativities are narrower in Australia. (1986: 199)

To a significant extent the same conclusion holds a decade later: that earnings dispersion and the structure of earnings between skill and demographic groups in Australia are consistent with the hypothesis that the wage regulation system in Australia has acted to narrow earnings relativities, in particular for low-wage workers.

The distribution of earnings

Most cross-country studies of the distribution of earnings have involved static comparisons between Australia and either the United Kingdom or United States. These studies uniformly find lower levels of earnings dispersion in Australia than in the other countries, in particular for employees with below-median earnings. Less centralized wage-setting and a smaller role for third-party intervention in wage-setting in those countries is consistent with the existence of a relation between earnings outcomes and wage regulation. Comparisons with a broader set of countries preserve the ranking between Australia and the United States and United Kingdom, but also show that earnings dispersion is higher in Australia than in countries such as the Scandinavian bloc. But this ordering is still found to be consistent with the existence of a significant inverse relation between the degree of centralization in wage-setting and earnings dispersion (Blau & Kahn 1996b; OECD 1997). In other words, some countries have lower levels of overall earnings dispersion than

Table 3.1 The effects of wage regulation in Australia – Cross-country studies

Study	Details	Findings
Hughes (1973)	Inter-industry earnings differentials – a) Australia and UK – average annual earnings – male production workers – 63 industries – 1962–63 b) Australia and US – average annual earnings – all workers – 69 industries – 1962–63	Little difference between dispersion in Australia and UK; Significantly wider dispersion in US than Australia.
Brown et al. (1978, 1980)	Inter-plant earnings differentials – Australia, US, and UK – average standard earnings – 14 occupations – Aust (1974)/UK (1974)/US (1963)	Little evidence of significant differences in inter-plant earnings dispersion.
Norris (1980)	• Inter-industry earnings differential – Australia and UK – average hourly earnings – nonmanual workers – 1976 • Inter-occupation earnings differential – Australia and UK – 1914–18 • Distribution of earnings – Australia and UK – weekly earnings – adult males – 1971–78	Little difference in inter-industry earnings dispersion between Australia and UK; Differences in changes in inter-occupation earnings differentials between Australia and UK reflect effect of wage regulation in Australia; Lower dispersion in distribution of earnings in Australia than UK.
Rowe (1981)	Inter-industry earnings differentials – Australia and UK – average annual earnings – male production workers – 1931/32, 1935/36, 1947/48 and 1955/56	Little difference between Australia and UK.
Mitchell (1984)	Inter-industry earnings differentials/Dispersion in changes in average earnings by industry – Australia and US – weekly earnings – Aust (award)/US (average total) – 1969–90	Greater inter-industry dispersion in US than Australia; Greater variation in changes in earnings by industry in US than Australia; Greater dispersion in distribution of earnings below median in US than Australia.

Study	Topic – data	Findings
Gregory & Ho (1985)	Gender earnings differential – Australia and US – weekly earnings – Aust (full-time adult private sector) / US (full-time) – 1965–85	Earnings differential in US stable cf. in Australia decreases; Period of divergence matches timing of implementation of equal pay policy in Australia.
Gregory et al. (1986)	Gender earnings differential – Australia and UK – weekly earnings – Aust (full-time adult non-managerial) / UK (full-time) – 1965–85	Earnings differential narrows in both countries at time of implementation of equal pay policies; Differences in size of narrowing due to differences in method of implementation of equal pay policy.
Blanchflower (1989)	Experience-earnings profiles – 10 OECD countries – weekly earnings – 1980s	Increase in earnings for an extra year of experience (at 10 years and 20 years) smaller in Australia than United States, Canada, Japan and most European countries.
Gregory et al. (1989)	Gender earnings differential – Australia, US and UK – weekly earnings – Aust (full-time adult non-managerial) / US (full-time wage and salary earners)/UK (full-time adult employees) – mid 1960s–mid 1980s	Implementation of equal pay policy has large effect on gender earnings differential in Australia, and smaller effect in UK and US. Differences in effects explained by differences in other institutions and in nature of labour market segmentation.
Gregory & Daly (1990)	Gender earnings differential – Australia and US – weekly earnings – Aust (full-time adult non-managerial) / US (full-time wage and salary earners) – 1967–88	Earnings differential in US stable cf. in Australia decreases; Period of divergence matches timing of implementation of equal pay policy.
Gregory et al. (1991)	Average earnings – Australia and US – weekly earnings – full-time workers in TCF industry – 1980/81	Earnings of TCF workers relative to male average weekly earnings higher in Australia than US; Effect is particularly evident for immigrants.
Blau & Kahn (1992)	Gender earnings differential – 8 OECD countries – workers aged 18–65 years – annual/monthly earnings – 1980s	Earnings differential relatively low in Australia (especially cf. US and UK); Main cause of difference is effect of returns to observable and unobservable skills.

Table 3.1 (cont.)

Study	Details	Findings
Bradbury (1993)	Distribution of earnings – 6 OECD countries – annual earnings – full-year full-time male workers aged 25–54 years – mid-1980s	Lower dispersion in Australia than US or UK, and similar dispersion to Sweden, Canada and Germany.
Gregory and Woodbridge (1993)	Changes in distribution of earnings – Australia and US – weekly earnings – full-time male workers – 1975–90	Larger overall increase in earnings dispersion in US than Australia; Main cause is greater increase in above-median earnings dispersion in United States than Australia.
Hawke (1993)	Average hourly earnings of full-time and part-time employees – Australia and US – 1986/87	Relative average hourly earnings of part-time to full-time workers significantly greater in Australia than United States. Difference is not explained by inter-country differences in the skill endowments of full-time and part-time workers.
Coelli et al. (1994)	Inter-industry earnings differentials – 14 OECD countries – average compensation per employee – 1975–90	Little systematic relation between inter-industry dispersion and centralisation in wage-setting.
Gregory & Daly (1994)	Determinants of individual weekly earnings – Australia and US – full-time workers aged 15–54 years – 1981	Earnings increase less rapidly with age in Australia than US; Mixed evidence on relation between education and earnings; Industry effects slightly compressed in Australia compared to US; Gender earnings differential larger in US than Australia.

Saunders & Fritzell (1995)	Distribution of earnings – Australia and Sweden – full-year full-time workers – annual earnings – Aust. (1981/82 and 1989/90) and Sweden (1980 and 1990)	Earnings dispersion for males similar in Australia and Sweden in early 1980s but greater in Australia than Sweden in late 1980s; For females earnings dispersion larger in Australia than Sweden in both periods.
Blau & Kahn (1996)	Distribution of earnings – 10 OECD countries – male wage and salary earners aged 18–65 years – annual/monthly earnings – 1980s	Relatively high level of overall dispersion in Australia; Mainly due to larger 50–10 percentile differential; Difference due to 'unobservable' factors such as degree of centralisation in wage bargaining.
Kidd & Shannon (1996)	Gender earnings differential – Australia and Canada – wage and salary earners aged 16–64 – hourly wage – 1989/90	Smaller differential in Australia than Canada; Differences in wage structure explain about one-half of the cross-country difference.
OECD (1996)	Changes in distribution of earnings – 19 OECD countries – wage and salary earners – 1981–94	Change in below-median and overall earnings dispersion in Australia smaller than in US, UK or Canada, and similar to Sweden and Japan.
OECD (1997)	Distribution of earnings – 19 OECD countries	Earnings inequality inversely related to degree of centralisation in wage bargaining, and to trade union density.
Gregory et al. (1998)	Distribution of earnings – Australia and US – weekly earnings – full-time male workers – 1975–95	No difference between change in 50–10 percentile earnings difference in Australia and US.

Table 3.2 The effects of wage regulation – Australian studies

Study	Details	Findings
Panel A		
Gregory & Duncan (1981)	Gender earnings differential – award wages and weekly earnings – 1914–77	Decrease in earnings differential due to implementation of equal pay policy; Effect independent of market factors.
Miller (1994)	Determinants of gender earnings differential – hourly wage – workers aged 30–64 – 1973–89	Decrease in earnings differential mainly due to decrease in wage discrimination; Timing coincides with implementation of equal pay policy.
Panel B		
Brown et al. (1980)	Determinants of over-award pay – 18 occupations – metal industries – 1974	Semi-skilled/Unskilled workers – Establishment effect significant/Occupation effect insignificant; Skilled workers – Establishment effect and occupation effects significant.
Brown et al. (1984)	Determinants of over-award pay – 44 occupations – manufacturing/construction/trade – 1974	Establishment and industry effects generally significant; Occupation effect generally insignificant.
Mitchell (1984)	Correlation between award wage and over-award payments – 18 occupation groups – metal industries – 1982	Positive correlation between level of award wages and percentage of total weekly earnings in over-award pay.

Australia, but this appears to be partly because their wage-setting institutions exert a stronger influence on earnings outcomes than do those in Australia.

There have been fewer cross-country studies of changes over time in earnings dispersion, and their findings have been somewhat mixed. Gregory and Woodbridge (1993), Gregory (1996), and Gregory et al. (1998) examine movements in below-median earnings dispersion for male employees in Australia and the United States from the mid-1970s to the 1990s. These studies find that changes in both countries have been very similar. Taken together with the 'static' evidence of differences in the level of earnings dispersion between Australia and the United States, this might suggest that the effect of wage regulation systems in these countries is to cause a fixed time-invariant difference in earnings dispersion, rather than affecting the extent of adjustment that occurs over time in the relative earnings of low-wage workers. However, comparisons with other countries reveal different changes in earnings dispersion across time that appear to be correlated with the degree of centralization in wage-setting (OECD 1996). And the findings from comparisons between Australia and the United States can be sensitive to the period of the comparison; for example, in the mid-1980s where Australia had a relatively centralized wage-setting system with a signficant role for the AIRC, below-median earnings inequality in Australia appears to have increased more slowly than in the United States (Gregory & Woodbridge, 1993).

Having concluded from available evidence that the wage regulation system in Australia does appear to reduce earnings dispersion, there remains the issue of the magnitude of that effect. This of course is far more difficult to establish. One approach, which follows Gregory (1996), is to take the United States as the 'unregulated' benchmark. Deregulation of wage-setting for low-wage workers in Australia might then be expected to shift the distribution of earnings in Australia to be equivalent to that in the United States. Blau and Kahn (1996b) show that for male (full-time and part-time) workers in Australia in 1986 the 50–10 percentile earnings difference is about 30 per cent higher than in the United States. About one-third of this difference, however, is due to cross-country differences in the dispersion of observed skills. Hence the maximum effect on the 50–10 earnings difference that it seems reasonable to attribute to the effects of wage regulation is about 20 per cent.[6] Moreover, it is important to note that not all of the differences in earnings dispersion between Australia and the United States due to 'unexplained' factors and differences in returns to observed skills will occur as a result of differences in wage regulation. Some part is also likely to be due to cross-country differences in the dispersion of unobserved skills and job conditions. Evidence for this argument is that Blau and Kahn (1996b) find that including extra explanatory variables for earnings – such as industry and occupation variables that may proxy for unobserved skills and job conditions (see Topel 1989) – lowers the cross-country difference in earnings dispersion that is attributed to 'unexplained' factors and to differences in returns to observed skills.

The structure of earnings

The structure of earnings in Australia – differences in average earnings between groups of employees in different skill or demographic categories – appears to some extent to reflect the effects of the wage regulation system. These effects are evident, for example, in analysis of earnings across different gender, occupation, and age groups.

Perhaps the strongest finding from the cross-country studies relates to the gender earnings differential. This is lower in Australia than in the United Kingdom or United States. Time-series evidence from these countries suggests that institutional changes such as the implementation of an equal pay policy in Australia in the early 1970s have been very important in explaining cross-country differences in the evolution of the gender earnings differential.

Industry effects on earnings tend to be highly correlated between Australia and the United States and United Kingdom, and early studies concluded that there was little cross-country difference in the overall dispersion of relative earnings by industry. But there does appear to be evidence that relative earnings in some low-pay industries are higher in Australia than in the United States (Hughes 1973; Gregory & Daly 1994).

Cross-country studies of occupational earnings differentials between Australia and the United Kingdom and United States have found lower dispersion in Australia than those other countries; in particular, this effect is evident between low-wage and middle-wage occupation groups (Norris 1986). This would appear to be consistent with an effect of wage regulation systems on inter-occupational earnings differences. However, analyses of the determinants of over-award payments reach quite different conclusions on the effects of the wage regulation system. These studies begin from the hypothesis that, where the wage regulation system has the effect of compressing earnings differentials between workers in different skill or occupation categories, the size of over-award payments should be positively correlated with the award wage rate by skill or occupation groups. Although there is some evidence that such a relationship does exist, probably the most convincing evidence is from studies that control for industry and firm effects on over-award payments. In these studies occupation is not generally found to be a significant determinant of over-award payments (Brown et al. 1978, 1984).

Finally, there is some evidence that relative earnings of some specific groups of low-wage employees are higher in Australia than in other countries. It appears that immigrants in low-wage industries such as textile, clothing and footwear have higher relative earnings in Australia than the United States (Gregory et al. 1991), and so also do young employees (Blanchflower 1989; Gregory & Daly 1994). Further, the ratio of the average hourly earnings of part-time to full-time workers is higher in Australia than the United States, even after correcting for differences in skill endowments (Hawke 1993).

Australia and the United States – full-time male employees

In this sub-section findings from research on differences in earnings outcomes between Australia and the United States are presented (for further details see Borland et al. 1996). Samples of full-time male workers in the private sector aged 16–64 who worked at least 40 weeks during the previous year were chosen for Australia and the United States for 1982 and 1990.[7] Self-employed workers, employees who earned less than $60 per week (in 1982 dollars), and those working in the agriculture sector were also excluded from the samples. Weekly earnings are defined for the United States as annual wage earnings over the calendar year divided by weeks worked, and for Australia as current usual weekly earnings. Earnings are adjusted using a GDP deflator to obtain real earnings measures. Some variables such as education and industry classification have been regrouped to achieve comparability between countries (see Borland et al. 1996: Appendix 1).

Table 3.3 presents various measures of dispersion in the log of real weekly earnings in the United States and Australia. Rows 1 to 3 show information on overall earnings dispersion. Clearly the distribution of earnings is wider in the United States than Australia. For example, in 1982 a worker at the ninetieth percentile of the earnings distribution in the United States earned approximately 137 per cent more than a worker at the tenth percentile. In the same year the 90–10 earnings differential in Australia was 93 per cent. A similar pattern is evident in the late 1980s.

Although Australia has a narrower distribution of earnings than the United States, the distributions do not differ in all dimensions. Row 4 of Table 3.3 displays the variance of average weekly earnings by industry in Australia and the United States (using seven industry groups). Consistent with the findings of previous studies, inter-industry earnings dispersion in Australia and the United States are very similar. Clearly the

Table 3.3 Measures of male earnings dispersion – Australia and the United States

| | United States | | Australia | |
	1982	1990	1982	1990
90–10 Difference in log real weekly earnings	1.370	1.504	0.932	0.981
75–25 Difference in log real weekly earnings	0.713	0.799	0.457	0.530
Variance of log real weekly earnings	0.287	0.342	0.152	0.176
Weighted variance of average industry log real weekly earnings	0.015	0.017	0.013	0.015
Weighted variance of average occupation log real weekly earnings	0.036	0.058	0.020	0.039

Source: United States, *Current Population Survey*, 1983, 1991; Australia, *Income Distribution Survey, Unit Record File*, 1981/82, 1989/90.

greater degree of earnings dispersion in the United States is due to greater earnings variation within industries, rather than across industries. Interestingly, the same pattern is not evident across occupations. Row 5 of Table 3.3 shows that the variance of earnings across eight occupation groups is greater in the United States than in Australia. In fact the greater variability of earnings across occupations is in proportion to the greater overall variability of earnings.

To shed light on the sources of differences in intra-industry earnings dispersion between Australia and the United States, the decomposition method of Juhn et al. (1993) is applied. This method allows a decomposition of inter-country differences in earnings dispersion into components that represent differences in observed skill characteristics, differences in the return to observed skill characteristics, and differences in unobservable factors.

Findings from decompositions of differences in earnings dispersion for Australia and the United States are reported in Table 3.4. The measures of earnings dispersion are the 90–10, 90–50, and 50–10 percentile differences in log real weekly earnings. Results are presented for the average contribution of each component to the inter-country difference in earnings dispersion.[8] Observable characteristics included in the regression analysis are educational attainment, years of experience, and industry status. Including industry status allows the results to be interpreted as the decomposition of differences in intra-industry earnings dispersion.

A number of findings are evident from Table 3.4. First, in both periods the difference in the 50–10 percentile earnings difference between

Table 3.4 JMP decomposition of inter-country differences in intra-industry male earnings dispersion – United States minus Australia – log real weekly earnings

	Overall	Observed characteristics		Observed returns		Unobserved characteristics/ returns	
1982							
90–10	0.442	0.055	(12%)	0.138	(31%)	0.249	(57%)
90–50	0.109	–0.026	(–24%)	0.041	(38%)	0.124	(86%)
50–10	0.333	0.082	(25%)	0.095	(29%)	0.157	(46%)
1990							
90–10	0.511	0.071	(14%)	0.153	(30%)	0.287	(56%)
90–50	0.113	–0.048	(–42%)	0.066	(58%)	0.095	(84%)
50–10	0.398	0.120	(30%)	0.087	(22%)	0.188	(48%)

Source: United States, *Current Population Survey*, 1983, 1991; Australia, *Income Distribution Survey, Unit Record File*, 1981/82, 1989/90.

Australia and the United States is smaller than the 90–50 percentile earnings difference. This holds for total average earnings, but also for differences due to 'unexplained' factors and for differences in returns to observed skills. This is consistent with evidence from previous studies that the effect of wage regulation in Australia is to reduce overall earnings dispersion, in particular in the range of below-median earnings. Second, the magnitude of the difference between the 50–10 percentile earnings difference between Australia and the United States is around 25 per cent using the sum of the differences in 'unexplained' factors and returns to observed skills. These numbers are slightly larger than in Blau and Kahn (1996b), probably mainly due to the smaller set of controls for observable skills included in the earnings analysis described in this sub-section. As with Blau and Kahn's estimates, differences between Australia and the United States in the distributions of unobserved skills and job conditions mean that it would not be sensible to interpret the numbers as reflecting purely the effect of differences in wage regulation between those countries.

Australia and the United States: other employees

It is also of interest to consider how differences in systems of wage regulation between Australia and the United States might affect earnings outcomes for particular low-wage groups of workers. Table 3.5 presents information on average hourly earnings of specific groups of low-wage workers expressed as a ratio of average hourly earnings of all male employees aged 16–64 years for each country in 1995. The sample of

Table 3.5 Relative earnings of low-wage workers –
Australia and the United States – 1995

	Australia	United States
All		
Female	0.876	0.701
Male, part-time	0.973	1.274
Female, part-time	0.896	0.636
CHS/NCHS		
Male	0.876	0.723
Female	0.793	0.412
Male – Immigrant	1.116	0.527
Female – Immigrant	0.744	0.415
Age 16–20 years		
Male	0.522	0.467
Female	0.548	0.380
Male, part-time	0.554	0.524
Female, part-time	0.580	0.383

Source: Australia, ABS, *Income and Housing Survey 1994/95,*
unit record file; United States, *Current Population Survey,
March 1996,* unit record file.
Note: Wage and salary earners: ratio of average hourly
earnings for specified group to average hourly earnings
for all males aged 16–64 years.

employees is restricted throughout to wage and salary earners. The low-wage groups examined are employees who work part-time, who have a highest educational qualification of high school completion or below (disaggregated by country of birth), and who are aged 16–20 (disaggregated by hours of work).

The results in Table 3.5 provide strong support for previous empirical research which has shown that relative earnings of low-wage workers are higher in Australia than the United States. For example, average hourly earnings of a female immigrant whose highest educational qualification is to have completed high school or below – relative to average hourly earnings of all male employees – are 74 per cent in Australia and 42 per cent in the United States. The same pattern holds for all groups except for male part-time employees, although since male part-time employees earn close to average male earnings in Australia, and well above average earnings in the United States, they should probably not be considered low-wage workers.

Examining the distribution of hourly earnings for the sample of male and female full-time and part-time employees provides similar results to the analysis for male employees from Blau and Kahn (1996b) and to the analysis described in the previous sub-section. The difference between

Australia and the United States in the 50–10 percentile earnings difference in 1995 is 35 per cent for all employees, 38 per cent for male employees, and 34 per cent for female employees. These differences are very similar to the cross-country 50–10 percentile earnings differences for full-time male employees in 1982 and 1990 reported in the previous sub-section. Hence these results seem consistent with the conclusion that, correcting for differences in the distribution of skill characteristics, low-wage workers in Australia have relative earnings between 20 and 25 per cent higher than their US counterparts. Once again though, not all of that difference can be interpreted as representing the effects of wage regulation.

Summary

The effect of wage regulation on earnings outcomes in Australia is to reduce the relative gap between low-wage and high-wage employees from what would otherwise exist. This effect is evident from static cross-country comparisons. But it also seems that, over time, changes in earnings dispersion and in the structure of earnings between countries are to some extent correlated with differences in the degree of centralization in wage-setting. The effect of the system of wage regulation on earnings outcomes is particularly apparent for groups of low-wage workers such as women, and less educated, younger, part-time and immigrant workers.

What is the magnitude of the effect on earnings of low-wage workers in Australia? If we take the United States as an 'unregulated' benchmark, and correct for cross-country differences in the distributions of skills, the evidence suggests that low-wage workers in Australia receive 20–25 per cent more than their US counterparts. Some part of this differential is likely to be due to cross-country differences in the distributions of unobserved skills and job conditions, and some part seems to be due to differences in wage regulation systems. On the basis of a crude estimate that unobserved worker skills and job conditions accounts for about 10 percentage points of this difference, the effect of wage regulation may therefore be to increase relative earnings of low-wage workers in Australia by about 15 per cent.

How Much is Employment of Low-wage Workers Affected by Changes to Labour Costs?

This section presents empirical evidence on the responsiveness of employment of low-wage workers to changes in their labour costs. Evidence from international studies (potentially relevant to the Australian situation) and available Australian studies are reviewed.

Evidence will be presented in terms of the own-wage elasticity of labour demand for low-wage workers; that is, the change in the employment of low-wage workers in response to a 1 per cent increase in their wages. Elasticities will be presented as negative numbers to represent that an increase in wages causes a fall in employment. However, in discussing the size of those elasticities we will be concerned with the absolute value of the own-wage elasticity; hence, for example, we will say that an elasticity of –1 is larger, or shows a greater degree of responsiveness, than an elasticity of –0.5.

International evidence

In the international literature there are two types of studies that provide micro-level information on the determinants of labour demand for low-wage workers; a number of studies have estimated the relationship between labour costs and employment for specific occupation, industry, or skill groups, and there is a large literature that has sought to estimate the effect on labour demand of changes to minimum wages in the United States.

Findings from the first type of study (relating to people employed in particular skills, occupation or industries) are summarized in Hamermesh: 'The overwhelming implication is that own-wage demand elasticities decrease with skill. This was generally true comparing white-collar and blue-collar, educated and less-educated, and older and younger workers' (1993: 126). This summary still leaves open the magnitude of the own-wage demand elasticity for low-skill and low-wage groups. Here it is more difficult to be precise. Studies that examine labour demand by education or skill category tend to find a relatively low own-wage elasticity for less educated or low-skill labour – around –0.5 (Hamermesh 1993: Table 3.8). Studies of labour demand by age category, however, often find quite large own-wage elasticities for younger workers, generally greater (in absolute value) than –1.0 (ibid.: Table 3.9).

Research on the employment effects of the minimum wage has a long history in the United States (for a review see Brown et al. 1982). But perhaps at no point has the topic attracted as much attention as during the past decade, when a major debate has occurred over new empirical evidence on the effects of the minimum wage (see for example, Card & Krueger 1995; Ehrenberg 1995). Although the debate should not yet be regarded as having reached a consensus, a reasonable summary is provided by Freeman:

> No study in the United States or United Kingdom has found that increases in minimum wages reduce total employment with an elasticity near unity: the

debate over employment effects is a debate of values around zero . . . Absence of noticeable employment losses in these studies does not, of course, imply that minimum wages much higher than those observed do not risk large job losses. (1996: 642)

In assessing the relevance of this minimum wage research for Australia it is important to take into account that the group of workers affected by US minimum wage laws is likely to be quite different from workers affected by Australian award wage changes and that, as a percentage of the average hourly wage, the US minimum wage is set far below the level of award wages which apply to most occupation groups in Australia.

Australian evidence

Compared with all workers, low-wage workers in Australia are younger, have less formal education, and are more likely to be female part-time workers (Richardson 1998; Richardson and Harding in this volume). Some evidence on the responsiveness of employment to changes in wages exists for the first two of these groups in Australia. This evidence is reviewed below.[9]

Youth

It is difficult to come to a strong conclusion on the magnitude of own-wage elasticities for young workers in Australia from existing research. Only a few studies have been undertaken, the results of those studies have varied quite widely, and their methodologies have been subject to considerable criticism.

Perhaps the best known study is that of Lewis (1985), which found quite large own-wage employment elasticities for young males and females (−1.80 and −4.58 respectively). Problems relating to model specification and data quality, acknowledged in Lewis' article, have raised doubts about the robustness of those results. More recently, Daly et al. (1998) use workplace-level data to examine the determinants of youth employment and find similarly large own-wage employment elasticities of −2 to −5 in industries with relatively high proportions of youth employment. However, this study has also been subject to some criticism, in particular relating to construction of the wage variable used in regression analysis. There is one other study (Vella & Mackay 1986) which finds relatively large own-wage-type elasticities for youth employees (equal to −2.1 in the long run). This study appears more satisfactory from a methodological point of view, but its limitation is that it is an analysis of the effect of a change in wage subsidies on commencements in a training program for unemployed youth. Hence it is difficult to know to what extent the findings can be extended to the whole youth labour market.

Estimated elasticities from other studies that analyse responsiveness of employment of apprentices and youth to changes in wage subsidies are much smaller. A study by Merrilees (1984) is a careful disaggregated analysis of the effects of changes in labour costs on the employment of five types of apprentices. In this study, for only one group of apprentices is there found to be a significant effect of labour costs on employment. Similar to the Vella and Mackay study, the question about this study by Merrilees must be the extent to which it has application outside the labour market for apprentices. Other aggregate-level studies of youth employment by Merrilees (1979) and Mangan and Johnston (1997) find elasticities that are around or below −1.0, and McCormack (1993) finds evidence of a significant negative own-wage employment elasticity only for part-time female workers. But these studies appear to have some of the same types of problems as the aggregate-level study by Lewis.

To claim to provide a definitive opinion on the magnitude of the youth own-wage employment elasticity would be most foolhardy. Probably it is not possible to do better than Merrilees (1985: 7) who states: 'In summary, the indirect studies point to a teenage wage elasticity of −0.5 to −1.5 with higher elasticities for females, less skilled occupations and private sector employees. Furthermore, it seems likely that the wage elasticity for younger youth (aged under 18) is somewhat higher than for all teenagers.'

Women

The employment consequences of the equal pay policies implemented in Australia in 1969 and 1972 have been examined in several studies. In the first major study for Australia, Gregory and Duncan (1981) found that changes in relative wages of male and female employees – occurring as a result of the equal pay cases – reduced the growth rate of female employment relative to male employment by 1.5 per cent per annum over the six years during which the equal pay policy was introduced. Most of this effect was due to a reduction in employment in female-dominated industries rather than a decrease in the share of females employed within industry groups. Gregory and Duncan interpret these findings as evidence of the high degree of labour market segmentation by gender. Killingsworth has also examined the effects on employment of the Australian equal pay policy of 1972, and concludes in a similar vein that 'the effects of EPEV [equal pay for work of equivalent value] on private wage and salary employment and on full-time employment were quite similar: a negative (and not insubstantial) initial effect that, however, wore off fairly quickly' (1990: 263).

McGavin (1983a, 1983b) has criticized Gregory and Duncan's findings on two main counts. First, he argues that including both public sector and private sector employment in the measure of male/female relative employment causes the effect of relative wage changes in the market sector to be underestimated. Second, it is suggested that by using a measure of employment that is equal to jobs rather than hours worked, Gregory and Duncan overestimate the growth rate in female employment relative to male employment.

Although there is a substantive point in each of McGavin's criticisms, whether his criticisms are empirically important is less clear. Gregory and Duncan (1983b: 62) in a rejoinder argue that even taking account of the criticisms the employment consequences of the equal pay policies are still 'very small'. Gunderson's interpretation of the debate also favours Gregory and Duncan but is a little more cautious: 'Clearly the Australian experience has led to different interpretations of the behavioral responses to what are indisputably dramatic wage gains on the part of females. Perhaps a balanced conclusion is that there was some adverse employment effect but not a substantial one, given the dramatic increase in female relative earnings. Whether this reflects a conscious policy to sustain female employment by increasing their employment in the public sector remains unresolved' (1989: 67).

Summary

A paucity of evidence means that caution is required in seeking to draw conclusions on the effect of a change in labour costs on employment of low-wage workers. Nevertheless, it does seem possible to make some general comments.

The effect on employment of low-wage workers of an increase in their wages will, at least in the long run, be negative. There is no evidence for Australia to suggest that there is a positive relation between wages and employment of low-wage workers, and the most common finding from empirical research is that a statistically significant negative relation exists. Even in the United States, where for some time debate over the effects of changes to minimum wage rates seemed to be about whether those effects were positive or negative, the main issue is now the magnitude of the negative effect (see Debelle & Borland 1998: 138).

Evidence for Australia and from international studies suggests that own-wage employment elasticities are higher for low-skill workers than for high-skill workers. Recent aggregate-level studies of the demand for labour in Australia tend to find wage-employment elasticities of around

–0.5 (for example, Debelle & Vickery 1998; Dungey & Pitchford 1998). So it seems reasonable to expect that own-wage elasticities for low-skill workers should be greater (in absolute value) than –0.5.

International research has found that low-wage workers are a heterogeneous group. The magnitude of the own-wage employment elasticity of low-wage workers is therefore likely to vary depending on how that group is defined. Empirical research on low-skill workers in Australia has mainly concentrated on younger workers (aged 20 years and less); this research generally finds own-wage elasticities that are greater (in absolute value) than –1.0.

Should We Have Wage Regulation for Low-wage Workers?

The introductory section of this chapter described the current debate over the effects of wage regulation for employment of low-wage workers. What can we say about these effects from the review of evidence undertaken thus far?

Research on the magnitude of cross-country differences in below-median earnings dispersion suggests that, relative to the United States, the wage regulation system in Australia may raise the earnings of low-wage employees by about 15 per cent. If we adopt a value of the own-wage employment elasticities for low-wage workers of –0.8 (as an approximate average from the review of Australian empirical studies), this implies an overall negative effect on employment of low-wage workers of about 12 per cent. We take as the population of low-wage workers those people on minimum wage rates, and use the estimate by Richardson and Harding in Chapter 4 that about 500 000 workers were in this group in 1993/94. This gives the net negative effect of wage regulation on employment of low-wage workers of around 60 000 jobs at that time. Expanding the definition of low-wage workers to include workers with earnings in the range just above the minimum wage – this is appropriate where changes to minimum wage rates have spillover effects on wages of other low-wage workers – Richardson and Harding estimate that in 1993/94 there were about one million low-wage workers. Assuming that the reduction in wages for low-wage workers not on minimum wage rates is on average one-half of the reduction for minimum wage workers, then it is estimated that removing wage regulation would have increased employment of low-wage workers in 1993/94 by about 90 000 jobs.[10]

Of course, estimates of the employment effects of wage regulation are very sensitive to changes in any of the assumptions that have been made. For example, increasing the assumed effect of wage regulation to 25 per cent and the own-wage elasticity to –1.5 would raise the estimated net employment effect for low-wage workers to 187 500 to 281 250 jobs; on the other hand, lowering the assumed effect of wage regulation to 10 per cent and the own-wage elasticity of employment to −0.5 would reduce the estimated net employment effect of wage regulation to 25 000 to 37 500 jobs.

What would be the consequences for unemployment of the estimated employment gains from deregulation of wage-setting? Suppose that the estimate of a gain in employment of 60 000 to 90 000 jobs is correct. Assume also that labour force participation will rise by about 0.75 per cent for every 1 per cent increase in employment (Dixon 1994). Then the effect of wage deregulation will be to reduce unemployment by 15 000 to 22 500 persons. This represents about 2–3 per cent of average total unemployment (915 000 persons) in 1993/94. Taking what appear to be the most optimistic estimates of the employment effects of wage deregulation – a gain of 187 500 to 281 250 jobs – gives an estimate of a reduction of 5–8 per cent in the number of persons unemployed.

Is this size of possible gain in employment (and corresponding reduction in unemployment) enough to suggest that wage-setting for low-wage workers should be deregulated? Those in favour of deregulation would argue yes, and make two alternative types of arguments to support their case. One approach is to argue that as well as having negative employment consequences, wage regulation for low-wage workers also has other adverse efficiency consequences and worsens equity, so its overall effect is unambiguously to lower social welfare. An alternative approach, while accepting that wage regulation may have desirable equity consequences, suggests that it is possible to achieve the same equity goals through the social welfare system without having the same adverse employment consequences as wage regulation. Those who oppose deregulation, should they accept that wage regulation has negative employment consequences, would still argue that it provides an overall net benefit to society. The main arguments made against deregulation are that wage regulation for low-wage workers improves equity, that there are reasons why it is better to seek to achieve equity goals in part through the labour market than to rely wholly on the social welfare system, and that there are other efficiency benefits of wage regulation that must be taken into account.

All this suggests there are three main extra questions that need to be answered to make a well-informed judgement on the effects of wage regulation for low-wage workers: what are the effects of wage regulation for low-wage workers on the distribution of income? Should we seek to achieve equity goals through the labour market or instead rely entirely on the social welfare system? What are the efficiency consequences, apart from on employment, of wage regulation for low-wage workers?

Each of these questions is addressed briefly in the remainder of this section. The first two questions are considered at more length in Chapters 4 and 7.

Does wage regulation for low-wage workers improve equity?

Recent research on the distribution of income in Australia provides two main findings of relevance for assessing the consequences of wage regulation (Richardson 1998; Richardson & Harding 1998): unemployed people are disproportionately concentrated at the bottom of the distribution of household income; and low-wage workers are spread fairly evenly throughout the distribution of household income, though somewhat concentrated at the bottom end.

These findings appear to have quite strong implications for the equity consequences of wage regulation. The second finding implies that large reductions in wages of low-wage workers will have only a small effect on household income inequality. (In Chapter 4, Richardson and Harding report that a 30 per cent wage cut for low-wage workers would increase the Gini coefficient from 0.323 to 0.326.) Together with the first finding, this suggests that there would only need to be a relatively small positive effect on the distribution of household income from people who shift from unemployment to employment in order for the wage cut to cause an overall reduction in inequality.

The finding on the position of low-wage workers in the distribution of income is perhaps surprising and merits further comment. One reason for this is that in thinking about the distributional consequences of wage regulation we have been continuing to apply an outdated image of the Australian labour market. In a labour market such as that which prevailed up to the mid-1960s, where most households had only one person employed (the 'male breadwinner') and almost all jobs were full-time, then it seems reasonable to think of the distribution of income between households as being fairly closely related to the distribution of wages and labour market earnings. However, in the labour market that prevails today, with many households having several members employed and a large supply of part-time jobs to facilitate employment by members other than the main earner, it is less sensible to expect a close correlation between the distribution of wages and the distribution of family income.

Equity: using labour market or social security instruments?

One argument in favour of deregulation of wage-setting for low-wage workers suggests that equity outcomes should be achieved through the social security system rather than through the wage regulation system.

Potential benefits of this approach are the absence of an adverse effect on efficiency through wage regulation, and the capacity to target low-income workers and households more directly than through wage regulation (Dawkins & Freebairn, 1997).

But there are counter-arguments for why society might prefer to achieve equity outcomes through the labour market:

1 Political economy factors: the institutional structure of industrial tribunals and trade unions may mean that the wage regulation system is a more credible mechanism than the social security system for ensuring continuing income support for low-skill workers.
2 Coverage of the wage regulation system may be greater than the social security system. This will depend on eligibility criteria for benefits and benefit take-up rates compared to coverage of minimum wage rates.
3 Psychological factors: the utility benefit to a worker from a given amount of labour market earnings may be greater than from receiving an equal amount in social security benefits.
4 Deadweight losses from raising taxation revenue: Campbell and Bond (1997), for example, have estimated that the marginal cost from raising an extra dollar of tax revenue may be as high as twenty cents (see also Freebairn 1995).
5 Capacity to manipulate income measures for social security reporting purposes.

Other efficiency consequences of wage regulation

Efficiency considerations are broader than just the effects of wage regulation on employment. Those in favour of wage regulation tend to argue that a variety of market failures means there is scope for government intervention, through wage regulation, to improve economic efficiency, whereas those against wage regulation adopt the perspective that such intervention is likely to impede the operation of what would otherwise be an efficiently functioning labour market. Some examples follow of debate over the efficiency consequences of wage regulation.

First, centralized control over wage-setting means that it is possible to remove external effects that may arise in wage-setting where decentralized wage-bargaining units do not take account of the overall inflationary consequences of wage outcomes to which they agree (Calmfors & Driffill 1988). Hence one efficiency rationale for wage regulation that allows the scope for centralized wage-setting is the macro-economic benefits. Empirical research in Australia tends to conclude that periods of centralized wage-setting can achieve reductions in the rate of overall wage inflation, though this evidence is not entirely unambiguous (for example, Gregory 1986; Blandy 1990; Chapman et al. 1991). It is also important to note that some theoretical studies have suggested that increases in product market competition due to an expansion in international trade mean that external effects in wage-setting are less important in Australia in the mid-1990s than was the case, for example, in the mid-1980s (Danthine & Hunt 1994; Freeman & Gibbons 1994).

Second, the system of arbitration may have important consequences for transaction costs in the labour market. To the extent that the system is able to settle industrial disputes more quickly than would otherwise occur, this would reduce transactions costs. But it is also argued that by creating an adversarial culture between workers and employers the arbitration system may have actually caused an increase in disputes (Dawkins 1998).

Third, increases in the relative wages of low-wage workers will have various effects additional to any effects on employment. One will be on labour market search activity, whereby information imperfections mean that workers must 'search' for jobs and firms must 'search' for workers. Wage regulation (for example, increases in relative wages for particular types of workers) may affect incentives of workers and firms to undertake search activity and hence affect the job-matching process. Gregg and Manning argue that 'generally, increasing wages will increase the incentives of workers to undertake activities like job search . . . On the other hand, it reduces incentives for firms to engage in recruitment . . . The optimal amount of labour market regulation will be higher the more important are the actions of workers relative to firms in determining labour market outcomes and the more sensitive are those actions to economic incentives' (1996: 417).

Changes in wage rates may also affect workers' incentives to undertake training. One argument is that investment in training will be reduced by regulatory changes to the wage structure. For example, it is sometimes suggested that setting minimum wage rates for younger workers reduces the scope for them to finance general training (through lower wage rates). Alternative approaches, however, suggest that wage regulation may have beneficial effects on training outcomes. Where workers' decisions on how much training to acquire depend on the types of jobs that it is expected will be created by firms, and where firms' decisions on the types of jobs they create depend on expectations of the skill levels of workers, it is possible that there will be multiple equilibria – for example, where workers acquire low skill levels and firms create mainly 'bad' jobs, and where workers acquire high skill levels and firms create mainly 'good' jobs (Snower 1996). Wage regulation may provide one means of forcing the labour market to the high-skill/good job equilibrium.

An overall assessment

A best guess – and it is necessary to emphasize again the extent to which it is a guess – about the employment consequences of deregulating wage-setting for low-wage workers is that such a policy would yield a moderate increase in employment. Using the case of the United States as the benchmark for wage outcomes in the absence of wage regulation, and based on available estimates of the elasticity of labour demand for low-wage workers, it seems that the overall effect of deregulation might be to increase employment of low-wage workers in Australia by about 10–15 per cent. Recent studies suggest that such an increase in employment – deriving from deregulation of wage-setting for low-wage workers – would reduce unemployment and inequality in the distribution of income in Australia, though perhaps by only small amounts.

That is the good news about wage deregulation. The bad news comes in two parts. First, achieving an increase in employment from wage deregulation is likely to be a slow process, and to get an increase of the magnitude described above it will be necessary to deregulate all aspects of the system of wage regulation. Second, there are other adverse consequences from deregulation of wage-setting that seem sufficiently important for them to be weighed against the positive employment and distributional consequences.

Deregulation of wage-setting – or shifting wages of low-wage workers from their current levels to a 'market' level – would not occur overnight. Rather, political factors suggest that deregulation is much more likely to occur as a slow process, as, for example, where relative wages of workers relying on safety-net wage adjustments would fall in each year by the amount of wage adjustments received by other workers. Slow adjustment of wages of course means that employment gains from wage deregulation will be correspondingly slow in coming. Moreover, to obtain the magnitude of employment gains from wage deregulation that have been suggested in this chapter, all aspects of the system of wage regulation would need to be significantly deregulated.

Three main types of adverse consequences from deregulation of wage-setting – already described in the main part of the chapter – appear particularly important in undertaking a cost-benefit analysis of wage regulation. One is the removal of centralized wage-setting as a policy option for responding to periods of high wage inflation. A second is the costs associated with relying entirely on the social security system rather than also using wage-setting institutions to achieve equity goals. The third, and perhaps most important, is the significant shift in bargaining power towards employers and away from workers that would occur following the type of deregulation necessary to achieve a significant improvement in employment. Regulatory or institutional factors, such as trade unions, affect wage outcomes but also have a plethora of other effects on the nature of the employment arrangement between a worker and employer. The shift in bargaining power towards employers that is necessary to achieve 'market' wage outcomes will also inevitably mean that employers have the scope to change working conditions in a range of other ways (for example, unpaid overtime, unjust dismissals, discriminatory behaviour).

Notes

The views expressed in this chapter are those of the authors cited, and should not be attributed to the Australian Competition and Consumer Commission.

1 See also Committee of Review into Australian Industrial Relations Laws and Systems 1985; Dawkins 1997, 1998; Gregory 1996; and Lewis 1997.

2 Adopting a broader definition of regulation – as rules designed to control the actions of individuals and groups who are a party to the production of goods and services – implies that regulation will always be present in an industrial relations system. In this case government regulation might be referred to as external regulation, and the rules associated with firms' internal labour markets as internal regulation (Buchanan & Callus 1993: 518–19).

3 This description of the system of wage regulation necessarily involves some omissions. For example, it might be argued that an important part of the system of wage regulation has been promotion of collective organization of employers (Plowman 1996). One particular area of simplification in our description of the wage regulation system is the abstraction from differences between state and federal systems. Although these systems have generally evolved in a similar manner over time, at any particular point there are likely to be differences between states, and between the state and federal systems in regulation of wage determination and trade unions. A further point is that the scope of the system of wage regulation in Australia is not universal. Not all workers are covered by decisions of arbitration tribunals, and for those workers who are covered, enforcement may be imperfect (for example, Bennett 1994). In May 1990 about 80 per cent of workers should have been covered by wage regulation (ABS, *Award Coverage, Australia*, May 1990, catalogue no. 6315.0). Hancock (1983), Plowman (1986) and Dabscheck (1995) present more comprehensive descriptions of the details of wage regulation in Australia.

4 The Accord was an agreement between the federal Labor government and the ACTU covering a range of economic policy matters, notably wage fixation. During the initial phase of the Accord (Mark I from 1983 to 1985) wage adjustments for workers covered by industrial tribunals were restricted to those obtained from National Wage Cases (for more details, see Lewis & Spiers 1990).

5 For evidence of spillover effects in wage-setting, following increases in minimum wage rates in the United States, see Card and Krueger (1995: 288–97).

6 Of course it is possible to argue that differences in the distributions of observable skills between Australia and the United States – to the extent that they are due to cross-country differences in returns to skills – may also reflect the influence of wage regulation systems in each country. Lower returns to skills in Australia than the United States may mean that, for example, workers in Australia have less incentive than in the United States to acquire extra years of education, so there might be less dispersion in education outcomes in Australia than the United States. But the effect could also operate in the opposite direction: if returns to education were very high in the United States all workers might choose to acquire a university degree, whereas with lower returns in Australia workers might be dispersed across different education levels. As well, other exogenous factors (such as supply-side constraints on higher eductaion in Australia) are likely to be very important in explaining differences in dispersion of observed skills between Australia and the United States. Hence we choose to use differences in returns to characteristics and in unobservable factors as the measure of the potential effect of the wage regulation on the earnings structure.

7 The unit record data used in this analysis were taken from the 1983 and 1991 March Supplement (Annual Demographic File) of the Current Population Surveys (CPS) for the United States, and the 1981/82 and 1989/90 Income Distribution Surveys (IDS) for Australia.

8 Alternative orderings are possible in undertaking the JMP decomposition. The findings presented in Table 3.4 represent the average results from undertaking all possible orderings. For further information see Borland et al. 1996: Appendix 2.

9 For an overall review of Australian studies of labour demand see Lewis & Seltzer 1996.

10 Note that the simulations undertaken are for the specific 'experiment' of deregulation of wage-setting for low-wage workers. Alternative policy changes, such as proposals to adjust award wage rates for youth employees, or the Dawkins–Freebairn plan to freeze safety-net wage adjustments, will affect different types and numbers of employees. Therefore the simulations presented in this chapter should not be seen as directly applicable to evaluation of those alternative policy proposals.

CHAPTER 4

Poor Workers?
The Link between Low Wages, Low Family
Income and the Tax and Transfer Systems

Sue Richardson and Ann Harding

*The main argument for regulation of the wage structure is to increase the wages
and well-being of people at the bottom of the ladder. This has a particular
relevance in today's environment, where real wages for full-time employees at the
bottom of the pay structure have been falling. This chapter takes a close look at
just who are the people whom regulation is, in large part, intended to benefit. It
also traces the effects of a substantial cut in the wages of low-wage workers, to
identify the income distribution and some other consequences of maintaining low
wages above the level they may sink to if left to the market.*

Today men at the bottom of the wage distribution are paid wages that
buy less than they did twenty years ago, while for the high-paid real wages
have risen substantially. Low-wage women workers have seen a rise in
their pay during this period, though inequality in the distribution of pay
among women has risen as it has among men (Borland & Wilkins 1996;
Harding 1997). This development is not confined to Australia, but is also
occurring in other OECD countries (Gottschalk & Joyce 1997).

At the same time, the protections afforded to low-wage workers by the
system of industrial tribunals and by reasonably strong trade unions are
diminishing. This is in the context of high overall unemployment, high
rates of structural change that include a reduction in the absolute levels
of employment in some industries, and increasing competitive pressure
in product markets.[1] In such an environment, individual contracts of
employment for workers whose skills are in excess supply are likely to
depress still further the real value of their wages. In brief, real wages for
low-paid men have fallen, inequality in the dispersion of pay is rising
and, given the current economic and policy environment, these trends
are likely to continue. A key question to which this chapter is addressed
is whether the falls in the real value of low wages and rising inequality of

earnings generates economic hardship among families in a way that warrants regulation to prevent it happening.

On the other side of this question are the calls for cuts in minimum wages and other restrictions on the terms of employment as a remedy for persistent high unemployment. This proposed remedy (discussed in Chapters 2 and 3) for unemployment is based on the simple premise that the demand curve for labour slopes down and externally imposed limits on low pay prevent wages from falling to the level that would equate supply and demand. The crucial element in this story is just how responsive is employment of the low-paid to moderate changes in the level of their pay? Most estimates of the elasticity of demand for low-wage labour conclude that it is low, if it differs from zero at all.[2]

However, this empirical judgement is based on modest movements in the value of minimum wages and does not necessarily hold for large changes.[3] And support for the idea of cutting low wages as a remedy for unemployment is found in the relatively low unemployment currently observed in several countries that now have few barriers to employer-determined wages (the United States, United Kingdom, New Zealand). So there remains a question whether a substantial cut in low wages would be effective in increasing the number of low-wage workers employed, in reducing unemployment and in improving the income position of low-income families. The second main purpose of this chapter is to simulate a large cut in low wages and track the impact of this cut on the distribution of family income, once account has been taken of the offsetting effects arising from the tax and social welfare systems.

The proposition that a cut in low wages and any consequent rise in employment will make workers better off requires that the gains in employment would more than offset the loss of earnings of the currently employed. For this to be true, the elasticity of employment would have to be at least 1 (even on the most favourable assumption that the incomes of those unemployed before taking a newly created job were zero and that the new jobs went entirely to the unemployed). Earlier chapters, in particular Chapter 3, explore this question at length. They conclude that there is no credible evidence that the elasticity of employment exceeds 1. Indeed, in Hancock's view it is close to zero, and Borland and Woodbridge put the upper bound at around −0.75. It is therefore most unlikely that the employment response would be high enough for a wage cut to increase the incomes of the relevant group. But it might be worth taking the risk if unemployment creates distress independent of its associated low income and/or people who receive low wages do not live in low-income families.

In addition, Freeman (1996: 642) makes the point that the level of wages at the bottom can affect who gets the associated jobs. Specifically, it may be that the labour supply of secondary income-earners in middle-income families is more sensitive to the wage level than is the labour supply of unskilled primary-income workers. If so, a fall in the value of low wages would cause a fall in the labour supply of workers from middle-income families, thus reducing the competition for jobs faced by the unskilled primary-income worker.

Note that we can turn on its head the argument that if low-wage workers are predominantly secondary-income earners then it does not matter much if their wages fall so long as employment rises. If most low-wage jobs are occupied by secondary income-earners in middle-income families, then any increase in jobs caused by a pay cut is also likely to go to such workers. Then those low-wage workers who are the primary income-earner (and nobody suggests that there are none of these) will face a pay cut to generate jobs for the secondary income-earners of the middle class. This corollary can only be avoided if the fall in wages changes the composition of labour supply (and employment) in the manner discussed in the preceding paragraph.

The strongest case that a cut in low wages would enhance overall equity and welfare is made where:

1 the elasticity of demand for low-wage workers is high;
2 the current recipients of low wages are secondary earners in comfortably-off families;
3 low-wage jobs are entry-level only and workers do not remain in them for long;
4 a cut in low wages would induce a change in the composition of labour supply, such that the proportion who were unskilled primary income-earners would rise;
5 there are no adverse efficiency effects from paying workers very low wages; and
6 any associated adjustments that must be made to the welfare system to retain an incentive to work are modest.

This chapter looks closely at point 2 and draws some inferences about points 3 and 4.[4]

There is convincing evidence from the United States and some also from the United Kingdom that now only a minority of low-wage workers are heads of families. The rise of the multiple-earner family has had a marked effect in reducing the link between an individual's wage and the income of the family in which he or she lives. So too has the extension of formal education, with many young people combining education and low-paid jobs in their preparation for independent adulthood.[5] Indeed, the US debate has concluded that the link between low wages and low family income (adjusted by an allowance for size of family) is so tenuous that raising minimum wages is a most inefficient way of improving the living standards of the poor.[6]

It is the purpose of this chapter to establish whether the same can be said for Australia, whether the relationship between low wages and low family income is changing, and to what extent the tax and transfer system might ameliorate any regressive effects of a cut in low wages.

Defining Low Wages

People and families can have low weekly or annual earnings either because they receive low pay per hour worked or because they work only a small number of hours. It is important to distinguish between these in understanding the sources of low earnings and in thinking about policy responses.

The debate that forms the context for the question at hand is over the role of imposed wage minima; wage in this sense refers to hourly wage. Thus the discussion will centre on those who have low hourly wage rates (as distinct from low weekly or annual employee earnings).[7]

There has been a long tradition in Australian wage-fixing of seeking to identify fair minimum rates of pay for the low-skilled. It began with the Harvester case in 1907, in which Justice Higgins was required to determine what were 'fair and reasonable wages' for unskilled (and skilled) workers, without any guidance from the legislature on how to interpret the phrase 'fair and reasonable'. In the end he interpreted it to mean 'a condition of frugal comfort estimated by current human standards' (2 CAR 1:4). Even this definition does not translate readily into a dollar figure. Higgins had to decide how much money was needed to provide this condition of frugal comfort and how many people it should be able to support in such a state. Family and employment relations were more homogeneous in Higgins' time and he was able to settle on the predominant family mode of full-time employed husband supporting a family of 'about five'. Of course, single men, of which there were many, would live well above frugal comfort on the same wage. Higgins received evidence on the expenditure levels of his standard family, covering food, rent, groceries and fuel. The information was supplied by workers' wives, by butchers, real estate agents and others (2 CAR 1:6). He concluded that the 3s 7d that was left from the prevailing unskilled wage of 36s per week after meeting these essential expenses was not enough to cover the remaining areas of necessary expenditure. In deciding to increase the minimum wage to 7s a day, he also took account of the wages paid to unskilled workers by reputable employers.

We see here some of the difficult issues that confront attempts to establish what is an unacceptably low wage. Whose expenses is it intended to cover? What items should a family reasonably be able to purchase (and what quality)? What are the wage norms into which any decision must fit? Any imposed minimum must be feasible as well as fair. The norms of an acceptable minimum will vary with the standards of the community, as Higgins clearly recognized. But precisely how?

Eighty years later, the contemporary face of Justice Higgins' court (the Australian Industrial Relations Commission) dealt with the same questions. The so-called 'Living Wage Case' heard by the AIRC during 1996–97 grappled at length with the question of what is an unacceptably low rate of hourly wage. Evidence was adduced on the number of people employed at different low rates and on the living circumstances of people who received low wages. The Commission was exhorted to establish a benchmark of adequacy, somewhat above the Henderson poverty line. In the end, the Commission rejected this approach, drawing attention to the following difficulties:

1 There is no accepted standard of living that constitutes adequacy, and no accepted margin on top of that which should apply to a wage-earner (as distinct from a person not in the labour force).
2 A benchmark approach requires that some norm be specified for the family unit for which the wage is to be adequate: in practice there is a large diversity of family circumstances, in terms of numbers of earners and numbers of people to be supported.
3 The adequacy of an earned income is affected by both taxes and transfers, which 'raises the question whether award wages should be increased or reduced to offset reductions or increases in social welfare benefits' (AIRC 1997: 66).

We agree with the Commission that it is probably not possible to specify a level of wages that would command wide assent as being the minimum amount necessary to ensure an adequate standard of living for workers.[8] In addition to the reasons given by the Commission, we note that a) increasingly people are not working a standard 38–40 hour week and that hours worked as well as wage determine a worker's standard of living and b) increasingly, workers live not only in families of varying size but also in families with varying numbers of paid workers. The total family labour supply, not just that of any one member, now has a large impact on where that family sits in the distribution of family income.[9]

For all these reasons, we do not seek in this chapter to establish a level of low wages that is deemed to be adequate to support a family in frugal or any other specific level of comfort. Rather, we use explicitly arbitrary criteria to choose the level of wages that we will call 'low'. For 1994–95 we choose the level of $10 per hour for an adult and $6 per hour for a person aged less than 21. In 1994–95, 14 per cent of adults and 16 per cent of all wage-earners received these or lower wages. For 1986 we choose an amount that is an equivalent proportion of average weekly ordinary-time earnings, namely $6.70 and $4. In 1986, 9 per cent of adults and 11 per cent of all wage-earners received wages at or below these levels.[10]

We chose $10 on the following grounds:

- it is a low wage, in that it is not much above the lowest adult award wage then available (about $9);
- there was a sufficient number of people earning this wage or less to have a perceptible impact on the distribution of family income;
- there was a sufficient number of people in the sample survey who earned this wage or less to enable decomposition of the low-wage groups into interesting subgroups.

The measure we have chosen is strictly relative. It does not purport to be low in any sense other than that it is at the bottom of the wage distribution. Its relative character is also implied by the manner in which we adjust its absolute value in moving from one period to the next.

The cut-off wage is set at a lower level for young people than it is for adults ($6 rather than $10 in 1994–95). This is in accordance with both the structure of awards and with custom.

In order to establish the sensitivity of our results to the level of wage chosen, we also use a 'minimum' wage, which is commensurate with the minimum rate set by the AIRC in its 1997 Living Wage decision. The AIRC rate was $9.50 per hour. The equivalent value (expressed as a constant proportion of average weekly adult ordinary-time earnings) was $8.50 in mid-1994–95 and $5.70 in mid 1986. We apply this minimum rate only to adults. In 1994–95, 6 per cent of adults received wages at or below this level. The figure for 1986 was 5 per cent.

Data and Method

The data we use come from the unit record files of the ABS survey 'Income and Housing Costs and Amenities, Australia', which we will refer to as the Income Distribution Surveys. These surveys have been conducted at approximately five-year intervals for several decades, though the different surveys are not fully comparable. The size of the survey sample has varied from about 33 000 in 1989/90 to about 14 000 in 1994–95. Since 1995 the surveys have been conducted annually.

These surveys have the uncommon feature, which is necessary for our purposes, of enabling the wage of a person to be matched with her or his family income.[11] They provide very detailed information on sources of income, together with demographic, housing and employment information. We use the 1986 survey in preference to the 1982 survey, because in the latter it is not possible to separate out the earnings of full-time students.

Since respondents were asked their weekly and annual but not their hourly earnings, it is necessary to impute an hourly wage. This is done by dividing usual wage and salary earnings by hours usually worked. Any errors in the data for either hours or earnings will find their way into imputed hourly earnings. About 2.5 per cent of employees had wages of less than $5 per hour in 1994–95, when imputed in this fashion. It is not possible to discern from the data whether these people genuinely had extremely low pay or whether these are data errors. We have retained those with hourly earnings of $1 or more in the analysis, in the interests of not arbitrarily censoring the data. It is possible, though not legal, that some people are indeed employed at very low wage rates; we do not wish to exclude the possibility of genuine very low pay and its growth or decline by deleting such observations from the data. It is also possible that in the black economy low cash wages are paid because their recipients intend to avoid income tax, and are perhaps also drawing social welfare payments. A third possibility arises from the fact that the 1994–95 survey defines as an employee a person who works for his or her own company. The problems of obtaining accurate information about the pay and income of self-employed people are well known. Unfortunately it is not possible to identify and hence delete such self-employed 'employees' from the 1994–95 sample.

For the surveys before 1994–95, hours worked were grouped into intervals.[12] This adds another imprecision, since we can only guess at the hours actually worked by people within the interval. For 1986 we have assumed that the average hours worked in each hour interval is the same as that for 1994–95 (which can be calculated from actual hours worked).

There are people who report working very long hours (50 or more per week). Other ABS surveys show that this group (and the group working a very small number of hours) has been growing as a fraction of the workforce (ABS 1995). Most of this growth in long hours has been in unpaid overtime, chiefly among managers and professionals. Because wage is calculated as weekly earnings divided by reported weekly hours worked, then a low wage can arise either from low earnings or from long hours. Our interest in the low-paid arises from a concern that they may not be earning enough to give them an adequate income. This is not an issue for people whose hourly wage is low solely because they report working very long hours. For this reason, in the calculation of hourly wage we impose a cap of 40 on the hours worked in a person's main job. Specifically, if a person reports working more than 40 hours, we calculate his or her hourly wage as weekly earnings divided by 40. It is therefore still possible for a person who works full-time to have a low hourly wage, but this must be caused by having a low weekly wage and not just arise from reporting working hours well beyond the standard working week.

We exclude self-employed workers (other than those describing themselves as an employee of their own firm), because of the unreliable relationship between reported earnings and actual material benefit derived from the business.[13] Thus the workers for whom wages are calculated are all employees who work for wages or salaries and receive $1 per hour or more. This includes youth and those who work part-time or part year.[14]

The purchasing power of a prime-age family is moderately well reflected by its income. But this income needs to be net of income tax and to take account of the number of people that it supports. Thus we use as the measure of income of the family, income from all sources, minus imputed income tax (as calculated by the ABS) and adjusted by an equivalence scale. There is no equivalence scale that commands wide assent as best reflecting the income needs of families of different composition. The choice of equivalence scale is therefore somewhat arbitrary, but it can make a difference to the results. We mostly use the OECD scale, which is widely used internationally.[15] It differs from the Henderson scale, which is widely used in Australia, in that the Henderson scale gives a lower weight to children and adjusts for workforce status.

For most of the subsequent detailed analysis, we relate the wage of the individual to the annual equivalent disposable income of the family in which they reside.[16]

Who Are the Low Paid?

We begin by assessing whether there is anything distinctive about the people who receive low pay. We would expect them largely to be employed in jobs that do not require high levels of skill. We look also at the family circumstances of low-wage workers. On the one hand, workers may be supporting more than just themselves on their earnings. On the other hand, they may benefit from the incomes of other members of their family.

Low-wage workers

Table 4.1 shows the proportion of low-wage workers (adults with a wage of $10 or less and juniors with a wage of $6 or less in 1994–95, or their equivalent for 1986) with specific workforce and demographic

Table 4.1 Characteristics of low-wage and all employees, 1994–95 and 1986

	Low-wage workers 1986			Low-wage workers 1994/95			All workers 1994/95		
	Female	Male	All	Female	Male	All	Female	Male	All
Number weighted ('000)	330	220	550	535	523	1058	2879	3795	6674
Number unweighted	548	365	913	547	493	1040	2923	370	6625
Per cent of all workers	16	7	11	19	14	16	100	100	100
Per cent part-time	53	17	38	44	17	31	38	8	21
Age									
age 15–20	10	17	13	11	17	14	11	9	10
age 21–24	14	19	16	16	18	17	12	10	11
age 25–34	25	22	23	20	18	19	25	26	26
age 35–54	46	33	40	47	36	42	47	46	46
Education qualifications									
still at school	4	4	4	5	7	6	2	3	2
none	67	62	65	68	58	67	54	45	50
certificate/diploma	24	28	26	21	29	25	31	40	36
degree	4	6	5	6	6	6	12	12	12
Marital status									
married	68	46	59	61	47	54	61	62	62
never married	28	49	36	30	47	39	31	32	31
separated, widowed etc	4	4	4	9	6	7	8	6	7
Industry									
whole & retail trade	24	25	25	26	32	29	22	21	21
finance & business	10	7	9	14	8	11	16	12	14
community services	24	10	18	19	5	12	27	8	17
personal & other services	13	12	12	18	11	15	12	8	10
manufacturing	17	12	15	12	17	15	10	20	15
Occupation									
managers	3	15	8	3	9	6	4	12	8
professionals	5	8	6	4	7	6	14	15	15
para-professionals	3	5	3	2	1	2	8	6	7
tradespersons	5	22	12	4	25	14	3	22	14
clerks	21	4	14	24	5	14	31	8	18
sales & personal service	27	13	21	33	12	23	25	9	16
plant and machine op	8	8	8	5	10	7	2	11	7
labourer	29	26	28	25	32	28	13	18	16

Table 4.1 (Cont.)

	Low-wage workers 1986			Low-wage workers 1994/95			All workers 1994/95		
	Female	Male	All	Female	Male	All	Female	Male	All
Family relationship									
husband+dep									
children	–	29	12	–	24	12	–	37	21
wife+dep children	48	–	29	34	–	17	34	–	15
other husband	–	17	7	–	22	11	–	24	14
other wife	20	–	12	27	–	14	27	–	12
lone parent+dep									
children	2	0	1	5	1	3	4	1	2
full-time student									
child age 15–24	4	7	5	7	9	8	5	3	4
other child aged									
15+	12	26	18	14	23	19	12	14	13
unrelated group	7	12	9	4	9	6	7	9	8
live alone	3	6	4	5	11	8	8	9	9
other	4	3	3	4	2	3	3	2	2

characteristics. It also shows how these differ from the whole population of wage and salary earners.

The first point to note is that the proportion of wage and salary earners whose wages are below the thresholds has risen over the eight years, from 11 to 16 per cent. This is another symptom of rising inequality, though in itself it says nothing about whether low-wage workers are worse off in real terms.[17] In fact the real value of our threshold level of low wages has risen by about 2 per cent over the period 1986–94. The increase in the proportion of low-wage earners has been particularly pronounced for men. The proportion of men whose wage is below the threshold has doubled from 7 to 14 per cent, and the fraction of low-wage workers who are men has increased from 40 to 49 per cent.

There has been little change in the age distribution of low-wage workers, which continues to look much like the age distribution of wage-earners in general. People under the age of 25 comprised 31 per cent of low-wage workers in 1994–95 (29 per cent in 1986) and 21 per cent of all workers. Thus while young people are disproportionately likely to be low-wage, 70 per cent of low-wage workers are prime age. This last point is important, for it makes it clear that low wages are not confined to new entrants to the workforce, or to young people who are living at home. It suggests that people are at risk of low wages at any stage in their working lives, and it cannot be assumed that low wages will be transitory for them.[18]

There has been little change in the educational qualifications of low-wage workers, with about two-thirds having no qualifications, compared to only half for all wage and salary earners. What has changed for women is the proportion who are full-time workers: these now are a majority of low-wage women. Indeed, 70 per cent of all low-wage workers work full-time: we are not describing a group who have a marginal attachment to paid employment or who give such work a low priority in their lives.

There has been little change in the marital status of low-wage workers, aside from some fall in the proportion of women who are married. This fall is reflected in the rise in the proportion who are separated or divorced. Nearly half the low-wage men and over 60 per cent of the low-wage women are married.

There has been some change in the industries in which low-wage workers are mainly found. Over the period the share found in wholesale and retail trade, and for women, in personal and other services, rose; low-wage workers are disproportionately to be found in these two industries. The share found in community services fell. Wholesale and retail trade continues to be the predominant employer of low-wage workers. It is not surprising then that by 1994–95 one-third of low-wage women were employed as sales and personal services workers. In contrast to the women, almost one-quarter of low-wage men were tradespersons, and this share has risen. While the trades are not generally well paid, there is a particular poignancy about the high representation of these skilled men among the low-paid.[19] Between them, labourers and tradespeople make up well over half the low-paid men. The low-paid women are predominantly labourers, clerks and sales and personal service workers. Whereas less than one-fifth of all male employees were labourers, they represented a third of all low-paid men.

Parents with dependent children declined as a proportion of all low-wage workers between 1986 and 1994, from 41 to 32 per cent (including sole parents). The principal change was in the sharp drop in the proportion of low-wage women who were married with dependent children. But even by 1994–95, they still represented a third of low-wage women. There was also a doubling, though from a small base, of the proportion who lived alone.

The low-paid in 1994–95 can be characterized as evenly divided between the sexes, spread across the age groups, married, with relatively little formal education, employed full-time, in wholesale and retail trade and working as tradespersons, labourers, clerks and personal service workers. About a quarter of low-wage men live at home with their parents but are not students. This broad characterization has changed from 1986 only in the increased proportion who are male.[20]

In sum, the major changes over the period have been the rise in the proportion of all wage and salary earners who are paid below the threshold used in this analysis, and of men among the low-paid. There has also been a drop in the proportion of low-wage workers who are mothers of dependent children.

Minimum-wage workers

Table 4.2 gives the same information for people who receive a wage approximately equivalent to the federal minimum wage set by the AIRC in 1997. Unlike Table 4.1, it refers only to adults aged 21 years or more. Note that, for both periods, the absolute number of people in the sample who receive the minimum wage or less is quite small (403 and 373). This is the main reason for setting a higher threshold for much of the analysis.

The increasing masculinization of the low-wage group is apparent for minimum-wage workers but rather less strongly so. This apart, the description given for Table 4.1 is hardly changed when reference is made to Table 4.2 instead. The main difference between the two low-wage groups is that a higher proportion of those on minimum wages are married and have dependent children. This is mainly because the minimum-wage group excludes youth.

A Changing Composition of Supply?

A comparison of Tables 4.1 and 4.2 provides some tentative evidence on the character of the supply curve of labour at the low-wage end. It was argued above that the case for cutting low wages in order to assist the unemployed would be stronger if the composition of the supply of labour altered as wages fell: specifically, if middle-income secondary wage-earners had reservation wages that exceeded the new lower wage rates, but low-income primary wage-earners did not. We take the characteristics of primary income-earners to include working full-time and being of adult age (especially over age 25), and/or living in one's own independent family and/or having dependent children.

The workers who are observed to have jobs that pay $10 or less or jobs paying $8.50 or less do not necessarily represent all those who would be willing to work at those wages. Unemployment rates were high in both 1986 (over 8 per cent) and 1994–95 (around 10 per cent). Thus it is more likely that the observed employment is on the demand curve for low-wage workers than on the supply curve. For the purpose of exploring the hypothesis that those who would get very low wage jobs are more needy than those who get higher-paid jobs, it is equally useful

Table 4.2 Characteristics of adult minimum-wage employees, 1994–95 and 1986

	Minimum-wage workers 1986			Minimum-wage workers 1994–5		
	Female	Male	All	Female	Male	All
Number weighted ('000)	141	109	251	198	174	372
Number unweighted	244	159	403	208	165	373
Per cent of all workers	7	3	5	7	5	6
Per cent part-time	67	18	46	47	18	33
Age						
age 15–20	na	na	na	na	na	na
age 21–24	14	25	19	14	19	16
age 25–34	28	18	23	28	16	22
age 35–54	49	44	46	48	47	48
Education qualifications						
still at school	4	3	3	2	2	2
none	62	55	59	66	50	58
certificate/diploma	27	31	29	26	41	33
degree	7	11	9	7	6	7
Marital status						
married	79	58	70	69	59	64
never married	16	37	25	21	32	26
separated, widowed etc	5	5	5	11	9	10
Industry:						
whole & retail trade	21	17	19	18	23	20
finance & business	12	7	10	16	9	13
community services	24	13	20	20	7	14
personal & other services	18	14	16	25	12	19
manufacturing	12	12	12	7	11	9
Occupation						
managers	2	22	11	7	14	10
professionals	7	10	8	9	9	9
para-professionals	2	5	3	2	1	2
tradespersons	4	22	12	4	21	12
clerks	22	5	15	23	5	14
sales & personal service	29	7	19	29	9	20
plant and machine op	4	10	7	1	12	6
labourer	31	18	25	25	30	27
Family relationship						
husband+dep children	–	37	16	–	31	15
wife+dep children	57	–	32	39	–	21
other husband	–	21	9	–	27	13
other wife	22	–	13	29	–	16
lone parent+dep children	3	1	2	5	3	4
first student child aged 21–24	na	na	na	3	1	2

Table 4.2 (Cont.)

	Minimum-wage workers 1986			Minimum-wage workers 1994–5		
	Female	Male	All	Female	Male	All
other child aged 15+	7	20	13	11	16	13
unrelated group	6	11	6	3	9	6
live alone	3	9	2	6	11	8
other	2	1	2	3	2	2

Note: Cells containing 11 per cent or less of the minimum wage group are subject to relative sampling error of about 25 per cent or more and should be treated with caution.

to identify demand as it is to identify supply. The key issue is to identify who gets the jobs, rather than who seeks the jobs. And the concern to increase employment opportunities (e.g. by cutting wages) is strong only while unemployment is high (i.e. while employment is constrained by demand rather than by supply). The information contained in the two tables is thus appropriate to give some insight into whether those employed at very low wages are more heavily dependent on those wages for their standard of living than are those employed at somewhat higher wages.

The characteristics of minimum-wage workers which support the view that they have a higher proportion of primary income-earners than do low-wage workers are the larger proportion who are married with dependent children, and the lower proportion who are living in the parental home.

These differences, however, can be fully explained by the fact that Table 4.2 excludes workers under the age of 21 whereas Table 4.1 does not. The only other substantial difference between low-wage and minimum-wage workers is that the latter have a higher proportion who worked part-time in 1986 (but not in 1994–95). Thus the evidence of these two tables is that minimum-wage and low-wage earners look very much alike, allowing for the fact that only the latter incorporates young people. If people who currently earn low wages are generally not the primary income-earner for their family, then those who earn even lower wages are not either. Thus to sustain the argument that an expansion of very low wage jobs will disproportionately benefit primary income-earners, it is necessary to demonstrate that new occupants of such jobs will somehow be different from the current occupants.

This view is given further support by an examination of low-wage earners based on the 1990 Income Distribution Survey (Richardson 1998). There, low-wage workers were compared with workers who earned $1 an hour more. The lower-wage group were *less* likely than those earning a bit more to be primary income-earners working full-time and more likely to be living in the parental home and working part-time. The difference was substantial only in the propensity to work part-time.

On balance, the evidence presented here, tentative though it is, provides little support for the view that the socio-demographic characteristics of people who get jobs at the minimum wage are much different (specifically, that they are more likely to be primary income-earners) from those who get jobs at a wage that is 15 per cent higher. This in turn makes it more difficult to argue that a cut in the value of low wages will increase the proportion of very low paid jobs that go to primary income-earners.

Does Low Pay Mean Low Income?

The relationship between low pay and low family (equivalent, after tax) income has been extensively explored elsewhere (Richardson 1998). We here see whether this relationship has changed over the period 1986–94.

Figure 4.1 ranks all adult workers who received a wage at or below the minimum, according to the equivalent *annual* after-tax income of the family in which they live.[21] There are two sets of comparisons in the figure. One is between 1994–95 and 1986. The other locates minimum-wage workers in two different income distributions. The distribution labelled 'all' has divided the entire population into deciles, based on the annual equivalent disposable income of the family in which they live. The 10 per cent of Australians (including children) with the lowest equivalent family incomes are thus in the bottom decile. We refer to this as the 'family income distribution'. If minimum-wage workers were located across the distribution of equivalent disposable family income in the same way as were the population at large, then 10 per cent of them would be found in each decile.

The second distribution, labelled 'in lf', only includes a subset of the whole population, namely those individuals who live in families which have a member in the labour force (this includes unemployed and self-employed people, as well as wage-earners). We refer to this distribution as the 'workforce family income distribution'. Thus the bottom decile in this case consists of the 10 per cent of Australians, living in workforce families, who are at the bottom of the workforce family income distribution.

People can have an annual equivalent disposable income that ranks them differently from their wage for a number of reasons. The principal ones are:

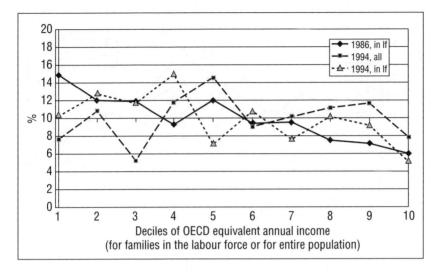

Figure 4.1 Proportion of minimum-wage earners in deciles of annual equivalent disposable family income, 1994 and 1986

1 that family income includes income from all sources for all members of the family adjusted by the equivalence scale;
2 that income is annual whereas wage is hourly: the number of hours worked at the imputed hourly rate may vary across the year; and
3 the two distributions refer to different points in time, with current low-wage earners not necessarily being low-wage earners in the preceding financial year; however, the intent of measuring annual income is to capture a better impression of the normal living standards of low-wage families.

As is to be expected, minimum-wage earners are concentrated more heavily in the bottom of the workforce family distribution than among the family distribution. The latter group includes people in families which rely on means-tested social welfare, such as the age pension and invalidity benefits, as their principal source of income.

Broadly speaking, the location of minimum-wage workers in the distribution of income among families in the labour force is similar for the two years depicted. Not much has changed. In both years, a disproportionate number are found in the bottom three or four deciles. At the same time, substantial numbers are found in all but the highest decile. An examination of the distribution by sex shows that the picture for men and women is very similar.

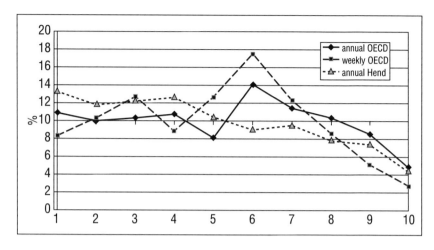

Figure 4.2 Proportion of low-wage earners in deciles of annual and current equivalent disposable family income for families in the labour force, by gender, 1994

Figure 4.2 extends the analysis in three ways. First, it examines the distribution for low-wage rather than minimum-wage workers (i.e. those earning $10/6 per hour or less, rather than those earning $8.50 per hour or less). Second, it examines whether using *current weekly* rather than *annual* equivalent disposable income would change our conclusions about the living standards of low-wage workers. Third, it looks at whether using the Henderson rather than the OECD equivalence scale would affect such conclusions. The conclusions from Figure 4.2 are that:

1 those on minimum ($8.50 or less) wages are more densely located at the bottom of the distribution of workforce family income than are those on the higher ($10 or less) wages;

2 the use of *weekly* rather than *annual* workforce family income does not greatly affect the picture, although somewhat fewer low-wage earners are in the higher deciles when current weekly family income is used; and

3 the use of the Henderson scale, which gives a lower weight to children and takes some account of the costs of working, produces a greater concentration of low-wage workers in the lower deciles of the workforce family income distribution.

Figure 4.3 gives the same information for an important subset of the low-wage group – those who are aged 25–55, have dependent children and are employed for at least twenty hours a week. This group is selected to contain only (but not all) people whose low wage is likely to be viewed as

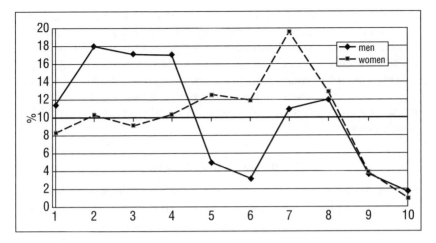

Figure 4.3 Proportion of low-wage workers with dependent children and working 20 hours or more per week by decile of annual equivalent disposable income, by gender, 1994

problematic. In order to have enough observations in the sample for the disaggregation embodied in Figure 4.3, it is necessary to use the higher ($10) definition of low wage. Even then, there are only about 250 survey respondents in the sample survey data, so the estimates should be treated with some caution. Such low-wage parents made up a smaller proportion of all low-wage earners by 1994 – down from 29 per cent in 1986 to 23 per cent in 1994. In addition to this encouraging decline, there was a small fall in the proportion of such low-wage parents in the bottom quintile of the workforce family income distribution (from 23 per cent in 1986 to 21 per cent in 1994).

Such low-wage fathers are concentrated much more heavily at the bottom of the workforce family income distribution than are the low-wage mothers. Low-wage mothers are predominantly found in the middle of the income distribution. The change over the period 1986–94 has been to make this difference between men and women less pronounced. A *quarter* of low-wage men (of prime age and with dependent children) were in the bottom *decile* of the workforce family income distribution in 1986. This had fallen to 11 per cent by 1994–95, while the proportion in deciles 2 and 3 had risen. Overall, the concentration of low-wage men in the lowest three deciles remained high, though it fell from 50 to 46 per cent. The movement out of the bottom decile presumably reflects the expansion of family social welfare payments during this decade – a shift which has also been revealed in other studies of income equality (Harding 1997).

Overall, the evidence presented so far does not give many grounds for
concern that low wages are increasingly precipitating families into the
bottom of the income distribution. Low wages are quite strongly linked
with low family income, but no more in 1994–95 than in 1986. The
correlation of low wages with low income is greater if the Henderson
equivalence scale is used, and if we focus on minimum wages (especially
for men with dependent children), and the distribution of workforce
family income.

Simulating a Cut in Low Wages

One of the principal reasons for being interested in whether low-wage
workers live in low-income families, and whether this is changing, is that
the level of wages which low-wage workers receive can be affected by
government policy decisions. State governments can legislate directly for
a minimum or other wage, and both the Commonwealth and the State
industrial tribunals set minima not only for the least skilled work but for
work of many types. Are policy-determined changes to legal wage
minima an effective way in which to alter the distribution of earnings
and income?

The previous section has shown that an increase in the level of minimum wages would make the workforce family income distribution
somewhat more equal, even though it is not a very tightly targeted form
of redistribution. This conclusion is based on a strong 'all other things
equal' assumption. But other things will change, including perhaps
some change in the number of jobs available and certainly some change
in the level and distribution of tax and welfare payments.

The Australian social welfare system is tightly targeted. This means
that eligibility for most benefits, and the level of benefits received, is
strongly linked to the level of private income received by the family. One
effect of this is to produce very high effective marginal tax rates for many
beneficiaries, especially those who have some employment income (see,
for example, Ingles 1997; NATSEM 1997; Gregory et al. in this volume).
Twenty years ago, families that received social welfare payments (apart
from the modest levels of child allowances) and families that had wage
income were almost separate groups. With the introduction of substantial means-tested payments to employed families with dependent
children, the overlap between families with earned income and families
with substantial welfare payments has increased. In 1990 almost half of
families with a low-wage earner received social welfare benefits of $500
or more in a year. These benefits, however, comprised only about 15 per
cent of their disposable income, on average.[22] In 1997 employed families
in the lowest quintile of the family income distribution were estimated to

have received also about 15 per cent of their income in the form of social welfare payments, while families in the top half of the distribution received almost nothing (Joint Governments' Submission 1998: 185).

One consequence of very high EMTRs, and the one that receives most attention, is that a rise in earned income does little to increase the disposable income of the family. The other side of this effect is that a *fall* in earned income, for example because of a cut in wages, does little to *reduce* the disposable income of the family. An assessment of the consequences of a cut, or rise, in the level of minimum wages needs to take the EMTR into account. It matters both for the distribution of disposable income among families and for the government budget. A cut in wages that is largely offset by a rise in welfare payments and/or fall in tax payable has the effect of transferring the responsibility for providing an adequate income for employees from business to the tax-payer. It is important to have some idea of the size of this transfer, in assessing the wisdom or otherwise of a deliberate change in the level of low wages.

We report here the results of a simulated cut in low wages, where account has been taken of the consequent effects on tax payable and social welfare benefits received. The simulation has been done using NATSEM's STINMOD model.[23] No behavioural responses are modelled, so that employment and unemployment are not altered in the simula-tion. The tax/transfer system is that which prevailed in 1997, while the characteristics and incomes of the population have been updated from the survey period of 1994–95 to match May 1997 benchmark data.

Three scenarios have been examined. In each of these, wages of $10 or less for an adult and $6 or less for those under 21 have been cut by a specified percentage, while wages of $10–15 for an adult and $6–9 for a junior have been cut by half that percentage. Note that in 1997 a wage of $10 per hour was only just above the AIRC minimum of $9.50.

- scenario 1: wages are cut by 10 per cent and 5 per cent
- scenario 2: wages are cut by 20 per cent and 10 per cent
- scenario 3: wages are cut by 30 per cent and 15 per cent.

The simulation assumes that wages of $10/6 or less are cut by decision of the industrial tribunals. If such a cut were to be fully reflected in the wages paid, then it is most unlikely that wages some small distance above these minima would remain unaffected. Indeed, the tribunals may consciously reduce these nearby wages as well, in the interests of comparative wage justice and to prevent sharp discontinuities in the wage structure. Whether through the market or through the tribunals, it is probable that wages only somewhat above those that have been cut will also fall. Thus the simulation incorporates falls in the wages of those who receive up to 50 per cent above the minimum that has been cut.

The simulated wage cuts are as high as 30 per cent. One reason to go this high is to see in magnified form the consequences of a wage cut for disposable income, taxes and transfers. The other reason is that it has been estimated that a cut of this magnitude may be required in Australia to have a substantial effect on boosting employment among the low-paid (Gregory 1996; Gregory et al. in this volume).

The simulation is unable to track any behavioural responses to the cut in wages, on either the supply or demand for labour or on prices and profits. Thus what it does is assume that the labour force status of all workers remains unchanged, as does their family status. The first-round effect of a cut in wages is tracked to its impact on family income and on tax payable and welfare benefits received. The money saved by employers is treated as if it just disappears from the economy, which of course is not what would actually happen. Rather, the reduction in labour costs would result in some combination of falls in prices (especially for products whose production is intensive in low-wage labour), rises in profits and perhaps some rise in employment. In the absence of a full computable general equilibrium model, these second- and subsequent-round effects cannot be quantified. What the simulation does enable us to do is to see who pays for any gains in profits and employment and the falls in prices, and how much it costs low-wage workers. It is worth noting that the main areas of employment of low-wage workers are in retail and wholesale trade and in business and personal services. A fall in the prices of these wholesale and retail services is *prima facie* likely to be mildly progressive in its impact, since low-income families spend a higher proportion of their income on goods and services than do high-income families (which are more likely to save). A fall in the price of business and personal services, in contrast, is likely to be of most benefit to higher-income families, who are more likely to eat out, employ home help, travel and so on.

Aggregate effects

Table 4.3 summarizes the effects of a wage cut under each of the scenarios on average (per family) total private income, cash welfare payments received, income tax payable and disposable income.[24] The values of these variables for the base (or pre-change) case are included to facilitate comparison. These variables are also reported in aggregate form, for the economy as a whole, in order to identify the effect on the Commonwealth Government budget. Just over 40 per cent of families (4.3 million) are affected by the wage cuts. Eleven per cent of all families

Table 4.3 Estimated impact of simulated wage cuts on families, 1997

	Average weekly value per family $				Total for all families: annual $m			
	Total income	Cash transfers	Income tax	Disposable income	Total income	Cash transfers	Income tax	Disposable income
All families								
Base	$664	$88	$136	$527	$327 751	$43 541	$67 356	$260 395
10/5% cut	$656	$89	$134	$522	$324 136	$43 818	$66 174	$257 963
20/10% cut	$649	$89	$132	$517	$320 526	$44 099	$65 033	$255 493
30/15% cut	$642	$90	$129	$512	$316 930	$44 394	$63 925	$253 005
Families affected by wage cuts only								
Base	$776	$35	$158	$617	$145 803	$6 630	$29 777	$116 026
10/5% cut	$757	$37	$152	$605	$142 188	$6 907	$28 595	$113 593
20/10% cut	$738	$38	$146	$591	$138 578	$7 188	$27 454	$111 123
30/15% cut	$718	$40	$140	$578	$134 982	$7 483	$26 347	$108 635
$ difference between scenarios								
10–5% cut	–$19	$2	–$6	–$12	–$3 615	$277	–$1 182	–$2 433
20–10% cut	–$38	$3	–$12	–$26	–$7 225	$558	–$2 323	–$4 903
30–15% cut	–$58	$5	–$18	–$39	–$10 821	$853	–$3 430	–$7 391

(1.3 million) have wage-earners who suffer the larger cuts, because they earn $10 or less if an adult or $6 or less if under 21.

The key points displayed by Table 4.3 are:

1 wage cuts of different magnitude have a proportional effect, so that the impact of a 30 per cent cut is about three times that of a 10 per cent cut;
2 the impact of a large (30/15 per cent) cut in low wages on average family private income is small, at 3.3 per cent, when considered across all families;
3 the tax and transfer system ameliorates by a small amount the fall in private family income, so that on average, disposable income falls by the lesser amount of 2.8 per cent;
4 most of the offsetting effect of the tax and transfer system comes through reduced personal income tax liability rather than through increased social welfare payments;
5 the overall effect on the Commonwealth government budget is a net $4.2 billion increased deficit or reduced surplus: $3.4 billion of this arises from reduced personal income tax revenue;
6 the fall in family private income is almost $11 billion and the fall in family disposable income is $7 billion; and
7 on average, in the 'pre-change' world, cash transfers comprise 13 per cent of family income and income taxes about 20 per cent.

The results of this simulation provide no support for the view that low-wage workers face very high EMTRs. On average, that rate is 40 per cent, in that the rise in welfare payments and cut in tax payments triggered by the cut in wages represent 40 per cent of the loss in wage income. Furthermore, most of the offset comes from reduced tax liability. Only 8 per cent of the loss in wage income is compensated for by a rise in welfare payments. The obverse of these results is that on average 60 per cent of a rise in wage earnings by the low- and medium-wage earner would be retained as disposable income. The fact that on average the EMTR is not high does not mean, of course, that it cannot be high for particular groups. Gregory et al. in Chapter 7 have shown that it is indeed high for families that have a number of children and who receive medium-level earnings.

The only respectable rationale for a deliberate policy to cut the value of low wages is that this is intended to increase employment and thereby to reduce unemployment. We raise but do not answer the question whether $4.3 billion 'spent' by the government via the consequences for its budget of a large cut in low wages would do more to increase employment than the same amount spent directly on employing people (even ignoring the value of the services provided to the government by the

extra people they employ). Chapman, in Chapter 6, produces parameters that suggest that $4 billion spent on a combination of wage
subsidy programs and public sector employment for the long-term
unemployed would generate, as a best estimate, about 700 000 jobs.

The lower panel in Table 4.3 provides the same information for only
those families that are affected by the wage cut (rather than all families,
both losers and non-losers). Again there is a uniform relationship
between the size of the wage cut and the size of the effects on total and
disposable income and on cash transfer payments and tax payable.

When the wage is cut by 30/15 per cent, the affected families on
average experience a 7 per cent (or $58) fall in their private weekly
income and a 6 per cent (or $39) fall in their disposable income. Income
tax liability falls by $18 per week and welfare payments rise by $5. This
reaffirms the earlier conclusions that the income tax system is much
more important in ameliorating the decline in wages than is the cash
transfer system and that EMTRs are not unusually high. The typical
affected family received 6 per cent of its disposable income from social
welfare benefits before the wage cut and 7 per cent after it. On the other
side, its income tax burden falls only slightly, remaining at about 20 per
cent of gross income.

The relative importance of the tax as distinct from the cash transfer
system is explicable by the fact that those families that are affected by the
wage cut must, by definition, contain members who are in employment.
The cash welfare payments for which they are eligible are largely confined to payments for children, and some rent assistance and rebates for
non-employed spouses.

Separate calculations reveal that the family which is worst hit by the
30/15 per cent wage cut loses $185 per week in disposable income. The
family that has the largest offsetting contribution from social welfare
benefits gains an extra $134 per week from that source. There are a few
families that see their disposable income rise (at most by $17 per week)
as a consequence of the wage cut. The fall in private income has brought
some families below the threshold that makes them eligible for several
forms of welfare assistance (including more-than-minimum family payment). Together these cash welfare payments (added to reduced tax
liability) more than offset the loss in earnings.

Effects on inequality

Who bears the burden of the wage cuts? We have already seen that low-
wage earners are found right across the distribution of working family
disposable income, but are overrepresented at the bottom end of that
distribution. People who earn an hourly wage of $10–15 look even more

Table 4.4 Estimated poverty rates before and after the wage cuts, 1997

Poverty rates	Base	10/5% cut	20/10% cut	30/15% cut
Income units	7.3	7.7	8.2	8.8
Adults and dependent children	6.7	6.9	7.4	7.8
Dependent children only	6.9	6.9	7.4	7.8

like the working population at large than do lower-wage earners. Thus we expect that the effects of a cut in low to medium wages will be felt across the whole income distribution, with some emphasis on those in the lower half of the distribution. It requires the more complex procedure of simulation, however, to track the net effects on the distribution of family income, once allowance is made for the induced effects of the tax and cash transfer systems.

One way of assessing the change in aggregate inequality is to examine Gini coefficients, which range between 0 when income is equally distributed and 1 when one person holds all the income in society. The Gini coefficient for OECD equivalent current disposable family income for all persons in the pre-change world is 0.323. The Gini increases steadily by 0.001 as each scenario progresses, reaching 0.326 after the 30/15 per cent wage cut. It is evident that the cut in wages increases overall inequality, but only by a small amount.

A second perspective is provided in Table 4.4. The data here are only for people who live in a family that has a member in the labour force. We take an arbitrary 'poverty' level, namely half the median income for the distribution of equivalent current disposable income in the pre-change world, and ask how many people have incomes below this level in each of the scenarios.

The proportion of people, of children and of income units below the poverty line rises as wages are cut, but the increases are not large. A wage cut of 30/15 per cent increases poverty among income units by 1.5 percentage points, or 21 per cent, after accounting for the offsetting effects of the tax and transfer system. The proportion of children living below the threshold also rises – by 16 per cent for the 30/15 wage cut – while the proportion of all persons living in working families that are in poverty increases by 13 per cent.

For a more detailed look at the redistributive consequences of a wage cut, we turn now to graphs of the entire income distribution. Figure 4.4 shows how the losses in income from the wage cut are distributed across the different deciles of the income distribution. After the wage cut the average income of families and the location of many families in the

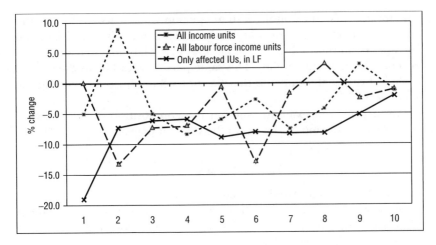

Figure 4.4 Estimated percentage change in disposable income for different types of families, by decile of OECD equivalent disposable current family income, 1997

income distribution changes. The distribution reported in Figure 4.4 is after this reshuffling has occurred. Thus the change shown for decile 1 compares the average income of families that were in the first decile in the base case with the average income of families that were in the first decile after the wage cut. The families need not be the same, and the income levels that define the decile boundaries have fallen in response to the wage cut.

With this in mind, we learn from Figure 4.4 that *affected families* in the first decile had substantial falls of almost one-fifth in their disposable income as a result of the wage cut. The losses were small for the top two deciles and about a constant proportion for the remaining deciles. For all families in the labour force the reshaping of decile boundaries clearly resulted in some strange effects as families shift deciles and average decile incomes vary.

The impact on the first decile of the distribution for the *whole population* is necessarily small, since not many people in that decile are in the labour force and hence at risk of a wage cut. On average, families in deciles 3 to 8 were worse off after the wage cut, after allowing for changes in income tax and social welfare payment, by about 5 per cent. If the wage cut were to be viewed as equivalent to a tax, it would be judged to be regressive in its effects on the working population.

In all the distribution stories told so far, individuals and families have been ranked by their equivalent income, using the OECD equivalence scale. It should be noted that the application of this equivalence scale can have a powerful effect on the ranking of families in the income distribution. As an example, a single person who earns a full-year full-time wage at $10 per hour would, on a ranking of equivalent disposable income, be in the sixth decile of families in the labour force and in the seventh decile of all families. This same person would be in the second decile of disposable income that has not been adjusted by an equivalence scale.

We turn now to examine whether the composition of the low-wage workforce is affected by the cut in the value of wages.

The new low-wage workers

As a result of the simulated wage cut of 30/15 per cent, the total number of workers who earn no more than $10/6 per hour rises by 900 000 to almost one-quarter of wage and salary earners. Does this more than doubling of the low-wage group change their general characteristics? Are the people who are newly added to the low-wage group very different from the people who were already there? Table 4.5 summarizes the characteristics of both the initial low-wage group and the new, post-wage-cut low-wage group.

The principal conclusion to be derived from Table 4.5 is that the two groups look quite similar. The new low-wage group is not very different from the original low-wage group. The comparison between the two is most apparent if the last column is contrasted with the third column. The last column examines the characteristics of the 900 000 additional low-wage workers, after the wage cut, and expresses the number in each category as a percentage of the total number of additional low-wage workers. This comparison shows that the new group has a higher proportion of women, married people, prime-age workers, people with no formal education qualifications and Asian immigrants. Most of the additional low-wage workers are sales and service personnel or labourers, though in proportional terms the biggest differences are that there are more clerks and equipment operators and fewer labourers, managers and professionals.

The industry where the new low-wage workers are most likely to be employed is wholesale and retail, followed by manufacturing. The proportion in agriculture and in recreation and other services is rather less than for the original low-wage group. Almost 300 000 of the new low-wage workers have dependent children, about two-thirds of whom are women. There is a noticeable fall in the proportion who are young people living at home. The proportion of low-wage earners who are parents aged 25–55 with dependent children and who work twenty hours per week or more and who have low equivalent family disposable incomes (in the bottom 20 per cent of the working family distribution)

Table 4.5 Characteristics of new low-wage workers after 30/15% wage cut, and comparison with existing low-wage workers, 1997

	Base			After 30/15% wage cut			Change	
	Male	Female	Total	Male	Female	Total	number	% of total
Number ('000)	357	359	716	769	848	1617	902	100
% of all w&s earners	5	5	10	11	12	23		
	%	%	%	%	%	%	No.	%
Sex	50	50		48	52	fem	483	54
Marital status								
married	42	56	49	46	58	53	506	56
divorced	3	12	8	5	10	7	56	6
never married	55	32	43	50	32	40	339	38
Country of birth								
Australia	81	77	79	80	75	77	679	75
Europe	11	14	13	12	14	13	117	13
Asia	3	6	4	4	7	6	68	8
Other	5	3	4	4	4	4	36	4
Age								
15–20	25	10	18	20	9	14	98	11
21–24	18	14	16	18	17	18	177	20
25–34	15	27	22	19	23	21	182	20
35–54	33	44	38	33	45	40	375	42
55–64	7	5	6	8	5	7	70	8
Highest qualification								
No quals	67	65	66	69	67	68	627	70
cert/diploma	27	27	27	25	27	26	227	25
degree	6	8	7	6	6	6	47	5
Occupation								
manager	9	4	6	7	2	4	22	2
prof	7	9	7	7	7	7	63	7
trades	21	4	12	23	4	13	124	14
clerk	3	22	13	4	25	15	149	17
sales/service	14	32	23	13	35	24	223	25
operator	7	1	4	10	4	7	85	9
labourer	39	28	34	36	24	30	242	27
Industry								
agriculture	15	3	9	9	3	6	33	4
manufacturing	14	6	10	18	13	15	171	19
construction	9	2	5	7	1	4	29	3
wholesale/retail	32	20	26	33	25	29	283	31
transport/storage	1	4	3	3	3	3	27	3
finan/business serv	7	13	10	8	14	11	106	12
community services	5	20	13	6	21	14	133	15

Table 4.5 (Cont.)

	Base			After 30/15% wage cut			Change number	Change % of total
	Male	Female	Total	Male	Female	Total		
recreation	13	27	20	11	17	14	83	9
other	4	5	4	5	3	4	36	4
Family relationship								
husband+dep child	21	na	11	23	na	11	99	11
wife+dep children	na	30	15	na	31	16	151	17
husband, no childn	20	na	10	22	na	11	106	12
wife, no children	na	26	13	na	27	14	133	15
sole parent	0	9	5	1	7	4	29	3
stud child at home	12	8	10	9	7	8	58	6
other child at home	25	15	20	24	14	19	164	18
unrelated group	8	6	7	10	6	8	79	9
live alone	11	4	8	9	4	7	56	6
other	1	3	2	2	4	3	34	4
Parents aged 25–55, with dep child, work 20 hrs+								
LF decile 1	10	2	5	6	2	4	6	3
LF decile 2	21	10	14	22	6	13	24	12
LF decile 3	20	21	20	24	13	18	32	17
other LF deciles	49	67	61	48	79	65	131	68

falls slightly, though the absolute number in this category rises substantially, from 143 000 to 275 000.

Thus a cut in the level of low and near low wages, as simulated in Scenario 3, brings almost a quarter of wage and salary earners below the low-wage threshold of $10 per hour for adults and $6 per hour for youth. The people affected look much like the workforce at large and could be characterized as mainstream battlers. They are typically married, Australian, relatively uneducated women, of prime working age, employed as clerks, sales and service personnel or labourers in wholesale and retail and community services. Almost one-third have dependent children. The age distribution and family relationships of the new low-wage group are more like those for all employees than is true for the initial low-wage group. But they are less like the average worker in being more female and less formally educated.

At this point we can say that a cut of 30/15 per cent in low wages would leave low-wage workers $7 billion worse off after taking account of the offsetting falls in income tax liability and rises in cash social welfare payments. In order for the combined group of low-wage and unemployed workers to be no worse off, in financial terms, as a result of the wage cut, an additional $7 billion – plus the value of forgone unemployment benefits – must be generated in the form of additional jobs or reduced prices of goods that they buy. If additional jobs generated by the wage cut paid on average $6 per hour for an adult (a cut of 30 per cent on the minimum wage), then the weekly wage for a full-time employee would be $230. This is around the current level of unemployment benefit for an adult. But suppose that some of the unemployed who got jobs were previously not eligible for unemployment benefit, because they lived in families where others were working. To be conservative, suppose that the average level of unemployment payment, across all the unemployed, was $150 per week. The net income gain to a person from moving from unemployment to a paid job would on average be $70 per week or $3500 per annum.

To recover the $7 billion lost to low-wage workers from the wage cut, there would therefore have to be two million new full-time jobs or a large fall in prices. There were, in 1997, about 1.6 million workers earning $15 per hour or less and only about 400 000 earning the minimum wage or less. It seems quite clear that a substantial cut in low wages will make the combined low wage/unemployed group worse off financially, even after taking account of the offsetting changes in tax liability and welfare receipts.

Should We Worry about Low Wages?

Low-wage workers are not disproportionately to be found in the bottom few deciles of the distribution of equivalent family income among all people. Indeed, they are spread rather evenly across this distribution. They are concentrated more heavily, however, at the bottom of the distribution of workforce family income. They are concentrated even more densely at the bottom of the income distribution among wage and salary earners, since a high proportion of people in the bottom two deciles of the workforce family distribution are in unemployed and self-employed rather than wage and salary earner families (Harding & Richardson 1998). About 140 000 low-wage workers have dependent children and are in the bottom quintile of the workforce income distribution. This figure would rise to 275 000 if medium wages were cut by 15 per cent. A cut in low and medium wages would impact much more heavily on workers in the bottom decile of the income distribution than on the rest. A 30 per cent cut in wages reduces the incomes of affected families in the bottom decile of the income distribution by 20 per cent.

We thus have a mixed picture. While many people who receive low wages live in comfortably-off families, hundreds of thousands do not. Protection of low wages benefits many low-income workers, but is not tightly targeted as an instrument of redistribution. Overall, it is some-what equalizing, and in our view should not be dismissed unless a superior alternative is identified and is equally liable to be implemented. But if it could be shown convincingly that a reduction in low wages would generate substantial numbers of jobs for the unemployed (which we think is unlikely), then the egalitarian case against a wage cut would be harder to sustain.

The fact that low-wage workers are mostly better off than people who are not in the labour force is largely irrelevant to the question of what is the appropriate level of low wages. Fairness among workers and fairness among the population at large are not the same thing. They are not commensurate groups. A concern about the distribution of (and in particular, low levels of) income among families is different from a concern about the distribution of wages and earnings. The two may or may not intersect. The criteria for fairness, the nature of the concern and the instruments for effecting change differ in the two spheres. There would still be a concern about fairness in the distribution of wages even if every family that had a full-time worker had a higher (equivalent) income than every family that did not. And there would be a separate concern about the efficiency of the wage structure.

Fairness in the distribution of pay centres around two ideas. One is that workers should not be exploited, or paid such a low rate that they cannot maintain an acceptable standard of living. The other is that workers should be paid an amount that reflects their contribution to the value of output – not a lot more and not a lot less (see Evans and Kelly [1996] for survey evidence that this latter is a typical view of Australian citizens).

The employment relationship is one of *quid pro quo*. The worker is compensated by her or his employer in return for the application of time, skills and effort in the interest of the employer. In a *quid pro quo* relationship, what is exchanged on each side of the bargain must be of approximately equal value in order to be seen as fair. In a perfectly competitive world, this condition is likely to prevail. But in the reality of multiple little pockets of market power and substantial ignorance, in both product and labour markets, there are opportunities for both workers and employers to obtain rents in the labour market. Rents which strongly favour one side or the other are unfair.

The *quid pro quo* nature of wages leads to them being seen as reflecting worth, and much flows from this. Very low wages are degrading because they imply that their recipients are almost worthless, and very high wages puff up the recipient by implying that she or he is of extraordinary value. In a society that values equality of people as citizens, degradingly low wages or indecently high wages are an affront to that equality of the person.

Workers expend effort and time to earn their wage. These are judged on balance to constitute a burden. Concerns about the maintenance of an incentive to work, in the form of ensuring a higher income if one does so, imply the judgement that work does on balance generate disutility and that significant numbers of people would choose not to work if they could receive the same income without doing so. The greater the concern about disincentives, the greater the implied disutility of work and the more the minimum wage needs to exceed the gift of income available to the non-employed, to be both fair and efficient. (Fair, to compensate for the disadvantages of working, and efficient, to induce labour supply.) This is an additional reason why the incomes of the employed should be judged separately from the incomes of the non-employed.

The empirical question of whether or not low-wage workers live in low-income families is of interest mainly because it has implications for the instruments that may be used to alter the distribution of income. On the evidence of this chapter, the level of low wages has a modest role to play in affecting the distribution of equivalent family income.

Conclusion

Summary of key findings

Low-wage workers are not predominantly the sons and daughters of the affluent middle class, working a few hours each week to finance their holiday in Bali while studying law and business. Nor are they predominantly hard-pressed heads of families struggling to put food on the table to feed their families. There are some of each of these groups, but they are relatively small in number. The typical low-wage worker works full-time, is of prime age, with no formal education qualifications, probably married and equally likely to be male as to be female. One-third have dependent children. The men are more likely than the women to be found in low-income families.

Over the past decade the proportion of workers who earn low wages has risen from 11 to 16 per cent. But the characteristics of people who receive low pay have not changed much. The principal changes to emerge clearly over the past decade have been the increased proportion who are men, and the fall in the proportion who have dependent children.

While the evidence is not decisive, it offers no support for the view that a cut in low wages would cause middle-income secondary workers to withdraw from employment in favour of low-income primary workers.

A simulated cut in wages of 15 per cent for people who earned between $10 and $15 an hour more than doubled the number of low-wage earners. The additional 900 000 people who were then earning no more than \$10/6 per hour were only slightly older, more female and more likely to be Asian immigrants than the initial low-wage group. In other respects they looked much the same.

Low-wage workers reflect the diversity of the Australian working population. They are not a mirror image, but the similarities are greater than the differences and the differences are in large part what you would expect given that they are concentrated in relatively unskilled work.

The simulated wage cut also showed that low- and medium-wage earners typically do not face high effective marginal tax rates; that welfare payments were much less important than reduced tax liability in offsetting the fall in wage income; in its first-round effect, about 40 per cent of the cost of a cut in wages would be felt as a deterioration in the Commonwealth Government budget; for families affected by the wage cut, those in the bottom decile of the income distribution lost about 20 per cent of their disposable income, while those in the top decile lost about 2 per cent; the wage cut caused a rise in poverty among workforce families of up to 20 per cent and a small rise in inequality.

Are low-wage workers poor?

The American discussion of the position of low-wage workers in the distribution of family incomes concludes that, sole mothers aside, a shrinking minority of low-wage workers are poor. This point is established by identifying what proportion of low-wage workers live in families that have incomes below the US poverty line. It follows that raising minimum wages is a poorly targeted strategy for raising the incomes of people who are below the poverty line It is not a surprising conclusion, since even in the United States people below the poverty line do not rely predominantly on private earnings for their income. A high proportion are not in the labour force, or are unemployed. This is even more true for Australia, where the relatively compressed wage distribution and relatively high minimum wages have meant that families that rely on wage income mostly have higher incomes than families that are not in employment and that receive their income mainly from social welfare benefits (see, for example, Harding & Richardson 1998). Raising minimum wages is not and could not be expected to be a well-targeted way to compress the distribution of overall household disposable income, or to reduce the numbers of households with very low incomes. The welfare system, insurance against earnings loss and superannuation are the instruments to look to in order to assist most of the poorest 20 per cent of households, not wages.

It is for this reason that much of the material displayed in this chapter focuses on where low- and minimum-wage earners lie in the distribution of equivalent disposable income among families that are in the labour force (though not necessarily in employment). When looked at from this perspective, the evidence suggests that low-wage workers are found throughout the distribution of equivalent disposable family income; that this is particularly true for women; that they are nonetheless substantially overrepresented in the bottom few deciles; and that the lower the wage the greater the concentration at the bottom. This overall picture has not changed much since 1986.

Should low wages be cut?

There is of course no justification for a cut in low wages for its own sake. The only respectable argument for such a cut is that it would generate a substantial number of new jobs and that these would be taken by people who are currently unemployed. The policy is desirable only if the gain to the newly employed exceeds the losses to the low-wage workers. The measure of gains should include the psychological benefits of gainful employment, as well as any increase in income.

While this chapter presents a good deal of information about low-wage workers and how much they would suffer if there were to be a substantial wage cut, it is silent on a number of other crucial pieces of information. These include the number of new jobs that are likely to be generated by a wage cut; the proportion of them that would go to previously unemployed people, and the disincentive effects that would be generated if the value of low wages were cut but the level of social welfare benefits were to remain unchanged. These issues are dealt with in other chapters.

It has been argued that a wage rise is not a well-targeted instrument for improving the distribution of family income, because many of the beneficiaries are not low in the income distribution. Thus much of the increased wage payment would not go to those whom the wage rise is intended to benefit – low-income families. A similar argument can be made that a cut in the value of low wages is a poorly targeted instrument for assisting the unemployed. First, to the extent that a wage cut generates extra jobs, it is highly likely that many would go to people who were previously out of the labour force, rather than to the unemployed. Second, it costs the Commonwealth Government budget and takes income from low-wage earners and disperses it widely across the economy, to profits and consumers of products that are produced by low-paid labour. The proportion of the total loss to low-wage workers that ends up benefiting the unemployed is likely to be quite low. And while not all of the low-wage workers are struggling on low incomes, hundreds of thousands are.

There is no doubt that the average unemployed worker is financially and psychologically worse off than the average low wage, and even minimum wage, worker (see, for example, Harding & Richardson 1998). But it is obvious that their disadvantage is even greater when compared with high-wage workers. The efficacy and fairness of a policy that cuts low wages in order to reduce unemployment thus depends on the answer to two crucial questions. Would a cut in the value of low wages generate a large number of jobs, which were taken by the unemployed rather than those who were previously out of the labour force? Is there a fairer way to assist the unemployed than 'taxing' people who already have low wages? In our judgement, the best wage policy to assist the unemployed is one that reduces the average level of wages (or wage growth), rather than one that focuses on reductions at the bottom end of the wage distribution.

Notes

1 Chapters 1, 2 and 3 provide extensive discussion of these points.
2 See, for example, Freeman 1996 and Card & Krueger 1995. In his review of the redistributive effects of the minimum wage, Freeman concludes that the central tendency of empirical estimates of the employment effects of increases in minimum wages in the United States and the United Kingdom 'has shown that the elasticity of demand for minimum wage workers hovers around zero' (1996: 642).
3 Borland & Woodbridge, in Chapter 3, opt for the rather higher figure for the wage elasticity of demand, for Australia, of around 0.75.
4 Chapter 3 in this volume deals with the first and fifth points. Chapter 5 has some evidence on the third point and Chapter 7 looks closely at the last point.
5 See, for example, Mincey 1990; Burkhauser & Finegan 1989, 1993; Bell & Wright 1996.
6 Thus, for example, Ehrenberg & Smith, in their textbook on labour economics, instruct students that 'the minimum wage is a relatively blunt instrument with which to reduce poverty: most of its benefits go to workers in non-poor families' (1997: 127).
7 Chapter 5 adopts the alternative position, and defines low wage in terms of low weekly earnings, i.e., less than $400 per week in 1997.
8 The Social Policy Research Centre at the University of New South Wales recently published the results of a large project to identify and cost in detail the expenditure necessary to achieve the same standard of living for families of different composition. This is know as the 'budget standards' approach. It is a sophisticated form of Higgins' enquiry of housewives and butchers and of Rowntree's initial budget standards. But even this approach cannot avoid making myriad judgements about what families 'need' (e.g. what is the life expectancy and cost of a pair of false teeth?).

9 For a detailed examination of the difficulties of basing low wages on some definition of need, see Hancock 1998.

10 These percentages are derived from the unit record data of the Surveys of Income and Housing Costs of the ABS. In 1986 there were 913 people in the sample who received low wages, as defined. The absolute number for 1994–95 is 1040. The Harvester rate of pay of 7s per day for an unskilled man was about half the average rate of pay for a full-time male employee in manufacturing. For comparison, $10 per hour was, for a man employed full-time, about 60 per cent of male average weekly ordinary time earnings in November 1994.

11 In this chapter, family and income unit are used synonymously, unless the text makes their distinction obvious. Technically, the unit that we work with is the ABS income unit, which is essentially a 'nuclear family'. This comprises an adult, a partner if there is one and any dependent children. Dependent children are those under age 16 and full-time students up to age 21 (in 1986) or age 24 (in 1994–95). An unemployed 18-year-old still living in the parental home is thus counted as a separate income unit.

12 The ranges were no hours worked, 1–9 hours worked, 10–19, 20–24, 25–29, 30–34, 35–39, 40–44, 45–49 and 50 hours a week or more.

13 See Bradbury 1996 for some interesting support for this view.

14 Saunders looks only at full-time full-year adult workers when he concludes that 'What emerges most clearly from this analysis is that the degree of inequality among the primary labour force has a substantial impact on the overall income inequality profile' (1995: 232).

15 The OECD equivalence scale that we use is as follows: the first adult has a weight of 1, a second person has a weight of 0.7 and additional people (all of whom are children because of the income units that we use) have a weight of 0.5.

16 In both years we have deleted from the analysis income units with zero or negative annual incomes.

17 Recall that the 1994–95 values are adjusted to 1986 by expressing them as a constant proportion of average weekly ordinary-time earnings. The values for 1986 were 67 per cent of the values for 1994–95. Over the period there has been about a 2 per cent increase in the real value of average weekly adult ordinary time earnings.

18 This conclusion is supported by the work of Mitchell, in Chapter 5.

19 Although note that it is possible that a significant proportion of low wage tradespeople are 'employees' working for a company that they own.

20 Note that Mitchell, in Chapter 5, finds that 70 per cent, rather than our 50 per cent, of low-wage workers are women. One reason is that she defines as low-wage a person who earns up to $12 per hour but works only part-time, and women are much more likely to work part-time.

21 The OECD equivalence scale is used. People who live in income units which reported zero income for the year have been deleted from the sample.

Note that there are several differences in the way in which the distribution of income is constructed in this chapter, compared with Richardson 1998. In this chapter, wage and salary earners include 'self-employed' employees who work for their own company; whereas in the earlier paper the self-employed were excluded – a step which is not possible with the 1994–95 data. The distribution of income ranks all people, including children, according to the equivalent annual disposable income of the income unit in which they reside (the OECD equivalence scale is used): in the earlier paper, only people over the age of 15 were included in the income ranking; the equivalence scale used in the earlier paper gave less weight to children.

22 These figures are derived from the 1990 Survey of Income and Housing Costs, ABS, unit records.

23 See Lambert et al. 1994 for an introduction to the STINMOD model.

24 Disposable income is private income for the family, plus cash welfare payments less personal income tax. It is not adjusted by an equivalence scale.

(Australia)

CHAPTER 5

Labour Market Regulation and Low Wages: Taking a Lifetime Perspective

Deborah Mitchell

J31
J38   J53
L51

One argument against regulation to raise the level of wages at the bottom is that low-wage recipients are overwhelmingly young people with their foot on the first rung of the jobs ladder, which they are about to ascend. Chapter 4 has rejected this characterization, on the basis of cross-section evidence on who low-wage workers are. This chapter looks at the issue by drawing on an important new set of data, which enable the author to construct the work histories of low and other wage-earners. The results support the view that a majority of low-wage earners are not beginners but are established workers. The chapter shows too that low wages are associated with other poor conditions of employment and with difficulty in establishing income security.

Over the past decade it has become increasingly apparent that the standard employment relation (SER)[1] was fast becoming the exception rather than the norm of employment patterns in Australia. The driving force behind this change is largely related to a shift away from the manufacturing base of the economy towards the service sector. Service sector employment lends itself more readily to contractual employment. It is characterized by small-to-medium rather than large enterprises, has a less unionized workforce, requires more flexible responses to down-turns in demand, and therefore leads to less secure tenure of employment within both the firm and the particular industry. In place of the SER, we now find a new set of employment patterns described as transitory employment relations (TERs), characterized by work that is casual and non-permanent, part-time or part-year. In order to maintain continuity of employment, labour market participants may also have to retrain and move into several different areas of employment rather than along a single career track (Mitchell 1998a).

159

In addition to these longer-term shifts in the Australian economy – and partly reflecting the institutional accommodation of these shifts – a radical reorganization of the wages system and the industrial tribunals that governed working conditions has taken place in two stages. First, under successive Labor administrations of the 1980s, a series of Wages Accords were negotiated as agreements between the ACTU and the Commonwealth Government. These had the effect of holding down real-wage growth, partly as a trade-off of wages for benefits (the social wage). These accord processes commenced the gradual dismantling of the regulation of wages (and to some extent employment conditions) by the federal and state industrial tribunals. The second stage of change came with the policy shifts of the Howard conservative government, which completed the weakening of the centralized wage-fixing system by limiting the role of the Australian Industrial Relations Commission in favour of individual contracts.[2]

In the wake of these major changes to both the security and 'one career' nature of employment, we also find that up to a third of primary breadwinners can now expect at least one lengthy spell of unemployment during their working lives (Keating & Mitchell 1999). Thus the proportion of the workforce who face both lower real wages, as a result of the deregulation process, and longer durations on low incomes, as a result of the spread of TER to a larger proportion of the workforce, is increasing rapidly.

It is in this context that this chapter seeks to analyse a set of conditions not seen in Australia in the postwar era: that of a considerable proportion of the workforce facing the prospect of a lifetime of low wages. While many social scientists and policy analysts are accustomed to dealing with the incidence and problems associated with low income, this research (in Australia) has mainly been conducted from a short-term perspective and is largely based on cross-sectional evidence. In the same way that research on unemployment has had to adopt a quite different set of approaches, analytical tools and data sources in order to understand the growth in long-term unemployment, there is a corresponding task to be undertaken in respect of long-term receipt of low market wages.[3]

This chapter is a contribution to that task. The first section starts with some theoretical considerations of why we need to distinguish between short- and long-term receipt of low wages. It moves on to link these concerns to labour market deregulation and what the shift away from wage regulation implies for low-wage earners. The next section provides a brief overview of the characteristics of low-wage earners as identified in standard labour market literature. This is contrasted with new empirical evidence drawn from a recent panel study that examines the characteristics and prospects of a group of current low-wage earners. The third section draws out the links between the theoretical issues and the empirical evidence. The final section concludes with some observations on the policy responses that may be required to overcome some of the possible impacts of labour market deregulation.

Earning a Low Wage: Theoretical Concerns

Earlier chapters in this volume discussed the minimum-wage aspect of labour market regulation in Australia. Several of these chapters set out some of the general concerns we might have about low wages, irrespective of the period over which a person might be receiving a low wage.[4] Many of the same concerns, especially those to do with social justice, are relevant here. But the primary focus in this chapter is on identifying additional concerns we may have when we take a lifetime perspective. There are two ways in which long-term considerations may differ from short-term concerns: first, does *starting* on a low wage lead to disadvantage in later life?

A similar question has been posed by Hutton (1991) in her cohort studies of youth unemployment in the United Kingdom. The aim of this research was to examine the longer-term outcomes of certain cohorts of young people who entered the labour market at times of very high youth unemployment (early 1960s and mid 1970s), in particular, to ascertain whether these cohorts were unduly affected by the early experience of unemployment, for example whether this had an impact on their subsequent employment histories and their wage outcomes, vis-à-vis adjacent cohorts. The findings of these studies showed that 20–30 years later, there were no appreciable differences on either of these counts.

In this context, we need to consider whether starting on a low wage has implications for a person's longer-term capacity to attain a standard of living enjoyed by those who start on middle to high wages. In other words, does the receipt of low wages early in someone's working life, even though they may eventually move up the wages ladder, have some lingering impact on their life course chances? If so, what are the factors most likely to be associated with such an outcome? And what sort of indicators might reasonably reflect such short-term disadvantage? As an example of the former, we might be concerned to discover whether low wages are associated with other labour market-related disadvantages such as a lack of access to training or promotion opportunities that might impede a person's rate of progress on the wages ladder. An indicator of the long-term impact, especially in the Australian context, might be the ability of the low-wage starters to begin home ownership at an early enough age to ensure completion of mortgage repayments by retirement.

These are matters for empirical investigation, and like the studies on youth unemployment cited above, the second section indicates that existing studies of the Australian labour market show that after 5–10 years very few of those who started on a low wage (especially in the past) are likely to show any major differences from middle- to high-wage starters on these counts. Thus the empirical evidence is likely to present a picture of degrees of difference, rather than disadvantage on all fronts (cf. Travers & Richardson 1993: 201–2).

One possible disadvantage, which stems from government-mandated changes to retirement savings, is that low-wage earners are unlikely to make up the differences in occupational benefits enjoyed by those who start on middle to high wages. Theoretically, this is one area in which we might expect disadvantage for low-wage earners, irrespective of the future course of a person's earnings profile. Moreover, it has implications for the specific design of superannuation schemes, for example whether low-wage earners are in defined or accumulated benefit schemes. Defined benefit schemes will clearly produce better retirement incomes for those earning low incomes even for short periods, while accumulated benefit schemes will magnify earnings differences over the life course, especially where those differences occur early in the working life.

A second set of concerns that arise from taking a lifetime perspective on this issue is: what is the impact of *persistent* low wages on well-being?

When people receive a low wage over a long time, does such disadvantage in the labour market accumulate, spilling over into other aspects of their lives? In the preceding discussion it was noted that a short duration on a low wage is the lot of many entrants to the labour market and is unlikely to lead to severe long-term disadvantage. But the same cannot be said of persistent low wages. Here our concerns should focus on more than the satisfaction of immediate material needs. It is possible that an extended duration on low wages may substantially alter someone's life course by reducing their capacity to form autonomous households, distorting their fertility intentions, inhibiting their social participation, and so on. Outcomes of this kind are of great concern and, following Walzer's (1985) notion of *blocked exchanges*, oblige us to consider whether government intervention in the wages system is justifiable on social justice grounds,[5] or whether governments should engage in some form of compensation for losers from the deregulation process (Argy 1998).

Whereas much of the economics literature that deals with regulation of the labour market tends to focus on the short-term impacts of government intervention, and generally does so from an individual perspective, the case of long-term duration on low wages may require us to consider outcomes that extend beyond the lifetime of a particular individual or cohort, taking into consideration the impact on those dependent on a low-wage earner, or future generations who may have to shoulder the public pension burden of those unable to save for their old age. Thus a second concern arising from persistent low wages is the intergenerational implications of cumulative disadvantage. The social science literature has identified such concerns in constructions of inter-generational transmission of poverty (Coffield 1980; Atkinson 1989) and, latterly, the notion of an 'underclass' (Jencks 1989; Hochschild 1991; Hunter & Gregory 1996).

A shift of focus to intergenerational concerns raises issues of social mobility. In the sociological literature, social mobility refers mainly to the degree to which a society is 'open', that is, where an individual's own attributes and achievements are the primary determinants of their life course chances rather than the inheritance of (dis)advantage from the parental generation. There are a number of institutions, policies and practices that encourage 'openness' in a society: access to education and health care of a socially acceptable standard; employment practices that are non-discriminatory and that reward merit and/or experience; an absence of barriers to social participation, and so on. In this sense it could be argued that one of the key components in maintaining social mobility in Australia in the past has been the wage-setting system, in particular the ability of the industrial tribunals to set and enforce the minimum wages that enabled a reasonable standard of living to be maintained.[6]

Regulation of wages in Australia

As Hancock's survey in Chapter 2 indicates, the institutions that have regulated the labour market in Australia have intervened on many fronts including wage-setting. Of particular interest here are the actions of these institutions to prevent the payment of unacceptably low wages, through the establishment of legally enforceable minimum wages and to ensure some progress over an individual's life course – however modest that progress may seem – through the award wages system, which previously recognized seniority (years of experience) in award wage structures.

Indeed, Australia's wage-setting institutions evolved historically as the major element of our equality strategies and have acted as a substitute for the redistributive mechanisms of the welfare state found elsewhere in the OECD nations (Castles 1985). That this strategy succeeded in bringing about favourable outcomes for most workers is clear from both time series evidence in Australia and in historical comparisons with other OECD nations (Castles & Mitchell 1994). This reliance on these institutions to deal with equality in the wage distribution allowed the Australian welfare state to address only poverty alleviation, which enabled it to develop a fairly low-cost but reasonably effective social security system. However, as the progressive dismantling of the wages system occurred over the 1980s and real-wage growth – especially for those at the bottom end of the wages distribution – was held down, a rising number of low-income earners found themselves increasingly reliant on social security transfers to top up their wages (Mitchell 1997).[7]

In effect, the deregulation of the wages system has left a gap in our policy arrangements that deal with income inequality and relative living standards, relying instead on the social security system to maintain the 'working poor'. The implications for low-wage earners are more than just a repackaging of their income, which is the way some analysts have viewed this shift. It is possible that the passive receipt of transfer top-ups may discourage younger low-wage earners from actively investing in their human capital, for example through additional training, thereby trapping them in low-wage jobs. Becoming reliant on the social security system as a means of putting together a reasonable family wage may also affect a breadwinner's perceptions of their ability to meet mortgage repayments or to plan their future with any certainty.[8]

These are fairly speculative views on the impact of wage deregulation, and so the following sections will examine the empirical evidence on the characteristics and prospects of low-wage earners. In particular, they will seek to identify those earning low market incomes for a lengthy part of their working lives. It is this group of people that are likely to be most at risk of cumulative disadvantage, leading to measurable deficiencies in occupational, material and social benefits when compared with those who earn middle to high wages over their life course.

Identifying Low-Wage Earners: Empirical Evidence

In the past, low wages in the Australian labour market were mainly associated with new entrants to the labour market and institutionalized wage discrimination against women.[9] In the case of recent entrants to the labour market, cross-sectional data show that the returns to experience are highest over the first five years of employment and this seems to be a fairly consistent finding. Table 5.1 shows the average wage rise for an additional year of experience after one, five, ten and twenty years in the labour market. The table shows very similar outcomes in 1981 and 1991, indicating that while the Accord processes may have reduced real wages over this period, the returns to experience have not changed markedly over the decade. Thus we may reasonably assume

Table 5.1 Effect on wages of one additional year of
experience, full-time males, 1981 and 1991

Current labour market experience	1981 % increase	1991 % increase
1 year	4.8	4.7
5 years	4.1	4.0
10 years	3.2	3.2
20 years	1.5	1.4

Source: Preston 1997

that, on average, new entrants to the labour market can expect their
wages to rise by 4–5 per cent for each year of their first decade of
employment, after which their wage growth begins to slow.

In the context of this study, the cross-sectional evidence suggests that
the first ten years in the labour market is the period in which most wage-
earners should move out of the ranks of the low-paid. The exceptions,
those who have been in the labour market for ten or more years and are
currently receiving a low-wage, may be part of the group of persistent
low-wage earners who are the focus of this study.

Second, because of wage-setting traditions that have disadvantaged
women relative to men, gender may also play a part in identifying low-
wage earners. While the rapid closure in the gender wage gap over the
1980s – at least on an hourly-wage basis – has no doubt reduced the
potential size of this part of the low-wage population, women who are
unskilled or spend lengthy periods out of the labour market for family
reasons may also endure low wages for long periods after re-entering the
labour market (Rimmer & Rimmer 1994). While it is true that many of
these women live in households with another wage-earner and may
benefit from a higher joint income, it is also the case that when partners
separate, the wages of these women put them below the poverty line.[10]
For this reason, we should not give any less weight to the potential
impact of deregulation on women's long-term earnings and the disadvantages they may suffer as a consequence.[11]

While this cross-sectional evidence does point us towards the groups
that may be most likely to receive low wages for extended periods, it is
only longitudinal data on individuals that will most clearly establish the
existence and size of a persistent low-wage group – their demographic
and employment characteristics – and indicate whether the deregulation
of the wages system has contributed to their status of persistent low-wage
earners. At present such a data set does not exist in Australia. The closest
data available for this purpose form the first round of a panel study of

the life course completed in 1998.[12] This data set is used in the following sections to identify a group of current low-wage earners, to describe their demographic characteristics, to examine their labour force histories, and to identify their access to occupational welfare, training and promotion opportunities.

Life course data

The primary source material of the Life Course Project is a panel study that will follow a random sample of approximately 2400 people, currently aged between 18 and 54 years, over a ten-year period. The first survey, carried out in 1997–8, comprised nearly 300 questions covering issues such as demographic, educational, labour market, all sources of income, superannuation, family relationships, household time-use, childcare arrangements, and tenure status, as well as asking a series of attitudinal questions on workplace, family relationships, household organization and responsibilities. The survey also gathers basic demographic, educational, employment and income characteristics of the respondent's partner. A central feature of the survey is the compilation of a complete employment, educational and training history of the respondent from 15 years of age. On average, around 450 separate items of data were collected from each respondent.

For the purposes of this study, 'low-wage earners' were defined as those whose take-home pay in the survey period was less than $400 per week. In choosing this figure, the aim was to identify wage-earners on less than $10 per hour (after tax) for a standard 40-hour week.[13] The sample discussed below does include some part-time workers who earned slightly above this on an hourly rate (up to $12 per hour) but whose total earnings were well below $400 per week. This approach allows us to identify those on low wages both in terms of hourly pay and total take-home pay.

In selecting the low-wage sample and the base wage/salary comparison group, the self-employed were excluded mainly because their wages are not affected by wage regulation. Empirically, this group also raises two operational problems: first, it was difficult to separate wages and business income for many in this group; and second, their reported hours of work made it difficult to calculate reliable hourly wage rates. The sample also excludes the unemployed.

Characteristics of low-wage earners in the NLC data

Using the above definition, we identified a 'low-wage' group of 230 people from a total wage/salary sample of 1382 people, around 17 per

Table 5.2 Comparison of selected characteristics of low-wage earners with all others

		All other wage earners	Low-wage earners
Sex		48% female	75% female
Average age	(F)	36 years	35 years
	(M)	35 years	29 years
Average salary	(F)	$571 per week	$231 per week
	(M)	$773 per week	$294 per week
Av. hours per week	(F)	34 hours	25 hours
	(M)	46 hours	40 hours
Employer		70% private	80% private
Employment status		72% permanent	54% permanent
No. of years of full-time	(F)	3.9 years	2.4 years
education since 15	(M)	4.1 years	2.7 years
Proportion of full-time	(F)	45%	34%
work since 15	(M)	70%	57%
Proportion of part-time	(F)	17%	24%
work since 15	(M)	3%	8%
Self contribution	(F)	48% cont. super	33% cont. super
to superannuation	(M)	62% cont. super	45% cont. super
Employer contribution	(F)	90% emp. cont. super	83% emp. cont. super
to superannuation	(M)	90% emp. cont. super	87% emp. cont. super

cent of those who worked for wages in the week before the interview. Table 5.2 provides a brief summary of key differences between the low-wage group and other wage/salary earners. The table confirms the findings of other cross-sectional studies on the characteristics of the low-wage population: low-wage earners are predominantly women and younger men; the majority of the low-wage group did not complete secondary education; both men and women in this group work significantly fewer hours than other earners, though the men in this sample did work close to what is considered full-time hours; on average, both women and men in the low-wage group earn well under half the wages of the comparison group; low wage earners are more likely to be employed in the private sector; and only 54 per cent of low-wage earners have permanent employment, compared with a 72 per cent permanency rate for other earners.

In addition to these characteristics, the Life Course data also allow us to consider some of the longer-term issues which were discussed in the first section, for example whether low pay is associated with other disadvantages such as the ability to save for retirement. Table 5.2 indicates that in this respect, low-wage earners are mainly reliant on their employer's contributions to their superannuation savings. The real difference between this group and middle to higher earners is that their own contribution rates are far lower. Only one-third of women low-wage earners contribute to their super funds, compared with nearly half of women on middle and higher wages; while 45 per cent of low-wage men self-contribute, compared with 62 per cent of all other male wage-earners.

Using the work history data, we can also begin to gain a picture of whether these current low-wage earners have a history of regular, full-time employment (the SER). We find that women in the low-wage group have spent only one-third of their working lives in full-time employment, and low-wage men around 60 per cent.

Low-wage sub groups

While Table 5.2 covers only a small part of the Life Course data, we see a number of areas in which the low-wage group appears to be substantially different from all other wage/salary earners. But it is also the case that within the low-wage group there is substantial variation in these characteristics. In analysing the various aspects of the labour force histories of the low-wage group, four subgroups were identified for further analysis:

1 *recent entrants* to the labour market, defined as those under 25 years of age (N=51);
2 *married women working part-time* formed the largest subgroup (N=82);
3 a group of 25–34-year-olds who should be reaching the *peak* of their earnings growth (N=46); and
4 *others*, mainly older men who were formerly in blue-collar occupations and older women who no longer have dependent children (N=51).

Table 5.3 gives a more detailed breakdown of the labour force participation histories, wages, education and other job characteristics for each of these groups.

Those defined as recent entrants have spent an average 3.5 years in the labour market and only a small percentage have had one break in their employment. They were the second lowest-paid group in terms of their weekly earnings, but worked on average 34 hours per week. This group has the highest permanency rate (similar to the rest of the wage and salary earners in Table 5.2). Reflecting the general trend to higher school retention rates, only 40 per cent of recent entrants have incomplete secondary education.

Married women working part-time naturally have much lower hours and consequently the lowest weekly earnings; they also have the lowest rate of permanency among these groups and, surprisingly, they are the

Table 5.3 Work and education history, wages and hours

Low-wage group	Sub group %	Yrs in lf Mean	Yrs out lf Mean	1 break lfp %	2 break lfp %
Recent entrants	22	3.5	0.3	12	0
Married women part-time	35	16.1	7.1	38	40
'Peak' earners	20	10.2	2.1	25	18
Others	22	20.1	5.7	49	24

Low-wage group	$ per week Mean	Hrs p.w. Mean	Incomplete secondary	Permanent %	>1 paid job %
Recent entrants	269	34.2	40	70	14
Married women part-time	154	16.5	63	33	19
'Peak' earners	296	36.7	53	60	9
Others	321	37.2	67	64	13

Notes: lf – in the labour force; lfp – labour force participation

group most likely to have more than one paid job. Nearly two-thirds of the group did not complete their secondary education. Around 40 per cent of this group have had at least one break from work, while a further 40 per cent have had two breaks. On average they have spent seven years out of the workforce.

For the peak earnings group, most were working close to full-time hours, earning around $8 per hour, after tax. Around 60 per cent were permanent employees and over half did not complete their secondary education. Just over 40 per cent of this group have had one or two breaks in employment, and these breaks average around 10–14 months' duration.

For the remainder of the sample, who have been in the workforce longest, half have had at least one break, and a further 24 per cent, two breaks. The most striking aspect of this group is the very low levels of completion of secondary education (around two-thirds did not complete), reflecting the older average age of this group. This group had the highest weekly earnings, though on an hourly basis their pay rates were similar to the peak earnings group, and they were slightly more likely to have permanency.

In summary, the majority of the low-wage group exhibit the characteristics of *transitory employment* discussed at the outset of this chapter. In particular, the dominance of casual and contract work among this group and the lengthy breaks in employment (with the exception of recent entrants) suggest that many of these workers have earned low wages for much of their working life. In the following section we examine whether low wages are associated with other disadavantages of both a short-term and long-term nature.

Low Wages and Associated Disadvantage

While public debate surrounding the deregulation of the labour market has mainly focused on wages, it is important to recall that a second major element of the regulatory framework of the various industrial tribunals was concerned with occupational benefits and other working conditions. The determinations of the industrial tribunals resulted in widespread access to paid annual holidays, sick leave and long service leave among the Australian workforce. As a result of negotiations under the Accord processes, superannuation entitlement was added to the range of occupational benefits in the late 1980s. As deregulation proceeds, concerns have been raised by the trade unions as to whether these basic occupational entitlements will be lost. In the top panel of Table 5.4, we consider the extent to which the low-wage status of each group is associated with lack of access to customary occupational benefits.

Access to paid recreation and sick leave for these subgroups is strongly associated with permanency. Around 70 per cent of married women working part-time do not have access to paid recreation or sick leave. In the remaining groups, around 30–40 per cent do not have access to these entitlements. It would appear that the casualization of jobs, which has increased as deregulation has proceeded, has resulted in a 'double disadvantage' for many in this group: low wages combined with a loss of paid leave entitlements.

As noted earlier, self-contribution to superannuation is quite low across these groups, but most notably among the recent entrants and peak earners groups, which both work nearly full-time hours. Although working part-time, the married women group have similar levels of coverage. The older workers in the remaining group are much more likely to have coverage through their own contributions, which may reflect heightened awareness of approaching old age.

In the bottom panel of Table 5.4 we report the respondents' views on their job security, training and promotion prospects, as these will have a significant bearing on future earnings. When asked about their job security, the peak and older earners were most likely to express feelings of vulnerability. Similarly, these two groups were most dissatisfied with their earnings. In terms of future outlook, lack of access to training opportunities was felt most strongly by recent entrants to the labour market, while peak earners were more concerned about their promotion opportunities. When asked to evaluate promotion prospects in their

Table 5.4 Access to occupational benefits, training and promotion prospects

Low-wage group	Subgroup %	Super contributions		Paid rec. leave %	Paid sick leave %
		Self %	Employer %		
Recent entrants	22	27	87	72	75
Married women part-time	35	28	72	34	28
'Peak' earners	20	28	83	55	60
Others	22	51	94	66	57

Low-wage group	Not expect promotion %	Dissatisfaction with access to		Dissatisfaction with	
		Training %	Promotion %	Job security %	Earnings %
Recent entrants	41	26	22	6	24
Married women part-time	68	18	15	10	23
'Peak' earners	56	16	31	28	35
Others	67	21	23	28	38

current job, nearly 70 per cent of married women working part-time felt that they were unlikely to be promoted; two-thirds of the older workers did not expect promotion, nor did more than half of the peak earners; while 40 per cent of the recent entrants did not expect promotion.

In the current climate of deregulation, it may not only be these low-wage earners who feel less secure in their job or dissatisfied with their opportunities for promotion and training: these assessments of the future may also be shared by middle- and higher-income earners. To test this, Table 5.5 compares the responses of the 'peak earners' subgroup with their middle- and higher-paid counterparts. The table also reports a number of other differences that may give some indication of whether the low-wage status of this particular group may be affecting the achievement of important life-course events. This group has been chosen as it represents the age-band in which most major life-course events occur, for example establishment of independent living arrangements, marriage, birth of children. The table reports chi-square tests of significance for all variables except wages and social security benefits.

In this sample of 25–34-year-olds, around 10 per cent of the 450 respondents were in the low-wage category. The average age of both groups is identical (29.9 years). The wage difference between the two groups is sizeable: on average, nearly $400 per week. Social security

Table 5.5 Comparison of 25–34-year-old low-wage earners with reference age-group

Characteristic	Low-wage group N=46	Other 25–34-year-olds N=404
Never married *	58%	39%
Still living at home **	23%	6%
Receives social security	40%	33%
Wage/salary	$297 per week	$696 per week
Social security benefits	$44 per week	$16 per week
Permanent employee **	60%	83%
Paid recreational leave **	55%	83%
Self cont. to super **	28%	43%
Emp. cont. to super *	83%	93%
Dissatis. with access to promotion	31%	23%
Dissatis. with job security *	28%	15%

Notes: * Chi square significant at 5%
         ** Chi square significant at 1%

benefits add around $44 (or 13 per cent) to the net income of the low-wage group. Given these financial considerations, it is not surprising that the low-wage group differs significantly from other earners in their marriage rates (de jure and de facto) and their ability to establish independent living arrangements.

As noted earlier, low-wage earners are less likely to have permanency and consequently have less access to a range of occupational benefits. There are also significant differences between the two groups in respect of superannuation contributions made by both the employee and employer. Should this pattern persist, around 20 per cent of the low-wage group will have no retirement savings at the end of their working lives and a further 50 per cent will have only their employer's contributions.

In relation to the dissatisfaction with employment, training and promotion prospects the low-wage group did not vary markedly from the middle- and higher-income earners, although they were slightly more likely to feel that their jobs were less secure – again, an assessment strongly linked to the higher rates of casual employment among this group.

Earlier in this chapter I speculated on some of the possible effects that might be observed among persistent low-wage earners. The evidence in this section clearly suggests that the 25–34-year-old low-wage earners suffer a number of disadvantages compared with their middle- and higher-paid counterparts. First, the level of wages must have a strong effect on the ability of these workers to contribute to their own superannuation accounts. While this disadvantage may not be apparent at this stage of their lives, the longer-term effect will be seen on their reliance on social security pensions in retirement. There may also be a financial link with the much larger proportion of the group who are still living with their parents. Again, the low incomes earned by this group may not be sufficient for them to enter the rental market and/or they may be remaining at home until they have accumulated enough savings to enter into home ownership. Low wages also have a strong association with a lack of permanent employment status, and this in turn affects access to other benefits such as paid recreation leave and the lack of job security reported by the respondents. Taken together, these multiple disadvantages may partly explain why we observe a much higher never-married rate for this group (60 per cent) as compared with 40 per cent for the counterpart group.

Conclusions: Prospects and Policies

The findings of this study confirm a number of our expectations about the low-wage population. First, it is predominantly female, reflecting lower educational attainment for women, broken patterns of workforce participation due to child bearing/rearing, predominance of casual and part-time work, and probably some residual wage discrimination. Second, recent entrants to the labour market comprise just over 20 per cent of this low-wage sample. Third, as other studies have found, there is a substantial pool of older workers who, in their late forties, have experienced a substantial spell of unemployment for the first time in their working lives. Most of these people did not complete secondary education and very few have returned to study since leaving school. Finally, an unexpected group of low-wage earners emerged during the analysis who are in an age-group which, in Australia, is usually reaching the peak of growth in earnings.

The future prospects for these groups vary considerably. For the recent entrants, a great deal will depend on their level of education, if the peak earners group can be taken as a guide. The survey participants in this group remain comparatively optimistic: 60 per cent expect to be promoted in their current job and very few are worried about their job security. However, around a quarter of these recent entrants were dissatisfied with their access to training.

Married women working part-time have the lowest weekly earnings, even though it is this group that is most likely to have more than one paid job. Two-thirds are casual employees and they have the lowest levels of occupational benefits of the four groups. Around 70 per cent of these women do not expect to be promoted in the foreseeable future.

The prospects for the peak earners appear quite bleak. Most of this group have had at least one spell out of the labour market and more than half do not expect to be promoted in their current job. This group is most likely to feel insecure in their current job and one-third (mostly men) are dissatisfied with their earnings.

The prospects for the older workers in the sample are similarly poor. About half of both the men and women in this group have had at least one lengthy spell out of the labour market, and two-thirds do not expect to be promoted in their current job. Offsetting this, however, the Life Course data reveal that the majority of this group are currently owner-occupiers and most contribute to superannuation.

What do these findings imply for the push towards greater deregulation of the labour market? My comments here mainly address issues of deregulation from the viewpoint of the younger low-wage earners in the sample, as it is these workers who will bear the full effects of current changes.

The outlook for the group I have described as the 'peak earners' should alert us to problems that may spread to younger cohorts of workers. These entered the labour market in the mid-1980s and are essentially the first cohort to experience a deregulated labour market for most of their working lives. In addition to currently earning low wages, members of this group feel most dissatisfied with their lack of access to promotion opportunities and have a much lower rate of permanency and job security. The group also has a very low level of self-contributed superannuation savings. Taken together, the poor prospects for this group and their lack of savings for old age indicate that they are at risk of accumulating disadvantage over their working lives and that this may eventually spill into their retirement years. While a direct causal link cannot be established with low wages, it appears that some of this group are lagging behind their better-paid counterparts in the establishment of independent living arrangements and in their partnering rates.

For this particular group of low-wage earners, current policy arrangements offer very little in the way of either direct income support or labour market programs. On the income support side, this is partly a legacy of the fact that this age-group has traditionally experienced wage growth over this stage of their life course and, apart from child benefit transfers, has not been regarded as being in need as compared with other low-income earners. More recently, government policy has increasingly acted to further exclude young adults from income-support arrangements for both education and social security purposes, requiring parents to support adult children well into their twenties. Thus one of the policy issues that needs to be considered in this context is whether wage supplementation, especially for those without children, should be formally established as a legitimate function of the social security system.[14]

On the labour market side, past and present policies and programs have been designed primarily to deal with the unemployed. The upgrading of the skills of those currently in the labour market is not seen as a policy priority. But it is exactly this type of program that is most needed by this particular group of the low-paid, especially those who have not completed their secondary education. Increasingly, as transitory employment spreads, the ongoing need for retraining will spread to other age-groups. Essentially, our policy perspectives on the labour market need to be enlarged to enable all workers to anticipate their training needs and receive financial and service supports in order to maintain continuity of employment across the life course.

Notes

1　That is full-year, full-time employment within the one occupation or industry for most of an individual's employment history.
2　Hancock, in this volume, provides a detailed account and evaluation of these changes.
3　In other countries, studies using longitudinal data have been appearing over the past decade; see for example, Gregory & Elias 1994.
4　See also Gill 1990.
5　Walzer argues that no single sphere of life should be allowed to dominate others, for example 'wealth' should not be able to buy 'justice'; that there should be a boundary between advantage [disadvantage] in the marketplace and other spheres of life. See also the discussion in Travers & Richardson (1993: 1–13).
6　See Sloane & Theodossiou 1996 for a discussion of the impact of earnings mobility on family living standards.
7　See also Chapter 7.
8　These perceptions are reinforced by the fact that banks and other financial institutions do not include social security income in their repayment capacity calculations.
9　The evidence supporting this contention is extensive and well documented; see, for example, Gill 1994; Mitchell 1998b.
10　See Webb, Kemp & Millar 1996 for a fuller discussion of this issue. Richardson & Harding, in this volume, show that prime-age women constitute a large proportion of the group of low-wage earners.
11　It has been argued (Mitchell 1995; Bennett 1995) that one of the consequences of enterprise bargaining will be an increase in the 'gender wage gap'.
12　Data used in this study is drawn from the Negotiating the Life Course Project, Research School of Social Sciences, Australian National University.
13　This figure is similar to that used by Richardson & Harding, in this volume.
14　Cf. the United Kingdom, where this function was formally established under the 1986 Social Security Act (Webb, Kemp & Millar 1996: 2).

CHAPTER 6

Could Increasing the Skills of the Jobless be the Solution to Australian Unemployment?

Bruce Chapman

One of the most compelling arguments for deregulation of the labour market is that a system which keeps wages above levels that would be reached by market forces will condemn low-wage potential workers to unemployment, because they will not add enough value to justify the relatively high wage. This chapter examines the important question of whether it is possible to make wage and value added match for low-skill workers, not by reducing the wage but by increasing the value added. It does s o by taking the most difficult case – people who have been unemployed for a long time – and seeing whether wage subsidies, subsidized employment or more education can result in a high proportion being re-employed, at an acceptable public cost.

The argument that cutting low wages is the best way to reduce unemployment, canvassed in Chapters 1, 3 and 4, has another side to it. If low-skill people are not profitable to employ because the wage they must be paid exceeds their productivity, then an alternative solution is to raise their productivity and leave the wage the same. If this remedy could be implemented, it would avoid the worrying consequences of falls in low wages that have been explored in other chapters, including that:

1 there would be an increase in income inequality and particular hardship for blue-collar men and their families;
2 the additional employment created from lower wages is likely to be insufficient to counter this increased income inequality;[1]
3 governments lack the resources and/or commitment to expand social security payments to redress the potential adverse distributional influence of these forces, especially as a cut in low wages will reduce income tax revenue; and
4 social welfare benefits would have to be cut in order to retain an incentive for workers to take the lower-paid jobs.

Wage decreases and productivity increases are similar approaches to unemployment, since they are both attempts to make the value of a potential worker match the wage that must be paid to employ him or her, and thus to make the jobless more attractive to employers. Cuts to real wages achieve this directly, but increasing productivity has a comparable effect because it also decreases costs per unit of output.

However, there is a major difference. Wage cuts decrease the potential incomes of prospective workers and, as Chapter 7 shows, would produce serious disincentives to work. Skill increases, in contrast, should increase employment without reducing pay. Whether or not such skill increases could deliver this desirable outcome is the subject of what follows.

Put simply, the question is: if wage structures were kept unchanged, could the solution to Australian unemployment lie in increasing the skills of the least advantaged unemployed? The question is addressed through a series of simulations designed to assess the impact on net employment of different types of skill enhancement for unemployed workers.

The simulations leave unexamined a number of other approaches to reducing unemployment, including decreasing legal minimum wages (discussed in Chapters 3 and 4); changing the tax and spending arrangements of government; and instituting legislation aimed at minimizing monopolies in product and labour markets. Nor in what follows is there analysis of the potentially crucial role of monetary and fiscal policy, and what this means for economic and thus employment growth. Rather, the analysis in this chapter is focused exclusively on the labour cost–unemployment nexus. The essential innovation is that instead of asking how wage decreases targeted on the unemployed would improve the group's job prospects, the question is whether it is possible to increase the skills of the unemployed to the point where their productivity matches existing wage levels. The issue has not been addressed in this way before in the Australian context.

The method adopted is as follows. It is argued that understanding the dynamics – the flows – of the labour market is crucial to an assessment of the possible role of policy intervention. That is, policies targeted on the unemployed are modelled with respect to the longer-term job prospects of both those assisted directly and those displaced.

The analysis begins by presenting a 'policy-free' three-period model of labour market unemployment flows. This allows a reference point from which the effect of different government interventions can be judged. The strength of this method is that it takes into account the potential implications of targeted skills intervention over time. Previously these dynamic implications have not been considered in policy evaluation.[2]

Two broad policies, labour market programs and increases in formal education, are considered with respect to their potential for employment growth, with both interventions assumed to be targeted on those with long periods of unemployment. It is recognized that within these strategies there is considerable scope for different approaches and outcomes.

It is important to recognize that the question addressed is narrow, which has implications for the policy conclusions that might be drawn. For example, if the analysis suggests that increased investments in either labour market programs or formal education are not likely to solve the Australian unemployment problem, it does not mean that such policies are not worthwhile. There might be reasons for promoting these types of intervention that are unrelated to their potential for decreasing unemployment in the short run. Two such reasons are that increasing the skills of the unemployed is likely over the longer term to add to the economy's growth potential, implying improvements in income per capita,[3] and that there might be beneficial social implications as a consequence of a skills improvement policy targeted on the most disadvantaged, such as increased equality of opportunity. Some part of this is related to the potential for such policies to diminish the intergenerational transmission of economic and social opportunity.

While the consequences of such policies for unemployment are crucial and underpin this chapter, they should be seen as only one of several important parts of an assessment of the total economic and social case for such interventions.

In what follows the approach adopted is unusual. Apart from the modelling of Piggott and Chapman (1995), there is no comparable method that addresses these issues. The Piggott and Chapman framework was developed in response to a clear weakness in the labour market program evaluation literature. The approach offers new insights, but it has not yet been subjected to broadly based critique.

An important aspect of the chapter is the way in which it deals with the issue of assisting people who are already unemployed by providing them, not with tailor-made programs, but with additional formal education. The policy is analysed as if it had similar effects to labour market programs. Again, this is a new approach to understanding the connections between education and unemployment, and the results are therefore somewhat speculative.

With these qualifications in mind, the analysis delivers four main conclusions:

1 within the genre of targeted labour market programs there is a wide range of outcomes in terms of both employment creation and the costs to the budget;

2 labour market programs have a potentially important role to play in diminishing unemployment, but they cannot do the job on their own;
3 attempts to increase employment through targeted education policy seem to have little effect, at least in the short run; and
4 overall the results imply that the solution to high Australian unemployment, at least in the short term, must be multifaceted and cannot rely solely on policies designed to increase the skills of the unemployed.

Motivating a Flows Model of Unemployment

Why the adopted approach is useful

The framework underpinning the policy analysis is a flows model of unemployment that initially assumes no policy intervention. There are two main advantages in its use. The first relates to the importance of understanding flows in the labour market.

Much discussion of the labour market relies on measures of stocks – what is going on at a particular time. For example, the information most commonly used to describe the state of the labour market is the unemployment rate, which measures the proportion of the labour force that is jobless. But even though the rate dominates policy consideration, it is poor information in a dynamic context.

For example, if one wanted to know how many people experience unemployment in a given year, the stock (about 800 000 during 1998) understates the figure by over half; that is, more than 1.6 million people will have experienced unemployment during the year. In this case a stock measure does not come close to representing the incidence of unemployment over a given year. Very different perspectives arise if the focus is on measures of stocks rather than flows, and for many purposes, including those of this chapter, the flows perspective is superior.

The second advantage of the adopted approach is that it establishes a policy-free reference point. This allows the effects of different types of government intervention to be compared to the counterfactual of no government intervention. The basic structure is now explained.

A simple unemployment flows model of the Australian labour market

The three-period flows model of the labour market used comes from Piggott and Chapman (1995). They developed a model to evaluate the Job Compact, the previous Labor government's job guarantee for all those unemployed for eighteen months or more. The framework turns out to be suitable for analysing a broad range of labour market policies, including those explored in this chapter.

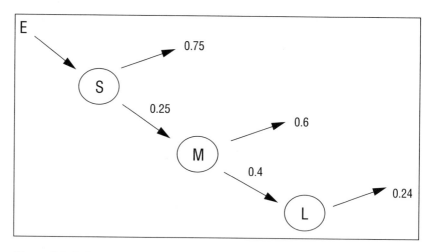

Figure 6.1 A three-period flows model of the Australian labour market

The model has the following characteristics. Those unemployed have three potential states defined by unemployment duration: less than nine months, nine to eighteen months, and greater than eighteen months. The structure is driven by 'exit probabilities', the likelihood that a person unemployed for a given length of time leaves unemployment to a job in the next period (nine months). The exit probabilities were derived from ABS gross flows data.[4]

The model is very stylized and implicitly assumes no business cycle and that the various parameters determining inflows to, and outflows from, unemployment do not change over time. There is a steady-state assumption, which means that inflows into unemployment are equivalent to outflows, and all outflows are assumed to be to employment, meaning that labour is 'permanently attached' to the labour force. Figure 6.1 illustrates the basic characteristics of the model.

The diagram should be understood as follows. There are four unemployment states: E, the number entering unemployment; S, the number unemployed less than nine months; M, the number unemployed between nine and eighteen months; and L, the number unemployed greater than eighteen months. The arrows pointing away from these categories represent the proportion of the stock exiting to a job, with the rest moving to the next unemployment duration period.

To illustrate, imagine that a group becomes unemployed and thus enters S. The exit probabilities mean that around 75 per cent find employment in the first nine months, with the other 25 per cent entering M. Of these, around 60 per cent exit to employment between nine and eighteen months, with the remaining 40 per cent moving to L. For those still unemployed after eighteen months a further 24 per cent exit to a job in the next nine-month period.

This is a useful tool for understanding what might happen in the labour market through policy intervention, for two reasons. The first is that labour market programs are typically targeted on the basis of unemployment duration, an essential part of the model. Second, policy interventions of the type to be explored are motivated essentially by the goal of increasing exit probabilities from unemployment to employment, which is also a fundamental aspect of the framework. These issues are now considered in the context of specific policies.

Understanding Targeted Skills Intervention

Background

The goal is to understand the employment impact of policies aimed at decreasing the real unit labour costs of the disadvantaged in ways that do not also affect the structure of wages. However, real unit labour costs will only be changed for program participants, and in this context it is important to understand 'targeting'.

Targeted labour market policy means that well-defined groups, such as the long-term unemployed or those at risk of unemployment, are offered special assistance. The two types of skills interventions considered, labour market programs and education intervention, are both assumed to be targeted to those with high unemployment duration. These policies are quite different in design and in their potential effects.

Labour market programs

Labour market programs are aimed at improving the employment and earnings prospects of targeted individuals. Apart from having a well-defined eligibility criterion (such as unemployment duration), a basic characteristic of programs is that they are temporary; that is, assistance to participants ceases after a short period.

There are many different forms of labour market assistance. In both Australia and the rest of the OECD, two quite different policies have been significant in expenditure terms, and are now described because they are the focus of later analysis. They are wage subsidy schemes and temporary public sector works programs.[5]

Wage subsidies involve the government offering employers payments for employing members of particular groups at going wages. They therefore decrease wage costs to the employer while keeping paid wages unchanged.[6] Thus they are ideal for exploring the question at hand.

Wage subsidy schemes started in Australia in 1978 with the Special Youth Employment Training Program. They became the dominant labour market program in the early 1990s through JOBSTART,[7] a general form of wage subsidy available to the long-term unemployed. JOBSTART was planned to be the major program of the previous Labor government's Job Compact project[8] (instituted in 1994), in which all people unemployed for eighteen months or more were guaranteed a short-term job. The project was discontinued when the government changed in 1996.

A second main type of program involves public sector community projects for the eligible unemployed. Like wage subsidies, the idea is to increase employment without decreasing wages paid to those targeted. The first of its type in Australia was the Regional Employment Development Scheme, which began in 1973 and was discontinued in 1975. Others of this genre were instituted in the 1975–94 period, with the most significant recent program being New Work Opportunities of the Job Compact, in which community works projects directed to the very long term unemployed were part of the Job Compact.

Wage subsidy and public sector job creation approaches are quite different in terms of their labour market consequences. But they share the important goal of increasing the employment prospects of those targeted when the policy support terminates. The reasons for the potential changes in employment prospects differ importantly between the policies.

In wage subsidy schemes those offered jobs have their long-term employment chances increased in two ways. The first is through the possibility that participants remain with the firm of initial employment after the subsidy stops. Continuation of the employment relationship is not hard to understand; the assisted employee has had time both to show his or her competence, and to acquire skills specific to the job.[9]

It is important to understand the role of specific skills. If an employer terminates previously subsidized workers, often new workers have to be hired to replace them. These new workers then need to acquire skills relevant to that particular work environment. Replacement of a wage-subsidized employee means that the associated training costs have to be incurred again.

The other way in which wage subsidy schemes improve the longer-term employment prospects of those targeted is less direct. Those who leave the initial job when the subsidy stops are likely to have acquired work skills, confidence and/or mainstream labour market connections that improve their prospects of finding employment, compared to their situation had they remained unemployed. At the very least, participants will not have been experiencing the atrophy of skills that would have happened if they had remained unemployed.

Work projects financed by the public sector seek to change longer-term employment prospects in a similar way to this second potential of wage subsidy schemes. While those employed in a short-term community job cannot continue after the designated period, the idea is that this employment experience changes the reality (or perception) of their productivity and, perhaps, participants' attitudes and commitment to job search.

Education intervention

The idea of targeting an educational increase on some of the unemployed is not conventional. Even so, in Australia over the last two decades there have been attempts to improve the educational opportunities of young people from backgrounds with low household income.

Means-tested grants in the form of AUSTUDY payments are the most important form this has taken, but there have also been education access programs motivated by various 'equity' concerns. These are best considered to be social policies aimed at improving the educational opportunities of the poor. The goal has been to redress social disadvantage rather than to decrease unemployment.

Nevertheless, there are some interesting similarities between labour market programs and education policies. The most obvious is that both can be seen to be attempts to decrease the future real unit labour costs of targeted groups without cutting wages. Much of the conceptual basis for labour market programs can be applied to targeted education expansion.

Evaluating Skills Intervention Policy

Conventional evaluation methods of labour market programs

There is an extensive literature on the effect of labour market programs on unemployment. Its intellectual basis is crucial to an understanding of the different approach of this chapter.

Measurement of the job creation effects of programs has typically used the following equation:

$$\text{Total new jobs} =$$
$$\text{Gross program jobs} - \text{deadweight loss} - \text{displacement} \quad (1)$$

'Gross program jobs' means the employment of participants and will be determined in part by the 'effectiveness' of the program in changing their employment prospects. 'Deadweight loss' refers to the number of targeted people who would have gained employment in the absence of the program, and 'displacement' refers to those who did not find employment because a program-eligible person was employed instead.

From the equation, if the goal is to increase net employment, labour market programs are more desirable: the more effective they are in increasing participants' probabilities of exiting from unemployment to employment (to maximize effectiveness), the more they are targeted on those with low exit probabilities (to minimize deadweight loss) and the less likely they are to substitute targeted labour for others (to minimize displacement).

The evaluation of labour market policies by governments and academics is typically based on the above broad understanding. However, this approach misses important aspects of the consequences of labour market policy. An alternative, dynamic, approach is necessary, for reasons now explored.

Towards an improved methodology for evaluating labour market programs

The most important limitation of the accepted methodology is that it ignores the dynamics of displacement, deadweight loss and effectiveness of programs. What happens over time is not accounted for, and this might very well be crucial to assessment of the value of a program.

The simple three-period model of Piggott and Chapman explained above provides a basis on which to account for the role of programs in changing the exit probabilities over time of participants and of those displaced.

With respect to displacement, for example, what matters is not that a proportion of those displaced become or remain unemployed, but rather what happens to their resulting employment probabilities as a result of this experience. It is important to work out to what extent displacement increases unemployment duration because this is a fundamental determinant of the probability of a person eventually finding employment. Similarly, the probability of finding a job after assistance ends for those targeted must be significant to an overall assessment of the efficacy of the program.

In summary, the conventionally accepted evaluation method does not account for crucial aspects of programs because it ignores effects beyond the initial. Since the dynamic consequences of policy intervention are fundamental to an understanding of what programs mean for employment over time, the case for a more sophisticated approach is clear. The

Piggott and Chapman flows model described earlier is very useful in this context because it can be modified to address some of these concerns; how this can be done is considered in the next main section.

The relevance of labour market program evaluation for targeted education policy

A targeted education intervention policy will have very similar effects to a labour market program because there will also be displacement, deadweight loss and effectiveness issues. This promotes the usefulness of the dynamic framework explained above for analysis of education policy. The issues of displacement, deadweight loss and effectiveness are just as pertinent for an education intervention as they are for other forms of labour market programs.

If a group of people are encouraged through policy intervention to undertake further education, there will be the following effects. First, once they re-enter the labour market there will be some displacement of those already employed or, more likely, some people not in the program will not receive jobs they otherwise would have. Second, some of those receiving the assistance would have been employed without the additional education, and these are a deadweight loss of the program. Third, the issue of effectiveness is also relevant, meaning in this context the extent to which higher levels of education improve the employment prospects of participants.[10]

Modelling Skills Intervention in the Flows Framework

The dynamic framework of pages 179–81 is used in the analysis reported below. It is assumed to have the following dimensions, chosen to reflect the contemporary Australian labour market.

The size of the labour force is assumed to be ten million, with an unemployment rate of 8 per cent. The exit probabilities described earlier mean that of the initial stock of unemployment (of 800 000), 480 000 will be in unemployment duration state S, 120 000 will be in M, and 200 000 will be in L. These numbers are close to 1998 Australian labour market circumstances.

The model is steady state, which means that without an exogenous change, the unemployment stock is constant over time – that is, inflows equal outflows. This means that at the beginning of each period 480 000 people flow into the shortest unemployment duration category, with 360 000, 72 000 and 48 000 respectively exiting into jobs from unemployment duration categories S, M and L. Labour market programs or a targeted education policy will impact on outcomes through their potential to affect the size of these flows.

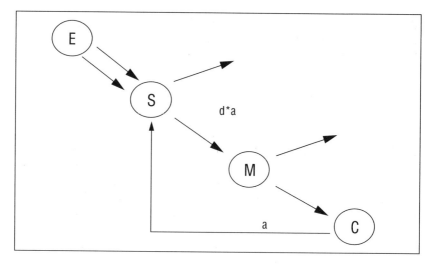

Figure 6.2 Modelling labour market programs in the flows framework

Applying the dynamic framework to an analysis of labour market programs

The way the flows model operates in an analysis of labour market programs can be illustrated by the following modification of the basic model, now shown in Figure 6.2. The figure shows how labour market programs with eligibility defined on the basis of unemployment duration can be incorporated into the flows model of unemployment described on pages 179–81. The policy assumes that those unemployed flowing from M to L (that is, those unemployed for more than eighteen months) all enter C, which represents program eligibility. But some proportion of those eligible for assistance – not shown in the Figure – would have become employed without it (deadweight loss).

A proportion given by 'a' (where $0 < a < 1$) will receive 'effective' assistance, which is defined to mean that their exit probabilities to employment are improved by the program to the extent that they will then be equivalent in employment prospect terms to those in S. At this stage and as a consequence, the proportion 'd*a' (where $0 < d < 1$) of those in S will then be displaced, which means in the model that they will then move to M. Once the displaced are in M, it is assumed that they experience the exit probabilities usually associated with unemployment duration greater than nine but less than eighteen months.

Thus the model takes account of deadweight loss, displacement, and program effectiveness. The size of these parameters is important to an assessment of possible program results.

The first parameter of interest is deadweight loss, the probability that targeted workers would have exited to employment over the duration of

Table 6.1 Parameter boundaries for labour market programs

	Public sector job creation	Wage subsidies
Deadweight loss	0.24	0.24
Displacement (d)		
Low	0.10	0.75
High	0.30	0.90
Average	0.20	0.83
Effectiveness (e)		
Low	0.12	0.41
High	0.31	0.71
Average	0.22	0.56

program assistance if the policy had not existed. From the ABS gross flows calculations this is 24 per cent,[11] and is assumed to be fixed in all simulations reported below.

The second parameter of interest is that of displacement. Wage subsidy schemes tend to have high, and public sector employment schemes low, displacement. The Piggott and Chapman analysis considered a very large number of international evaluations of schemes, and concluded that a reasonable range of displacement for wage subsidy schemes is of the order of 75–90 per cent, and for public sector schemes the range they found was between about 10 and 30 per cent.[12]

Third is effectiveness. In the modelling it is interpreted as the proportion of the targeted group who have their exit probabilities into employment changed from 0.24 to 0.75 (in other words, as if the effect of the program is to move participants from L to S). Piggott and Chapman concluded that effectiveness interpreted in this way lies between 0.41 and 0.71 for wage subsidy programs, and between 0.12 and 0.31 for public sector job creation programs.

The parameter sizes for these variables are summarized in Table 6.1.

How the framework applies to targeted education intervention

A stylized way to think about this particular policy initiative is as follows. Imagine the government is able to increase the education of a group of disadvantaged prospective workers, perhaps those who have been unemployed for a relatively long time. Further, assume that the policy increases the employment probability of those targeted.[13] Figure 6.3 illustrates how the education policy can be modelled in an

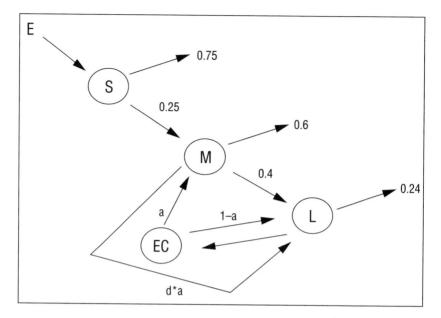

Figure 6.3 Modelling education intervention effects

unemployment flows context. The figure adds an 'education compact' (EC) to the original three-period flows model.

The education compact is assumed to take the following form. A proportion of those in the longest unemployment duration group are 'given' a number of extra years of formal schooling through participation in the education compact (EC), after which they re-enter the labour market and search for employment. The extra schooling is assumed to increase exit probabilities to employment for a proportion of participants, as if they were moved to unemployment duration state M, and is given in the diagram by 'a'. The program participants whose employment probabilities are not affected by the program have unchanged exit probabilities, and this group – (1–a) – is represented by the arrow returning them to L. Thus the division of the numbers between those entering 'a' and '1–a' depends on the effectiveness of the program, and is considered further below.

A consequence of the education intervention is that some of those in the unemployment duration category M will now be displaced from potential employment. Consequently, as a result of their longer unemployment, the displaced group d*a move to a lower exit probability, given by L.

The modelling of these effects requires simply that the relevant parameters be imposed in order to derive the new steady-state employment level. In the education intervention policy, deadweight loss is assumed to be the same as for the labour market program approach (0.24). Displacement boundaries are assumed to be the same as those reported above for wage subsidy schemes, meaning that the lower and upper levels are 0.75 and 0.90 respectively.

It is more reasonable to use the wage subsidy displacement boundaries, rather than those that could have been applied from public sector job creation schemes, because the education compact increases the competitive edge of participants, in a similar way that a subsidy acts. Effectiveness is more complicated, and is considered in the reporting of the education intervention results.

This simple method for analysing the possible consequences of a targeted education policy makes some strong assumptions. The first concerns the time framework, and is as follows. Obviously a higher level of formal education for a targeted group cannot be delivered instantaneously. This complication is ignored, which is an acceptable simplification because the focus of the steady-state modelling is on what transpires eventually, rather than what might happen in the very short term.

There are also budgetary implications from the policy since the government would need to offer financial inducements to encourage those targeted to take more formal education, and these are not considered. As well, the policy changes that would lead to increases in the education of the targeted group should take into account unemployment benefits, taxes and student income support. Because these issues are ignored, no attempt is made in what follows to work out the relative costs of the policy in budget terms; the focus instead is on the likely net employment effects of such an approach.

Assessing the Impact of Labour Market Programs

Policy description

The labour market program intervention is assumed to be targeted on those with very long unemployment duration (eighteen months or more), and offers only a wage subsidy or public sector job. Assistance is assumed to stop after nine months, and it is a 'reciprocal obligations' policy, in that those refusing the job are taken off unemployment benefit. This implies that those targeted take up an offer, given the high cost of not doing so.[14]

Three different variations are now considered: 100 per cent wage subsidy, 100 per cent public sector job creation, and 50 per cent wage subsidy with 50 per cent public sector job creation.

In reality, neither of the first two possibilities would eventuate. Employers would not be interested in offering wage subsidy jobs to the entire cohort of those who have been unemployed for more than eighteen months, since some of these will be considered to be poor prospective employees even with generous subsidies (for example, those unemployed for over three years). On the other hand, because of the relative costs to the budget (see below), governments would not be prepared to cover the entire eligible cohort with public sector employment. The scenarios are offered to illustrate possible boundaries of outcomes.

The cost calculations differ between scenarios because the wage subsidy is much less expensive than the public sector program.[15] Each wage subsidy job increases budget outlays by around $200 per week for nine months, or about $7000. On the other hand, a public sector placement costs about $350 in wage terms per week for nine months, or $12 500. But to this has to be added material and capital costs, which – in line with similar Australian government schemes – have been calculated to add about a further 60 per cent to outlays. That is, this category of program increases outlays by about $20 000 per job.[16]

The net budgetary costs per period include not only the outlays considered above, but the implications for both outlays and revenue from the higher employment resulting from the program. These take the form of outlays savings from decreases in unemployment and other welfare benefits and increased tax revenue. Conservative assumptions have been imposed in both areas, and per extra person employed these resulted in lowered unemployment benefits of about $6000, and higher tax revenue of around $3000.[17]

Labour market program results

Table 6.2 illustrates the outcomes for a range of program applications, all assumed to take up the entire cohort of those unemployed for eighteen months or more. The following points should be noted. The first is that the displacement and effectiveness parameters are important to the estimated effects of programs. For example, if the policy is entirely public sector job creation, having the lowest displacement and the highest effectiveness leads to a net job creation of about 107 000, and there are associated net costs to the budget of about $800 per job.

On the other hand, if displacement is at its maximum and effectiveness at its minimum for public sector job programs, the net employment creation is only about 25 000 and the net cost to the budget per additional job is around $48 000.

If the policy is entirely wage subsidy schemes there are also large differences in employment and net budget cost outcomes, again

Table 6.2 Labour market program results

	Public Sector100%		Wage Subsidy100%		50/50	
	Net Employ-ment creation	Budget cost per job created	Net employ-ment creation	Budget cost per job created	Net employ-ment creation	Budget cost per job created
Labour Market Programs						
Low d/ High e	107 340	$782	102 784	–$5478	105 023	–$1930
High d/ Low e	25 100	$48 207	–3900	*	10 974	$110 432
Average d/ Average e	73 437	$7462	60 900	–$281	67 216	$5445

Note: d – displacement; e – effectiveness

depending on the displacement and effectiveness parameters. With the most propitious combination of low displacement and high effectiveness, employment creation is about 103 000, and there is a net saving to the budget of over $5000 per job. However, with the highest displacement and the lowest effectiveness, net job creation is negative, and the costs to the budget are necessarily very high (and not easily computed with the parameters of the model).

It is clear that, for similar net job creation effects, wage subsidies are much cheaper than public sector schemes. For example, while the employment creation effects of the most propitious displacement and effectiveness parameters of wage subsidy and public sector approaches lead to similar employment creation effects, the per job net cost to the budget of the former is around $6000 lower.

Further, if the least propitious displacement and effectiveness parameters apply, the costs to the budget are very high no matter what type of scheme is used. For example, for a program that is 100 per cent public sector job creation, having the highest displacement in combination with the lowest effectiveness leads to a net employment creation of only around 25 000, and the net cost to the budget is about $48 000 per job. With the same displacement and effectiveness parameters with the 100 per cent wage subsidy policy, the net employment creation is around –4000.

For average displacement and effectiveness values there are also large differences in outcomes. For 100 per cent wage subsidy and 100 per cent public sector job creation respectively, between 60 000 and 75 000 extra jobs are created, with the net costs to the budget lying between zero and $7400.

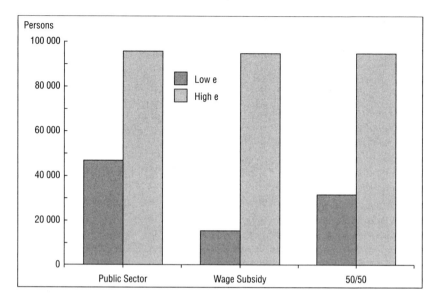

Figure 6.4 The importance of effectiveness for creating employment

A best guess would be as follows. If the policy is 50 per cent public sector job creation and 50 per cent wage subsidy, and there is average displacement and effectiveness, the program results in 67 000 extra jobs with a net cost to the budget of about $5500 per additional job. This should be considered a summary conclusion: in aggregate employment terms these results imply a modest, but potentially useful, role for labour market programs.

The importance of effectiveness

The modelling can be used to illustrate the importance of program effectiveness to the employment creation effects and net budget costs of labour market programs. By assuming that deadweight loss is 24 per cent (as is the case in all the above scenarios), and setting displacement equal to its average for both public sector creation and wage subsidy schemes, the role of effectiveness is now illustrated in Figure 6.4.

The important point from Figure 6.4 is that having an effective labour market program makes a very significant difference to employment creation. For example, if the scheme is 100 per cent public sector job creation, the increase in employment creation for an effective program is more than double that of an ineffective program, and for a 100 per cent wage subsidy scheme the job creation increase for effectiveness is

about sixfold. It follows for policy that there is perhaps no more important issue than program design and efficacious implementation.

The characteristics of effective programs are very much worth exploring further. They seem to include case management, flexibility of program rules to accommodate substantial heterogeneity of individual
needs, and early intervention for unemployed youth (Martin 1998).

Conclusions for labour market programs

There is a very large variation in the consequences of labour market
programs, on both employment creation and for the budget. In particular, if the nature of program design and delivery is such as to be fairly
ineffective in changing the exit probabilities to jobs of those in the
scheme, there is little reason for adopting such policies. Indeed, in some
circumstances intervention can actually decrease employment. On the
other hand, if the policies change the employment prospects of participants significantly, and displacement is relatively low, employment can
be increased considerably, and it is possible that there are net savings for
the budget. The wide range of outcomes illustrates just how crucial it is
that programs are formulated and targeted properly.

Even though there is a very large variation for labour market programs in terms of changing aggregate employment outcomes, there is a
bottom line. It is that with average expectations of deadweight loss,
displacement and effectiveness, labour market programs targeted on the
very long term unemployed do not result in a net creation of jobs that is
more than about one-third of the size of the targeted group. Given the
associated net budget costs, a circumspect conclusion is that while such
policies have a useful role to play, they cannot be seen to be a panacea
for the aggregate unemployment problem.

Assessing the Impact of Education Intervention

Description of the policy

Imagine that a large proportion of long-term unemployed people are
encouraged in some way to acquire an additional two years of formal
education. It is assumed that when they return to the workforce they
resume active search, and some proportion of the group has its probability of gaining employment increased as a result of having more
formal education. This is the basis of the conceptual framework of pages
187–9.

As noted, deadweight cost and displacement parameters are assumed
to be the same as those used in the analysis of wage subsidy schemes.

What differs relates to effectiveness, which in turn relates to the proportion of program participants who have their exit probabilities to
employment increased. What is crucial to the analysis is how much the
employment probability can be changed from additional education.

There is little broadly based Australian evidence on the effect of
education on exit probabilities, but the following two exercises using the
Australian Longitudinal and the Australian Youth Surveys help. The first
was done for this chapter, and the results are as follows.

Combinations of these surveys covering 1989–94 compared exit probabilities by unemployment duration (13, 26 and 39 weeks) for different
education groups. The analysis was restricted to those initially unemployed who eventually exited to a job, for two groups: those with only
ten years of formal schooling, and those with only twelve years formal
schooling.

The former group has a 15–30 per cent lower probability of being
employed in the next (nine-month) period. While the sample sizes were
too small to allow a focus just on those with very high durations, a
significant finding is that there was not much change in the relative
employment probabilities between education groups as duration
changed, which implies that the ratio can be used as an approximation
for what might be happening at higher unemployment durations.

Additional evidence is in Chapman and Smith (1992). They estimated
unemployment hazard functions controlling for a host of variables
including broad education categories. They found about a one-third
higher exit probability for those with Year 12 and beyond compared to
those with less than Year 12.

These two different sources suggest that an increase in formal education of two years after Year 10 increases the probability of exiting to a job
in the next period by between 15 and 33 per cent. These are the boundaries used for effectiveness in the simulations of the effects of education
intervention on job creation. Table 6.3 shows all the parameters used.

Job creation effects of education intervention: the case of a permanent change

The following policy design and parameters have been used:[18]

1 100 000 people in the highest unemployment duration category are
   given an extra two years of formal education (assumed to take them
   from having completed Year 10 to having completed Year 12);
2 the policy increases participants' search efficiency/labour market
   productivity commensurate with this higher level of education; and
3 deadweight loss and displacement are the same as those used in the
   wage subsidy analysis.

Table 6.3 Parameter boundaries for education compact

Deadweight cost	0.24
Displacement	
Low	0.75
High	0.90
Average	0.83
Effectiveness	
Low	0.15
High	0.33
Average	0.24

Table 6.4 shows the eventual net employment creation of an education policy intervention of the type described. The important point from Table 6.4 is that the job creation effects, compared to the size of the targeted group, are small. Although there are 100 000 participants in the program, even with the biggest increases in exit probabilities to employment as a result of higher levels of education, and assuming the lowest displacement, there are only about 8000 additional jobs. If effectiveness is low, and displacement is high, there is an increase in employment of less than 2000.

There is an issue of timing, because the changes in employment do not happen instantaneously. Figure 6.5 illustrates the dynamics of the employment adjustment to the scenario of average displacement (0.83) and overall effectiveness (0.24).

The time-path of the employment creation effect from the education compact is as follows. It takes seven periods (63 months) to reach the steady state of 6492 additional jobs. However, after just two years about two-thirds of the steady state is reached. This is illustrated in Figure 6.6, assuming the average displacement of 0.83. It is of interest to record that it does not seem to matter if education actually does increase exit probabilities to jobs, because the consequences of going from the lowest to the highest levels of effectiveness remain small.

Table 6.4 Education compact effects on job creation

	Net equilibrium job creation
Low d/high e	8216
High d/low e	1994
Average d/average e	6492

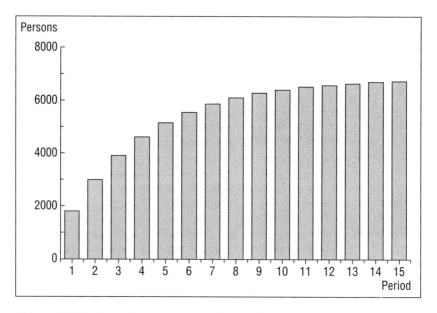

Figure 6.5 The dynamic employment effects of a permanent education compact

Results of education intervention: the case of a one-off change

The experiment reported above could take a different form. Imagine that the government chose to implement the policy for one cohort only, instead of permanently. Figure 6.6 illustrates this case for the scenario of average displacement and average effectiveness.

For the one-off education compact the effect is highest immediately after education levels are increased, and results in around 1600 additional jobs. However, the effect is reduced by about half after three years, and is less than 100 after about ten periods (just over six years). The effect washes out over time because increasing proportions of the targeted group re-attain average flow probabilities.

Conclusions and caveats

The results of the simulations imply strongly that a targeted education intervention of the type described has little job creation potential. The conclusion essentially reflects the fact that the search efficiency of the unemployed is not significantly increased by formal education. This suggests that the solution to aggregate unemployment, at least in the short term, does not lie in policies designed to increase the formal education of the long-term unemployed.

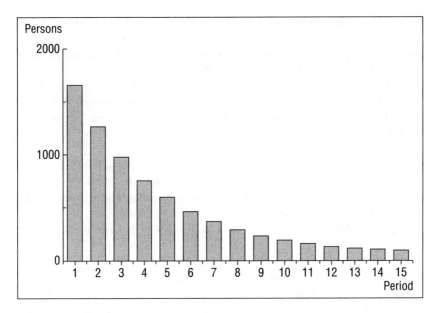

Figure 6.6 The dynamic employment effects of a one-off education compact

There are caveats to this result. It does not mean that education is irrelevant to economic performance, because higher levels of education could increase potential GDP through the provision of skilled labour resources, which might encourage increased physical investment.[19] And economic growth might well be higher because of a greater capacity of an educated labour force to adjust to external and new information shocks.[20]

Conclusion

The analysis of this chapter was motivated by the idea that Australian employment could be increased significantly through increases in the skill base of a large proportion of the unemployed. That is, instead of cutting wages, is there a potential for increasing aggregate employment by decreasing the real unit labour costs of the unemployed via improvements in skills? A stylized set of simulations have been used to illustrate some important relationships between formal skills and employment creation.

The main conclusion is that the answer to Australian job creation, at least in the short to medium term, cannot rely on increasing the skills of the unemployed. The combinations of deadweight loss and the displacement of non-targeted workers are such that even quite effective programs – in terms of changing participants' employment prospects – do not deliver enough extra jobs. In some circumstances with labour market programs, however, there is an obvious potential for gains. But at best, programs of the type simulated can be a significant though modest part of the solution to unemployment.

In terms of education intervention the potential seems much less. This is because the results are driven by the increases in search efficiency from higher levels of education. However, the presumed increases in search effectiveness are just too low to outweigh the effects of dead-weight loss and displacement.

That decreasing real unit labour costs in the ways considered is not the panacea for employment creation has two significant, albeit speculative, implications. One is that the other way of decreasing labour costs – wage cuts – might similarly have little effect on employment creation in the short to medium term. Moreover if such a policy is contemplated it is important to understand the mechanism to be used to reduce wages; in the Australian context this could only happen through real adjustments in the safety net, and few employees are now earning a minimum safety net.[21]

The other related point is that if much of the answer does not lie on the productivity and labour cost side, defined broadly, the case for looking elsewhere appears strong. For the contemporary Australian labour market, at least over the next short period, aggregate demand issues seem to loom large.

Notes

1 The link between wage and income equality is a crucial issue for this debate, and is considered by Richardson and Harding in Chapter 4. The other question, the extent of employment creation as a result of a wage cut, is indirectly an important aspect of what follows. It is explored by Borland in Chapter 3.

2 The exception is Piggott & Chapman 1995, and their method underlies the approach of this chapter.

3 Recent contributions in the area of endogenous growth theory imply that this is an important issue (Dowrick 1995).

4 The details are available in Piggott & Chapman 1995.

5 Martin 1998 examines this for the OECD.

6 First seen in the town of Lyon, France, in the sixteenth century (Betson 1982).

7 For the history of Australian programs to 1990, see Stretton & Chapman 1990.

8 See *Working Nation* (1994).

9 There is a considerable literature in this area, with the path-breaking theoretical contribution coming from Becker 1962. The author has contributed empirically (Chapman & Tan 1980).

10 Some part of this relates to the relative role of screening and human capital perspectives in education. The more important is the former, the less effective is the program in decreasing real unit labour costs. The more that education actually changes productivity, the greater is the likelihood of employment take-up of the targeted group.

11 See Piggott & Chapman 1995 for details.

12 See Piggott & Chapman 1995 for details.

13 This could happen either because the targeted group become more efficient in terms of search behaviour, or because the scheme leads to employers believing that members of the group have higher productivity than previously.

14 This part of the modelling reflects the approaches of both the Job Compact of the previous Labor Government and the apparent position of the current Coalition Government.

15 For a full explanation of the basis of the methods, see Piggott & Chapman 1995.

16 These assumptions are explained fully in Piggott & Chapman 1995.

17 Again, the details are available in Piggott & Chapman 1995.

18 Budget costs are not calculated because they would have required estimates of the cost of additional schooling, which are unavailable.

19 On this point, see Bartel & Lichtenburg 1987.

20 See Schultz 1976.

21 About 6 per cent of employees earn the federal minimum award rate or less, according to Richardson and Harding in this volume.

CHAPTER 7

Labour Market Deregulation, Relative Wages and the Social Security System

Bob Gregory, Eva Klug and Yew May Martin

The first six chapters have examined the arguments for regulation of the labour market, the consequences of regulation, the effectiveness of regulation and an alternative strategy for generating adequate incomes for the low-paid. This chapter considers whether the well-being of vulnerable workers can be adequately protected, not by regulation of the conditions of employment but by the provisions of the welfare system. It concludes that regulation of the labour market and the design and generosity of the social welfare system are intimately related, and that the dismantling of the former would lead inexorably to the undermining of the latter.

The Australian labour market has been subject to disappointing long-term trends since the early 1970s, in which the total number of full-time jobs has fallen by 20 per cent. This downward trend has quickened during economic recessions and slowed during strong periods of growth. The end is not in sight. There is something strange about the Australian economy. It just does not produce a sufficient number of full-time jobs for its citizens.

This lack of full-time job growth, over such a long period, has led many to suggest that the labour market might perform better if it were less regulated, so that wages and employment conditions could be more flexible. The reform strategy would be to weaken the role of trade unions and centralized wage fixing institutions and move towards a US-style labour market. It is argued that a less fettered labour market would allow wages to fall among those groups with high unemployment and, in this way, generate jobs for them.

The emphasis on deregulating the labour market derives partly from a simple micro-economic theory of demand and supply that ascribes unemployment to a wage that is too high, and partly from the rapid job growth in the less regulated US labour market. After a constant

200

employment–population ratio for most of the postwar period, the United States, from the mid 1970s, suddenly began to generate more full-time jobs relative to the population. The US labour market has been called the 'great job machine'. Since the early 1970s the adult full-time employment–population ratio has increased by 6 per cent in the United States and fallen just over 20 per cent in Australia.

But all is not perfect in the United States. Over the last two decades that less regulated labour market has also been subject to an undesirable trend towards greater wage inequality, with low wages falling substantially in real terms, especially for males. Since 1976, weekly income for male full-time workers at the tenth and twentieth percentile of the male earnings distribution has fallen 12 per cent relative to the median. The fact that wage falls for the low-paid have accompanied aggregate employment increases in the United States is taken as evidence that a less regulated labour market is necessary to re-establish full employment in Australia.

If Australia moves towards a substantially less regulated labour market, the extent of wage inequality might be expected to increase (as explored in Chapter 3) and, if the conjectures of those who advocate deregulation are right, full-time employment will begin to increase relative to the population. There is no free lunch however. Falling wages at the bottom of the wage distribution would be the price of additional employment.

This chapter explores some of the issues related to increased wage inequality and is structured as follows. In the first section the emphasis is placed on the different degree of US and Australian wage inequality, the relative wage flexibility of the two markets and the relationship between relative wage flexibility and employment growth.[1] We show that there is more flexibility in the Australian wage system to deliver relative wage falls for low-paid men and women than is commonly thought. Indeed, somewhat surprisingly, the Australian system has been producing falls in weekly earnings for low-paid adult men which are not all that different from the wage falls that have been occurring in the United States. Wage inequality is increasing at much the same rate in both labour markets.

The second section explores the interaction between the wage structure and the Australian social security and income tax systems. There are three themes. First, we explore whether the gap between low wages and social security payments will narrow, if wage inequality increases substantially. If the gap does narrow significantly this may reduce labour supply and increase the propensity for the unemployed to stay longer on social security payments.

Second, we explore whether the interaction of labour supply and the present social security system – which fully adjusts benefit and pension levels to keep them as a fixed proportion of average weekly earnings – provides a floor below which low wages will not fall. If there is a floor to low wages, a full employment strategy that relies on a less regulated labour market as a method of reducing the wages of the low-skilled may be ineffective unless the floor is lowered.

Third, for the employed workforce there are interactions between increased wage inequality and the social security and income tax systems that may affect labour market behaviour and that may protect a significant proportion of the labour market from an income fall associated with increased wage dispersion. For those with dependent children a fall in low wages may have little effect on income received. This phenomenon, whereby wage changes are largely offset by changes in taxation paid and welfare payments received, is often described as a system of high marginal effective tax rates. The phenomenon has important implications for judgements about the income and labour supply responses of greater wage inequality.

Wage Inequality in the United States and Australia

Earnings inequality before 1976

It is not possible to predict exactly what might happen to wage relativities if the Australian labour market were substantially deregulated. One difficulty is that it is not possible to forecast the degree of deregulation that might occur. Today unions are weaker, and less widespread, in terms of influence and membership than previously. Over the period 1976–96 trade union membership fell from 50 to 31 per cent of employees, and this trend is likely to continue. Centralized wage-fixing, which is probably the crucial feature of the regulated labour market, is also less important, but the old institutional framework remains intact and some centralized wage-setting still takes place. Because the present wage-setting system is a hybrid of centralized and deregulated labour markets, and likely to stay that way, there is always scope for more or less centralization of wage decisions depending on shifts in the political and economic climate.

Another difficulty is that apart from very broad associations, little is known about the links between a change in labour market regulation and a change in relative wage outcomes. There is no clearly articulated theoretical structure that can be applied, and the empirical work, which relates different degrees of labour market regulation to wage relativity patterns across countries, largely identifies the role of the institutional framework as the residual in the analysis. It seems from the research, however, that there is an association between more labour market regulation and more wage inequality and that institutional structures are not a veil behind which real forces are at work to *fully* determine the degree of wage inequality (Gregory et al. 1989; Blau & Kahn 1996a). The institutional structure influences the degree of wage inequality in its own right.

One way of handling the absence of a theoretical framework, and the difficulties of quantifying degrees of labour market regulation, is to go straight to a US–Australian comparison. The United States serves as the example of a less regulated labour market. We choose it not so much because its outcomes would necessarily be replicated here if there was a common degree of labour market regulation, but because a comparison gives some data to hold on to and provides a rough idea of the magnitudes of the key variables that are being discussed. The US data are easily accessible and US ideas, values and economic norms are becoming increasingly important influences on Australia.

We begin by focusing on the male pay structure. The first step for each country is to rank the 1975 full-time weekly earnings of male wage and salary earners from the highest to the lowest. The focus is on full-time weekly earnings because the Australian data do not allow adjustment for hours worked. The data are collected from household surveys in each country.[2] The second step is to divide the US weekly earnings at each decile boundary by the US male median full-time weekly earnings. The third step is to divide these US ratios by the equivalent ratios for Australia to illustrate the different degree of wage inequality in each country.

The more compressed Australian earnings distribution below the median is clearly evident. In 1976 Australian males at the tenth percentile earned 40 per cent more from a full week's work, relative to the median, than their US counterparts. In current Australian dollars the gap is $117 per week (Figure 7.1). This is quite a large sum. At the twentieth percentile the gap is 21 per cent, or $98 per week. There is also some compression above median earnings, but it is not very important. For example, Australian male full-time wage and salary earners at the eightieth percentile receive 4 per cent less per week, relative to median male earnings, than their US counterparts.

We perform similar calculations for the female pay structure (Figure 7.2) and once again divide by median male full-time weekly earnings to enable comparisons to be made across the two countries. The difference in the degree of inequality is even greater. At the tenth percentile women in Australia earned 76 per cent more than their US counterparts; at the twentieth percentile they earned 66 per cent more. The extent to which low-paid women were worse off in the United States is quite extraordinary by Australian standards. Furthermore, low pay spreads across most of the female workforce. In 1976, 88 per cent of US

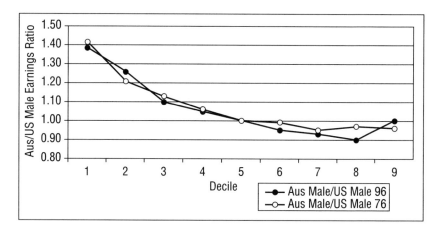

Figure 7.1 Australia to US male full-time weekly earnings ratio by decile, 1976 and 1996
Source: Based on US Current Population Survey and ABS 6310.0

women who worked full-time full-year earned less than male median earnings; in Australia the proportion was 78 per cent. If a less regulated labour market in Australia moved low pay down to US levels, Australian women would be the most adversely affected.

The pre-1976 puzzle: US and Australian wage and unemployment outcomes

It is not possible to take the Australian data back before 1976, but it is very likely that the United States has always had wider wage differentials than Australia, at least since the Second World War.[3] Throughout this period, despite narrower wage and earnings differentials, the Australian unemployment record was better than that of the United States. During the 1960s, for example, Australian unemployment averaged less than 1.5 per cent; US unemployment averaged over 4 per cent. In addition to achieving lower unemployment, the employment–population ratio in Australia was higher than in the United States and, as in the United States, varied over the cycle around a constant trend.

Before 1976, therefore, there appears to be something unsatisfactory about the US labour market in that it produced greater inequality of earnings than Australia but no better employment and worse unemployment outcomes. If one was interested in avoiding relatively low wages, low income, or an unemployment spell, Australia was a better place to live and work than the United States. Of course, the United States enjoyed higher average wages but, over the postwar period, the rate of growth of average income per capita increased at much the same rate in

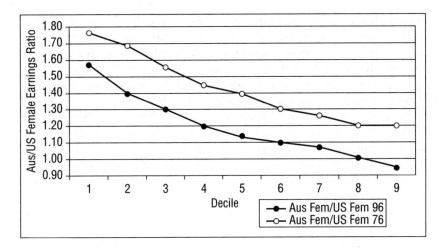

Figure 7.2 Australia to US female full-time weekly earnings ratio by decile, 1976 and 1996
Source: Based on US Current Population Survey and ABS 6310.0

both countries. Why was the US labour market performance in terms of wage inequality and unemployment worse than that of Australia? There are a number of ways of responding to this question.[4]

One way is to argue that unsatisfactory US outcomes before 1976 can be regarded, to some extent, as the cost of achieving higher *average* wages. This link has never been firmly established, however. Variants of this argument are often heard in Australia today. Sometimes it is said that greater wage inequality is necessary to produce incentives for individuals and firms to invest in training and to induce people to work harder. This argument that greater inequality is good for us might be reconciled with US outcomes before 1976 by asserting that the US labour market may have been inefficient and undesirable in the short run – it generated more unemployment and greater wage inequality before 1976 – but, in the long run, it is more efficient because it generates more income growth. But, since the early 1950s, US real-wage growth rates have been lower than real-wage growth rates in most of Western Europe and about the same as in Australia. The movement towards higher levels of US real wages, relative to Australia, appears to have occurred before the Second World War and seems closely linked to the development of the US manufacturing sector.

Another way to respond to the question why US wage inequality and unemployment outcomes were worse than Australia's is to argue that, by their nature, less regulated labour markets deliver greater wage inequality without significant employment and unemployment gains.

The higher *average* wage in the United States may be the result of other factors such as differences in savings rates, differences in technology levels, natural resource endowments and other non-labour market factors. Hence, in the full employment world of 1950–75, if Australia had changed towards a US system of labour market institutions this would have delivered greater wage inequality but no better employment or real wage growth outcomes. This response would then emphasize that the difference in labour market institutions between Australia and the United States primarily determines income distribution and not employment or growth. This is a radical position, but it is increasingly being accepted by labour economists who do research into international comparisons of labour markets.

A final response to the pre-1976 puzzle is to argue that the greater dispersion of wages in the United States is not related to US labour market institutions but the result of something outside the labour market, perhaps the result of greater regional variation of wages and prices, perhaps attributable to the difficult economic circumstances of Afro-Americans or perhaps the result of US education institutions, which produce greater variability in education quality. If this argument were correct the proposition that links greater wage inequality to the less regulated US labour market is exaggerated or perhaps wrong.

The lack of a clear understanding why US wage inequality outcomes were greater than those of Australia during 1950–75 is disappointing.[5] There is clearly a need for a better understanding of the economic history of the pre-1976 period as part of trying to establish more precisely the link between labour market institutions, relative wage variability and employment outcomes. Without this understanding we cannot be sure to what extent a less regulated labour market for Australia will produce a wider variation of earning, or whether a wider dispersion of earnings will produce better employment outcomes and increase average wages.

Earnings inequality since 1976

Since 1976 inequality of full-time earnings has increased in both countries, but the change, measured as the ratio between the ninetieth and tenth percentile, has been larger in the United States. In Australia this ratio has increased approximately 25 per cent; in the United States the increase has been about 40 per cent. For men and women in both countries the widening distribution has been generated by falls in earnings at the bottom of their respective earnings distributions and increases at the top. Male earnings at the tenth percentile have fallen approximately 14 per cent relative to the male median in both countries.

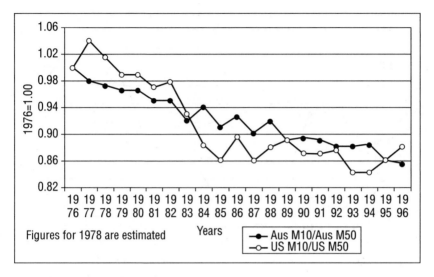

Figure 7.3a Australia to US male full-time weekly earnings ratio 10th to 50th percentile, 1976–96
Source: Based on US Current Population Survey and ABS 6310.0

Relative to the female median, female earnings at the tenth percentile of their earnings distributions have fallen 14 and 17 per cent in the United States and Australia respectively.

For our purposes we are more interested in changes in earnings relative to the male median. The changes are plotted in Figures 7.3a and 7.3b. For US women, earnings at the tenth percentile fall slightly until the mid-1980s, after which there are large increases concentrated on four years. For males, earnings at the tenth percentile fall in a fairly continuous manner between 1976 and 1984, after which the rate of fall seems more or less to have ceased.

It is the ability to deliver large falls in relative wages, such as occurred for low-paid males between 1975 and 1985, and large increases, such as those for low-paid females between 1988 and 1992, that is often presented as evidence for the employment-generating superiority of a less regulated labour market. Wages can vary more to facilitate employment adjustments to variations in demand and supply. The same calculations for Australia, and their comparison with the United States, suggest a puzzling and exciting research agenda.

First, the Australian labour market is widely regarded as a more regulated labour market and yet the falls in relative earnings for men at the tenth percentile (and also the twentieth and thirtieth) are almost exactly the same as in the United States and the falls are substantial. At the tenth percentile male full-time weekly earnings have fallen 12–14 per

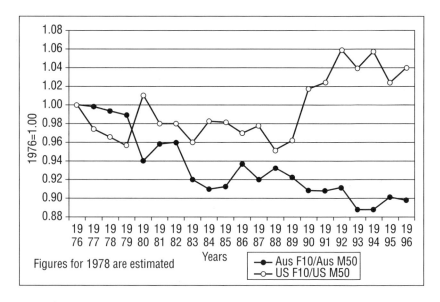

Figure 7.3b Australia to US male full-time weekly earnings, female 10th to male 50th percentile, 1976–96
Source: Based on US Current Population Survey and ABS 6310.0

cent relative to the median. If the Australian labour market is so regulated, how are such large falls in relative weekly earnings possible?[6] Why is the change in the dispersion of earnings so similar to that of the United States?

Second, the rate of fall of Australian low wages for men is continuous and proceeds at a fairly even rate through time. The rate of change is not simply a function of shifts in the level of employment or unemployment. When the Australian male full-time employment–population ratio falls most, 1976–85, full-time weekly earnings of low-paid men fall at much the same rate as when the male full-time employment–population ratio did not change (1982–89).

Third, the rate of fall of male low wages, relative to the median, seems to be independent of the degree of centralized wage-fixing that prevailed at different periods in Australia. Low wages, for example, continue to fall through the Accord period and at much the same rate as when there was less centralization.

Fourth, if such a large fall in Australian male wage relativities – 14 per cent at the tenth percentile – accompanied a 20 per cent fall in the aggregate male full-time employment–population ratio, what fall in relative wages would be required to generate sufficient jobs in Australia? Perhaps a very substantial fall indeed.

Fifth, Figure 7.1 produces the distribution of male weekly earnings relativities for Australia and the United States from 1976 to 1995. The relationship across countries has hardly changed. The country with the large loss of male full-time jobs has experienced much the same change in relative weekly earnings as the country with the small loss in male full-time jobs.

Sixth, women's earnings at the tenth percentile in Australia follow the earnings path of their male counterpart, and fall quite sharply between 1976 and 1982 – a fall of 9 per cent – then, after 1982, their earnings relativity stabilizes relative to the male median. For low-paid women the Australian earnings structure seems quite flexible. The Australian labour market seems not to be all that different from the United States in its ability to generate changes in earnings.

Each of the above propositions are very disturbing in that they do not agree with common beliefs. What does all this mean? How is it possible to argue that the more regulated Australian labour market compresses wage relativities and yet reconcile this belief with the proposition, at least with respect to changes in low pay, that the two labour markets seem similar in their degree of flexibility?

One obvious answer is that there appears to be no straightforward correspondence between these facts and the simple models that underlie the case for less labour market regulation by stressing links between relative wage changes and employment growth. The very different macro employment outcomes of the two countries seem independent of relative wage outcomes. The labour market deregulation case, which stresses relative wage flexibility, must be supported either by doctrine or an empirical analysis that is more subtle than this simple comparison of earnings outcomes. Yet it is not clear how a more subtle analysis could overcome the above interpretation of the basic facts. Further complicating the analysis to take account of the different distribution of education patterns, labour market experience and industry composition may explain a small proportion of the outcomes, but it is hard to see how the above simple facts could be overturned.[7]

Labour Supply, Relative Wages, Welfare Payments and Work Incentives

The payment structure of the Australian welfare system consists of four parts. First, there are a set of eligibility requirements that need to be satisfied before unemployment income support is paid. These requirements are based on income and asset tests, the nature of job separation, intensity of job-seeking behaviour and, for immigrants, the period of Australian residence. Second, there are standard base-rate payments that vary according to the marital status and age of the unemployed person. Third, there are additional income payments that include rent assistance, subsidized pharmaceuticals and numerous programs providing income for children such as cash payments (minimum rate family payments and more than minimum rate family payments), tax concessions (family tax initiative), childcare concessions (childcare assistance and childcare rebates) and a parenting allowance for those who wish to stay home and care for children. Fourth, there are different rates at which base rate and additional income payments are withdrawn as non-social security income increases. These withdrawal rates ensure that most low-paid workers with dependants receive some income support from the government.[8]

There are two important interrelationships between low wages and this welfare system. One is the provision of income support for those employed, especially the low-paid with a dependent spouse and/or dependent children. Government income support for low-paid workers can have a substantial impact on income distribution and perhaps on labour supply responses within the employed labour force, affecting mobility from one job to another and variations in hours worked.

The other important interrelationship is the change in government income support accompanying movements between employment and unemployment. Income support when not employed affects the general level of poverty of the low-paid, whose employment income may be interrupted by spells of unemployment benefits. Income support when unemployed can influence labour supply responses and, at very low wages, individuals who might normally be employed may choose to stay longer on welfare payments.

In principle, the analysis of these interrelationships should be undertaken within a full general equilibrium model in which all members of the population are able to respond to wage and welfare changes, but like most studies, this chapter analyses only EMTRs faced by a subset of hypothetical people. It is necessary in constructing hypothetical people to decide the family structure of the individual – such as a single adult family, sole parents with children – and the range of welfare benefits being received. For example, does the family access a rent subsidy? We assume that the wage is the only non-social security source of income and that the full range of welfare support available at that wage is taken.[9]

Wages and government income support among the employed workforce

Table 7.1 lists Australian income support for different family types at the tenth percentile of the male and female gross wage distributions. The 1997 pay rates for a single male and female employed full-time are $414

Table 7.1 Wages, welfare payments and taxation, tenth percentile, 1997

Family types	Full-time weekly earnings $	Gross income $	Net income $	Government income subsidy $	(%)[1]	Tax paid $	(%)[2]
Male	414	414	345	0	(0)	69	(17)
Female	367	367	312	0	(0)	55	(15)
Single with children, female							
1 child <13	367	505	474	138	(38)	31	(7)
1 child <13, 1 child 13–15	367	577	545	210	(57)	22	(4)
Married couple, no children							
One earner, male	414	478	434	64	(16)	44	(10)
One earner, Female	367	464	426	97	(26)	38	(8)
With children, one earner							
Male with 1 child <13	414	542	480	128	(31)	62	(11)
Female with 1 child <13	367	525	475	158	(43)	50	(10)
Male, with 2 children <13, 1 child 13–15	414	666	604	252	(61)	62	(9)

Notes: [1]As a percentage of gross F/T weekly earnings; [2]As a percentage of gross income.
Source: Authors' calculations.

and $367 a week respectively. These weekly wage rates are too high for single employed individuals to receive government income support, but income support is often available for the non-employed partner of a married couple household. At the tenth percentile of the male wage distribution this income support can reach 16 per cent of gross weekly earnings. At the tenth percentile of the female pay distribution income support can reach 26 per cent of the wage.

Most income support is directed towards families with dependent children. To illustrate this, and to simplify the exposition, we focus on income data for two family types: a married couple family with a male income-earner, dependent spouse and three dependent children, and a female sole parent with two dependent children. For these families direct government income support at the tenth percentile of the male and female wage distributions respectively is between 57 and 61 per cent of the gross wage.

Table 7.1 also adjusts income levels for tax liabilities, which at the tenth percentile of the gross wage distribution range between 4 and 17 per cent of the gross wage, depending on family structure (which affects tax concessions and taxable government income support). For all groups, except single adults, the government welfare subsidy exceeds taxation paid and has a substantial impact on income distribution. Consider an employed female sole parent with two dependent children. Government income support, which effectively adds 57 per cent to the wage, lifts her gross income from the tenth to just over the fiftieth percentile of the female gross wage distribution. Her low-tax liabilities are also important. Her after-tax income is just above that of a single female with no dependants at the eightieth percentile of the net wage distribution.

Family gross income for a married male with three dependent children and a non-employed spouse is lifted from the tenth to just over the fortieth percentile of the male gross wage distribution. This family at the tenth percentile of the male pay distribution receives an additional $252 of income per week and pays $62 in tax. On a net income basis the income of this family is increased to the net income of a single male at the seventieth percentile of the male net wage distribution. These calculations emphasize the importance of welfare payments for the income distribution of the employed. The ability of family structure to affect the income of the family is comparable to the effects on the expected wage of an individual moving from an education level of incomplete high school to a university degree.

Government income support is reduced as the gross wage is increased. One channel operates through increased taxation, the other through reduced welfare payments. As income increases from non-social security sources, each welfare payment (unemployment benefits, rent assistance and the various child assistance payments) is withdrawn from the family at different rates and usually without recognition of the withdrawal rates of other programs. Withdrawal rates stack on top of each other and are additive, so that over various income ranges the aggregate withdrawal rate can be quite large. The base allowance is withdrawn first. Thus low-paid families with a dependent spouse, but no dependent children, no longer receive income support once weekly income reaches the twentieth percentile of the male pay distribution. But, for a family with dependent children, government income support extends well up the wage distribution and often beyond the eightieth percentile (Table 7.2). If account is taken of tax liabilities for a family with one income-earner, a dependent spouse and three dependent children, the break-even point – where the gross wage is equal to the net income received and on balance a government neither taxes nor provides a subsidy – occurs at the fiftieth percentile.

The combination of additional income tax and social security withdrawal means that for many families the EMTR – the percentage of an extra dollar of non-government income that is lost either to tax increases

Table 7.2 Wages, government income support and taxes, deciles

Family types	10 $	20 $	30 $	40 $	50 $	60 $	70 $
Single female with 1 child <13 and 1 child 13–15							
Benefit	210	181	174	155	133	102	70
Tax	32	46	61	74	89	110	132
Additional net income	178	135	113	81	44	–8	–62
Net benefit as a percentage of full-time weekly earnings	49	31	24	16	8	–1	–10
Married couple, one earner (male) with 2 children <13 and 1 child 13–15							
Benefit	252	236	226	200	159	123	72
Tax	62	87	102	135	158	183	228
Additional net income	190	149	124	65	–1	–60	–156
Net benefit as a percentage of full-time weekly earnings	46	31	24	11	0	–8	–18

or benefit withdrawal – can be extremely high and sometimes over 100 per cent. High EMTRs may be encountered whenever there is a wage increase in the job, when moving from welfare payments to a job, or moving from one job to another.

The EMTR for a female single wage-earner with two dependent children is 69 per cent over the income range from the tenth to the twentieth percentile of the female wage distribution and 84 per cent over the income range from the thirtieth to the fortieth percentile (Table 7.3). The EMTRs for a married couple family with one income-earner and three dependent children is 61 per cent from the tenth to the twentieth percentile of male weekly earnings and 96 per cent from the thirtieth to the fortieth percentile. A wage increase of $66 a week over the tenth to the twentieth percentile increases family income by $26.

These EMTRs also matter when the wage distribution changes. Table 7.4 lists the average full-time earnings of men and women for the Australian and US 1997 wage distributions and illustrates how net income would respond, under the current tax and welfare systems, if the Australian wage distribution were to be replaced by that of the United States. All values are measured in 1997 Australian dollars.

For a single adult male at the tenth percentile the fall in wages accompanying a move to the US wage distribution is large, 28 per cent or $117 (Table 7.4). After taxes the net wage is reduced by $88 or 26 per

Table 7.3 Effective marginal tax rates

Family types	Income range decile boundaries		
	10–20 $	30–40 $	60–70 $
Single Female with 1 child <13 and 1 child 13–15			
Wage increase	62	38	66
Benefit reduction	29	19	33
Tax increase	14	13	22
Net income increase	19	6	11
Marginal effective tax rate	69%	84%	84%
Married Couple, one earner (male) with 2 children <13 and 1 child 13–15			
Wage increase	66	72	103
Benefit reduction	16	36	51
Tax increase	24	33	46
Net income increase	26	3	6
Marginal effective tax rate	61%	96%	94%

cent. Single adult males at this income level cannot access government income support, and the only offset to the wage fall is reduced taxation. Wages for women are very low in the United States and at the tenth percentile of the female pay distribution a movement to the US wage distribution would involve a larger reduction in the gross wage, $134 or 36 per cent. After tax adjustments, and access to welfare payments, the net income reduction is only $39 or 11 per cent. The Australian tax and welfare systems therefore impact differently on low-paid men and women. The higher EMTR for women arises because they can now access non-taxable income support. The tax and welfare system increases the total net income of low-paid women relative to that of men. For families with dependants, government changes in income support as the wage distribution changes is quite large and places a changing wedge between wage and income changes. At the tenth percentile the income fall associated with a $117 wage change that would be the result of moving to a US wage structure varies between $12 and $53 for the families listed.

These interactions between wages, welfare payments and income taxes have a number of important implications. First, as long as the current welfare and tax system remain in place, a family with dependent children can be largely isolated from relative wage changes over most of the wage distribution. If the average EMTR were 100 per cent, for example, each dollar fall in the market wage would be fully offset by a reduction in tax and an increase in government assistance. Hence, to a considerable degree, the income effects of a widening wage distribution below the median wage are predominantly of concern for single people, those

Table 7.4 Wages, welfare payments and taxation, Australia and the United States – tenth percentile, 1997

Family types	Australian pay structure Australian welfare system			US pay structure Australian welfare system		
	Full-time weekly earnings $	Gross income $	Net income $	Full-time weekly earning $	Gross income $	Net income $
Male	414	414	345	297	297	257
Female	367	367	312	233	297	273
Single with children, female						
1 child <13	367	505	474	233	438	421
1 child <13, 1 child 13–15	367	577	545	233	510	492
Married couple, no children						
One earner, male	414	478	434	297	443	408
One earner, female	367	464	426	233	424	401
With children, one earner						
Male with 1 child <13	414	542	480	297	504	478
Female with 1 child <13	367	525	475	233	485	461
Male, with 2 children <13, 1 child 13–15	414	666	604	297	628	592

without dependants and those with sufficient assets not to qualify for benefits. (According to Chapter 4, two-thirds of low-wage workers in the mid-1990s did not have dependent children.) The family types considered here are largely unaffected.

Second, the Australian welfare system ensures that relative wage changes are accompanied by *de facto* wage subsidies to a wide range of employees. As the wage falls, the labour cost to the employer is reduced, irrespective of family type, and the demand for labour may increase. But the link between the wage reduction and income received by the worker depends on the extent to which other members of the family are employed. Many low-paid workers with dependants could be largely indifferent to wage falls, and there may be no supply response (i.e. the amount of work they want) because the wage change is offset by changes in government income support and taxation.

Third, for a significant fraction of the labour force, those with dependent children, a change in relative wages effectively changes the proportion of their income derived from government. For them possible policy changes to the welfare and tax system may be more important than wage dispersion changes. This raises all sorts of issues about the 'need' for low-wage increases by workers with families and the degree to which they will attempt to seek wage increases.

Fourth, a simple demand-and-supply model to analyse wage and employment changes at low wages is clearly inadequate when the interactions between the wage, welfare payments and taxes are so important. The simple model needs to be generalized to take account of family types and the structure of social security. At this stage, the extent of the interactions are well documented (Ingles 1997; Beer 1997), but extensive research on labour supply responses to the system is yet to be undertaken; we do not know how work incentives are being affected. One issue, for a family with two or three dependants, is whether it is worth the primary earner accepting a full-time job at low wages. From a short-term perspective an occasional part-time job may be a better option because the EMTR is so high.

Fifth, we have directed attention towards single-earner families, but for families with secondary-income earners, especially those with dependent children, similar issues arise. Thus, in a recent study, Beer has shown that 'a low income family with three children is financially *worse off* if the mother works between 10 and 24 hours per week than if she works just 9 hours per week. By increasing her hours worked from 5 to 35 hours per week the family benefits by just $12 per week. For the same family with only one child, the increase is around $85 per week' (1997: 30).

Sixth, the rapid growth of welfare expenditure has often been seen as a response to the increase in unemployment benefit recipients and the associated growth of programs such as sole parent pensions and disability pensions, which can act as substitutes for unemployment benefits. The development of *de facto* wage subsidies for the employed with dependants means that the growth of welfare expenditure is now directly linked to the fall in low wages. It would be interesting to work out the changing balance between these two factors: the change in the social security budget generated by quantity adjustments in the labour market (job loss and unemployment) and the change generated by price adjustments (changes in relative wages, welfare payments and tax reductions).[10]

The movement between employment and unemployment: the replacement ratio

The first step is to calculate the level of unemployment benefits and sole-parent pensions for different family types and compare them to net income, if the individual is employed, at various points on the wage distribution. These calculations, often referred to as replacement ratios, provide an estimate of income gaps between welfare payments and full-time work that may affect labour supply choices.

As expected, replacement ratios differ between demographic groups and are largest for those with dependants. If a job is lost at the tenth

Table 7.5 Replacement ratios

| | Percentiles | | |
Family types	10th %	20th %	40th %
Single male			
Australia	57	51	42
United States	77	61	45
Single female			
Australia	63	56	49
United States	72	67	56
Single Female with 1 child <13 and 1 child 13–15			
Australia	64	62	59
United States	71	67	62
Married couple, one earner (male) with 2 children <13 and 1 child 13–15			
Australia	82	79	76
United States	84	83	77

percentile of the male pay distribution, welfare payments for a single male who qualifies for all assistance will replace 57 per cent of the after-tax income loss (Table 7.5). For a married couple family with a male earner, dependent spouse and three dependent children, welfare payments will replace 82 per cent of the after-tax income.

The fact that the replacement ratio is so high for married couples raises an interesting issue. There has not been much discussion in Australia about the extent to which welfare payments provide a floor under low wages. The data suggest that the greatest tension between low pay and welfare payments may occur for married couples with a dependent spouse and dependent children; this is the group with the highest replacement ratio. If their supply elasticity is not too low they may be the group whose supply responses act to support the wage floor. On the other hand this group is only a small proportion of the low-paid (see Richardson and Harding in this volume).

The next step is to calculate hypothetical replacement ratios if Australian welfare payments were to be combined with the US earnings distribution. These calculations enable us to develop a feel for the degree of incompatibility of the Australian welfare system with a US wage structure and, as a result, the scope for the Australian labour market to generate a wider distribution of earnings without changes to the structure of welfare payments.

For all groups, replacement ratios increase when welfare payments are combined with a US wage structure. For Australian single men at the tenth percentile the replacement ratio increases from 57 to 77 per cent. Under such a system some people might choose to accept welfare payments and combine them with small amounts of employment income that is not declared to the authorities. For single females, replacement ratios are higher because the wage at the tenth percentile of the female pay distribution is lower than the equivalent point on the male distribution. Finally, for married couples with dependent children, the change in the replacement ratio is quite small, increasing from 82 to 84 per cent.

These results suggest two conclusions. For single adults the relative wage falls associated with a move to a US pay structure significantly increases the replacement ratios. The question is raised whether supply-side effects, real or imagined, in response to such a narrow gap between employment and unemployed income would generate political and social pressure to reduce welfare payments. The other conclusion is a restatement of the results of the analysis of the previous section. For married couple families with dependants, the wage fall of moving to the US pay structure at the tenth percentile is 28 per cent, but the change in the replacement ratios is of the order of 2 per cent. The large wage falls are almost fully offset by increased government welfare payments and reduced tax liabilities. For these families the relationship between taxation, welfare payments and falling wages generates considerable demands on the government budget rather than a reduction in employment income and a possible labour supply response.

It has been recently suggested that the low-wage subsidy that now exists for families with dependent children should be extended to those without children to encourage low wages to fall further and isolate low-paid workers from the income effects of falling low wages (Dawkins et al. 1997). In this way it is argued that Australia can achieve more labour market deregulation by the taxpayer underwriting the wage falls and replacing lost income by government payments.

There are two important points to be noted. Earlier we showed that there have already been substantial falls in low weekly earnings, without noticeable increases in employment. Very significant falls in low wages may therefore be required to generate significant increases in employment. If so the budgetary costs might be substantial (and Chapter 4 suggests that they are: a 30 per cent cut in low wages costs the government budget $4 billion, if there is no offsetting increase in employment).

The current welfare system treats those with and without dependants differently, but does not distinguish between employed and unemployed people. One naturally wonders whether a significant extension of low-wage subsidies to those without children will generate sufficient budget pressure that a political response may be to introduce a welfare system that increasingly distinguishes between the employed and the unemployed. If this were to occur the costs of a widening wage distribution would be paid for in part by the unemployed and not by those in employment at low wages.

Conclusion

Growing wage inequality is gradually changing the nature of Australian society and challenging our understanding of the links between wages, employment and labour market institutions. The forces generating the changes are not clear and there are many puzzles. The fall in low wages for men, for example, has proceeded at much the same rate as in the United States without an obvious stimulation to employment growth. The data also seem to indicate that in many respects Australian wage flexibility is similar to that of the US although the degree of centralized wage-fixing is so different. Despite our lack of clear understanding of the forces generating these outcomes, it seems hard to escape from the proposition that wage inequality will continue to grow in Australia and increasingly present us with difficult policy choices.

First, there are likely to be increasing policy tensions between falling wages at the bottom of the pay distribution and the practice of setting unemployment benefits at around 25 per cent of average weekly earnings. One source of tension may arise from increasing replacement ratios for single people. The current replacement ratio at the tenth and twentieth percentile is around 57 and 51 per cent respectively. A US wage structure would generate replacement ratios of 77 and 61 per cent.

Another source of tension may arise from the increased budgetary cost of *de facto* wage subsidies for the employed with dependants. At the tenth percentile of the US male wage distribution the government subsidy for a married couple with three children exceeds the wage. At the twentieth percentile the government subsidy is 70 per cent of the wage. After taxes the net subsidy at the tenth and twentieth percentile are 100 per cent and 60 per cent respectively.

Finally, as low wages fall we would expect the real value of government income subsidies for children to increase relative to low wages paid for single people. Consider a sole parent in an environment of the US pay structure and the Australian welfare system. At the tenth percentile of the US female pay distribution a sole parent employed full-time, and with one dependent child, would receive a subsidy equal to 68 per cent of the net wage. At the twentieth and thirtieth percentile the subsidy would be 54 and 38 per cent respectively. This wage subsidy for children, relative to low wages, is almost twice as high as that currently paid in Australia. This arises because the structure and level of Australian welfare payments were set in the context of the more compressed

Australian pay distribution. They illustrate the interrelationships between the design of a welfare system and the wage distribution. This level of subsidy seems to overcompensate for children at least relative to the pay distribution, and it seems unlikely that a system could stay in place that almost allows a doubling of net income for a dependent child provided the mother remains in full-time work. It seems probable therefore that a large change in the wage distribution would change the welfare system. It would become less generous for the low-paid. Under these circumstances the earlier suggestion that single people and those without children would be most affected by a widening pay distribution may not be correct.

 These tensions suggest the following questions:

1 Will increased demands on government, generated by increased income support for those with dependent children, lead to less income support for those without children and without employment? Under the present welfare system more wage inequality may present government with increased welfare expenditure from two directions. From one direction increased welfare expenditure will be generated by falling wages of the employed, which will lead to an increased level of *de facto* wage subsidies. From another direction there may be a growing number of unemployment benefit recipients in response to significant increases in the replacement ratio for single adults. The direction of the current policy response seems clear. The process of tightening access to unemployment benefits is already under way, and at the same time support for those employed at low pay with dependent children is increasing.

2 Will a significant increase in inequality of the wage structure, which leads to increased income support for children relative to the low-paid, lead to a reduction in income support for children relative to the average level of income in the community? To date, the trend seems to be moving in the other direction and increasing child support rather than reducing it.

3 What are the more important supply responses to growing wage inequality? Replacement ratios are highest for those with dependants, but as wage inequality increases the changes in these ratios are marginal. But, among this group, are there important supply responses already occurring within the employed workforce which have not yet been documented? The high EMTRs for those with dependants suggest that for a large number of workers there is little to be gained from a wage increase and little to be lost from a wage reduction. The potential gains or losses from job mobility seem to be very low for those with dependants.

In response to increased wage inequality, the largest increases in replacement ratios occur among single people and those without dependants. This is the group that may choose to remain unemployed longer rather than to accept low-paying employment.

The concluding assessment of Chapter 3 suggests that the employment consequences of deregulating wage-setting for low-paid workers would yield only a small increase in employment (of 60 000 to 90 000 jobs). This assessment is consistent with the evidence of falling wages among the low-paid that has been described in this chapter and consistent with the view that although Australian wage falls among the low-paid are similar to those in the United States, Australian employment growth has been very much lower. Two things follow. First, that if wage reductions are to make a significant impact on unemployment, *large* falls will be needed. Second, labour market income of low-paid workers as a group will fall and poverty among the working poor will increase.

This chapter extends the employment–wage analysis and demonstrates that if there are significant wages falls in response to wage deregulation then consequent changes in the Australian welfare system will be set in train. These changes are likely to reduce the level of unemployment benefits, increase job subsidies for low-paid workers with children, and place further pressure on government expenditure, which will lead to reduction in access to income support.

The analysis of Chapters 3 and 7 suggests that the income distribution implications of wage deregulation are likely to be substantial, so substantial relative to employment gains that it seems unwise to place the policy emphasis on wage deregulation to solve the Australian unemployment problem. This suggests that the policy emphasis to create jobs should be directed primarily elsewhere, perhaps back to old-fashioned government involvement in job creation, job training schemes and good macro policies generally.

Notes

1 Of course, a deregulated labour market may create jobs without relative wage changes. Other proponents of a deregulated labour market may have in mind substantial labour productivity improvements. This has not happened in the United States however. Indeed fast employment growth in the United States has been associated with below-average productivity increases.

2 The Australian data are weekly income for the week before the interview. The US data are full-year full-time weekly income in the calendar year before the interview. Since 1981 US data are also available for weekly income last

week. A comparison of the two US series does not reveal a significant difference.

3 In the United States it appears that earnings inequality fell during the postwar period until the mid-1970s.

4 There was some discussion during these years about why the less regulated US labour market performed worse than other more regulated OECD labour markets in terms of employment, unemployment and wage dispersion, but the literature was not very extensive.

5 The degree of US wage inequality was not constant during this period. Wage inequality narrowed fairly continuously between the end of the Second World War and the mid-1970s.

6 The data refer to weekly earnings and not wages. Hence it is possible that the fall in low wages is generated by the job growth patterns (see Gregory 1996).

7 Of course, the important links between market deregulation and employment growth may not be between relative wages changes and relative employment responses. What may matter more is that in a more flexible labour market there is a lower nominal wage increase in response to an uplift in employment growth. But these relationships are outside the scope of this chapter.

8 The following describes the order of withdrawal of payment components. Allowances and pensions generally consist of different components. Some of these components are taxable (base age pension or base allowance) and others are non-taxable (Rent Assistance and Pharmaceutical Allowance). Taper income tests reduce payments from the maximum rate, based on the private income of the client. When calculating effective marginal tax rates, it is essential to know which components of a payment are withdrawn first as the taxation status of the components can differ. In calculating pensions and allowances, the different components are withdrawn in the following order: base pension or allowance, rent assistance, pharmaceutical allowance. Generally taxable components are withdrawn first and non-taxable components are withdrawn last. The components that make up Additional Family Payment are all non-taxable. This means that they can be combined into one payment and income-tested as such.

9 We include the base allowance, rent assistance, additional family payments, minimum family payments, parenting allowance, guardian allowance, family tax payment, spouse rebate, sole parent rebate, low income rebate and medicare levy. We did not include child care rebate, child care assistance and pharmaceutical allowances.

10 The situation has changed considerably over our period of analysis. The basic pension increased by 14 per cent in real terms between December 1982 and December 1997, while over the same period the real increase in assistance for a child was 141 per cent and the real increase in rent assistance was 120 per cent (Keating 1997).

References

N/A →

Abowd, J., and R. Freeman (eds), 1992, *Immigration, Trade, and the Labor Market*, Chicago: University of Chicago Press.

ABS, 1994, *Labour Force and Other Characteristics of Families*, no. 6224.0.

—— 1995, *Working Arrangements*, Australia, no. 6342.0.

Argy, F., 1998, *Australia at the Crossroads*, Sydney: Allen & Unwin.

Atkinson, A. B., 1989, *Poverty and Social Security*, London: Harvester Wheatsheaf.

AIRC, 1997, *Safety Net Review – Wages*, Canberra: AGPS.

—— 1991a, *National Wage Case April 1991*, Print J7400.

—— 1991b, *National Wage Case October 1991: Reasons for Decision*, Print K0300.

—— 1998, Safety Net Review: Wages, Print Q1998.

Bartel, Ann, and Frank R. Lichtenberg, 1987, 'The Comparative Advantage of Educated Workers in Implementing New Technologies', *Review of Economics and Statistics*, 69(1): 1–11.

Becker, Gary S., 1962, *Human Capital Theory*, Washington DC: Columbia University Press.

Beer, G., 1997, 'Is it Worth Working? The Financial Impact of Increased Hours of Work by Married Mothers with Young Children', paper presented at the 26th Annual Conference of Economists, University of Tasmania, 28 September–1 October.

Bell, D., and R. Wright, 1996, 'The impact of minimum wages on the wages of the low paid: evidence from the wage boards and councils', *Economic Journal*, 106(May): 650–6.

Bennett, L., 1994, *Making Labour Law in Australia: Industrial Relations, Politics and Law*, Sydney: Law Book Company.

—— 1995, 'Women and Enterprise Bargaining: the legal and institutional framework', in M. Thornton (ed.), *Public and Private: Feminist Legal Debates*, Melbourne: Oxford University Press, pp. 112–43.

Betson, David M., 1982, 'Comment on Robert I. Lerman', in Robert H. Haveman and John L. Palmer (eds), *Jobs for Disadvantaged Workers: The Economics of Employment Subsidies*, Washington DC.: Brookings Institution, pp. 180–3.

Blanchflower, D., 1989, 'International comparisons of wages and unionism', mimeo, London School of Economics.

Bland, A. E., P. A. Brown and R. H. Tawney (eds), 1914, *English Economic History: Select Documents*, London: G. Bell & Sons.

Blandy, R., 1990, 'Discussion', in S. Grenville (ed.), *The Australian Macro-Economy in the 1980s*, Sydney: Reserve Bank of Australia, pp. 66–72.

Blandy, R., and O. Covick, 1984, *Understanding Labour Markets*, Sydney: Allen & Unwin.

Blandy, R., and J. Niland (eds), 1986, *Alternatives to Arbitration*, Sydney: Allen & Unwin.

Blau, F., and L. Kahn, 1992, 'The gender earnings gap: learning from international comparisons', *American Economic Review: Papers and Proceedings*, 82: 533–8.

—— 1996a, 'International differences in male wage inequality: institutions versus market forces', *Journal of Political Economy*, 104: 791–837.

—— 1996b, 'Wage structure and gender earnings differentials: an international comparison', *Economica*, S29–61.

Bora, B., 1995, 'The implications of globalisation for Australian foreign investment policy', in Economic Planning and Advisory Commission, *Globalisation*, pp. 89–112.

Borkslund, S., 1993, 'Experimental Results from Sweden of Increased Intensity of Employment Services', in Denmark Employment Department, *Measuring Labor Market Measures*, Denmark, pp. 189–211.

Borland, J., 1996, 'Earnings Inequality in Australia: changes and causes', mimeo, Economics Department, Research School of Social Sciences, ANU.

Borland, J., and R. Wilkins, 1996, 'Earnings inequality in Australia', *Economic Record*, 72(216): 7–23.

Borland, J., F. Vella and G. Woodbridge, 1996, 'Earnings dispersion in Australia and the United States: do institutions matter?', mimeo, Centre for Economic Policy Research, ANU.

Bradbury, B., 1993, 'Male wage inequality before and after tax: a six country comparison', Discussion Paper No. 42, Social Policy Research Centre, University of New South Wales.

—— 1996, 'Are the Low Income Self-employed Poor?', Discussion Paper No. 73, Social Policy Research Centre, University of New South Wales.

Brotherhood of St Laurence, 1996, Submission in the Australian Industrial Relations Commission 'Living Wage Case, 1996–7'.

Brown, C., C. Gilroy and A. Kohen, 1982, 'The effect of the minimum wage law on employment and unemployment', *Journal of Economic Literature*, 20: 487–528.

Brown, W., J. Hayles, B. Hughes and L. Rowe, 1978, 'How far does arbitration constrain Australia's labour market?', *Australian Bulletin of Labour*, 4: 31–9.

—— 1980, 'Occupational pay structures under different wage fixing arrangements: a comparison of intra-occupational pay dispersion in Australia, Great Britain and the United States', *British Journal of Industrial Relations*, 18: 217–30.

—— 1984, 'Product and labour markets in wage determination: some Australian evidence', *British Journal of Industrial Relations*, 22: 169–76.

Browning, E., 1995, 'Effects of the Earned Income Tax Credit on income and welfare', *National Tax Journal*, 78(March): 23–44.

Buchanan, J., and R. Callus, 1993, 'Efficiency and equity at work: the need for labour market regulation in Australia', *Journal of Industrial Relations*, 35: 515–37.

Burdett, K., and D. Mortensen, 1997, 'Wage differentials, employer size, and unemployment', forthcoming, *International Economic Review*.

Bureau of Labour Market Research, 1984, *Public Sector Job Creation: Interim Report on the Wage Pause Program*, Canberra: AGPS.

Burkhauser, R., and A. Finegan, 1989, 'The minimum wage and the poor: the end of a relationship', *Journal of Policy Analysis and Management*, 8(Winter): 53–71.

—— 1993, 'The economics of the minimum wage legislation revisited', *Cato Journal*, 13(Spring/Summer): 123–9.

Callus, R., A. Moorhead, M. Cully and J. Buchanan, 1991, *Industrial Relations at Work*, Canberra: AGPS.

Calmfors, L., and J. Driffill, 1988, 'Bargaining structure, corporatism and macroeconomic performance', *Economic Policy*, 6: 14–61.

Campbell, H., and K. Bond, 1997, 'The cost of public funds in Australia', *Economic Record*, 73: 22–34.

Card, D., and A. Krueger, 1995, *Myth and Measurement: The New Economics of the Minimum Wage*, Princeton NJ: Princeton University Press.

Card, D., and T. Lemieux, 1997, 'Adapting to circumstances: the evolution of work, school and living arrangements among North American youth', Working Paper No. 386, Princeton University Industrial Relations Section.

Castles, F., 1985, *The Working Class and Welfare: Reflections on the Political Development of the Welfare State in Australia and New Zealand, 1890–1980*, Wellington: Allen & Unwin.

Castles, F., and D. Mitchell, 1993, 'A Radical World of Welfare: the welfare state and equality in the English-speaking family of nations', in F. Castles (ed.), *Families of Nations: Patterns of Public Policy in Western Democracies*, Dartmouth, UK.

—— 1994, *Designing for the Future: An Institutional View of the Australian Welfare State*, EPAC National Strategies Conference Paper, Canberra: AGPS.

Chapman, B., 1985, 'Continuity and change: labour market programs and education expenditure', *Australian Economic Review*, 3: 98–112.

Chapman, B. J., and H. W. Tan, 1980, 'Specific training and inter-industry wage differentials in US manufacturing', *Review of Economics and Statistics*, 62(3): 371–8.

Chapman, B. J., and P. N. Smith, 1992, 'Predicting the Long-term Unemployed: a primer for the Commonwealth Employment Service', in R. G. Gregory and T. Karmel (eds), *Youth in the Eighties: Papers from the Australian Longitudinal Survey Research Project*, Centre for Economic Policy Research, ANU, pp. 263–81.

Chapman, B., A. Hanlan, P. Lewis, W. Mitchell, C. Murphy, M. Upcher and M. Watts, 1991, 'Analysing the impact of consensual incomes policy on aggregate wage outcomes: the 1980s Australian experiment', Discussion Paper No. 253, Centre for Economic Policy Research, ANU.

Coelli, M., J. Fahrer and H. Lindsay, 1994, 'Wage dispersion and labour market institutions: a cross-country study', Research Discussion Paper No. 9404, Reserve Bank of Australia.

Coffield, F., P. Robinson and J. Sansby, 1980, *A Cycle of Deprivation? A Case Study of Four Families*, London: Heinemann.

Committee of Review into Australian Industrial Relations Law and Systems, 1985, *Australian Industrial Relations Law and Systems: Report of the Committee of Review*, vols 2 and 3, Canberra: AGPS.

Commonwealth Government of Australia, 1994, *Working Nation* (the White Paper), Canberra: AGPS.

Cook P., 1991, 'The Future of Wage Fixation', address to the Industrial Relations Society of New South Wales, 10 May.

Dabscheck, B., 1995, *The Struggle for Australian Industrial Relations*, Melbourne: Oxford University Press.

Danthine, J., and J. Hunt, 1994, 'Wage bargaining structure, employment and economic integration', *Economic Journal*, 104: 528–41.

Davies, P., and M. Freedland (eds), 1983, *Kahn-Freund's* Labour and the Law, 3rd edn, London: Stevens & Sons.

Dawkins, P., 1997, 'The minimum wage debate and policy developments in Australia, the UK and the US: an introductory overview', *Australian Economic Review*, 30: 187–93.

—— 1998, 'The economic effects of deregulation and decentralisation of wage determination', forthcoming, *Journal of Industrial Relations*.

Dawkins, P., and J. Freebairn, 1997, 'Towards full employment', *Australian Economic Review*, 30: 405–17.

Dawkins, P., G. Beer, A. Harding, D. Johnson and R. Scutella, 1997, 'Towards a Negative Income Tax System', Melbourne Institute of Applied Economic and Social Research, Melbourne University.

Debelle, G., and J. Borland (eds), 1998, *Unemployment and the Australian Labour Market*, Sydney: Reserve Bank of Australia.

Deery, S. J., and D. H. Plowman, 1991, *Australian Industrial Relations*, 3rd edn, Sydney: McGraw-Hill.

Department of Employment, Education and Training, 1993, *The Job Report*, 2(4).

Department of Industrial Relations, 1993a, *Small Business and Industrial Relations: Some Policy Issues*, Research Series No. 8, Canberra: AGPS.

—— 1993b, *A Survey of Small Business and Industrial Relations*, Canberra: AGPS.

—— 1997, 'The relationship between youth wages and employment: a review of the literature', Submission to House of Representatives Standing Committee on Employment, Education and Training.

Dixon, R., 1994, 'Apparent asymmetries in the relationship between the participation rate and employment rate in Australia', mimeo, Department of Economics, University of Melbourne.

Dolado, J., F. Kramarz, S. Machin, A. Manning, D. Margolis and C. Teulings, 1996, 'The economic impact of minimum wages in Europe', *Economic Policy*, 23, October 319–72.

Dowrick, S., 1995, 'The Determinants of Long Run Growth', in P. Andersen, J. Dwyer and D. Gruen (eds), *Productivity and Growth*, Sydney: Reserve Bank of Australia, pp. 7–47.

Drago, F. R., and M. Wooden, 'The BCA Report: a response to Frenkel and Peetz (II)', *Journal of Industrial Relations*, 32: 413–18.

Economic Planning Advisory Commission, *Globalisation: Issues for Australia*, Commission Paper No. 5, Canberra: AGPS.

Ehrenberg, R., 1995, 'Review symposium', Industrial and Labor Relations Review, 48: 827–49.

Ehrenberg, R., and R. Smith, 1997, *Modern Labor Economics*, 6th edn, Sydney: Addison-Wesley.

Elliott, R., 1991, *Labour Economics: A Comparative Text*, London: McGraw-Hill.

Epstein, R. A., 1985, 'In Defense of the Contract at Will', in R. A. Epstein and Jeffrey Paul (eds), *Labor Law and the Employment Market*, New Brunswick and Oxford: Transaction Books, pp. 3–38.

Evans, M., and J. Kelley, 1996, 'Job Complexity', World Wide Attitudes, International Social Science Survey, Research School of Social Sciences, ANU.

Forslund, A., and A. Krueger, 1994, 'An Evaluation of the Swedish Active Labor Market Policy: New and Received Wisdom', Working Paper No. 4802, National Bureau of Economic Research.

Freebairn, J., 1995, 'Reconsidering the marginal welfare cost of taxation', *Economic Record*, 71(213): 121–30.

Freeman, R., 1982, 'Union wage practices and wage dispersion within establishments', *Industrial and Labor Relations Review*, 36: 3–21.

—— 1995, 'Are your wages set in Beijing?', *Journal of Economic Perspectives*, 9(3): 15–32.

—— 1996, 'The minimum wage as a redistributive tool', *Economic Journal*, 106(May): 639–49.

Freeman, R., and R. Gibbons, 1994, 'Getting Together and Breaking Apart: the decline of centralized collective bargaining', in R. Freeman and L. Katz (eds), *Differences and Changes in Wage Structures*, Chicago: University of Chicago Press, pp. 345–70.

Frenkel, S., and D. Peetz, 1990a, 'Enterprise bargaining: the BCA's Report on industrial relations reform', *Journal of Industrial Relations*, 32: 69–99.

—— 1990b, 'The BCA Report: a rejoinder', *Journal of Industrial Relations*, 32: 419–30.

Fritzell, J., 1991, 'The gap between market rewards and economic wellbeing in modern societies', *European Sociological Review*, 7(1): 19–33.

Garvey, G., 1993, 'The Market for Employment: insights from traditional and modern economics', in Hilmer et al., 1993, *Working Relations*, pp. 239–354.

Gaston, N., 1998, 'The impact of international trade and protection on Australian manufacturing employment', *Australian Economic Papers*, 37(2): 119–36.

Gill, F., 1990, 'Social Justice and the Low-Paid Worker', *Australian Journal of Social Issues*, 25: 83–102.

—— 1994, 'Low Pay and Gender Under Wage Regulation: the Australian experience', in B. Caine (ed.), *The Woman Question in England and Australia*, Sydney Studies in History No. 5, University of Sydney, pp. 110–41.

Gottschalk, P., and M. Joyce, 1997, 'Cross-national differences in the rise in earnings inequality – market and non-market factors', Working Paper No. 160, Luxembourg Income Study, Luxembourg.

Gregg, P., and A. Manning, 1996, 'Labour Market Regulation and Unemployment', in D. Snower and G. de la Dehesa (eds), *Unemployment Policy: Government Options for the Labour Market*, Cambridge: Cambridge University Press, pp. 395–423.

Gregory, M., and P. Elias, 1994, 'Earnings transitions of the low paid in Britain, 1976–91: a longitudinal study', *International Journal of Manpower*, 15(2): 170–88.

Gregory, R., 1986, 'Wages policy and unemployment in Australia', *Economica*, 53, Supplement: 53–74.

—— 1996, 'Wage Deregulation, Low Paid Workers and Full Employment', in P. Sheehan, B. Grewal and M. Kumnick (eds), *Dialogues on Australia's Future*, Centre for Strategic Economic Studies, Victoria University, Melbourne, pp. 81–102.

Gregory, R., and A. Daly, 1990, 'Can economic theories explain why Australian women are so well paid relative to their US counterparts?', Discussion Paper No. 226, Centre for Economic Policy Research, ANU.

———— 1994, 'Who gets what? institutions, human capital, and black boxes as determinants of relative wages in Australia and the United States', in J. Niland, R. Lansbury and C. Verevis (eds), *The Future of Industrial Relations*, Thousand Oaks: Sage Publications, pp. 405–34.

Gregory, R., and R, Duncan, 1981, 'Segmented labor market theories and the Australian experience of equal pay for women', *Journal of Post Keynesian Economics*, 3: 403–28.

———— 1983, 'Equal pay for women: a reply', *Australian Economic Papers*, 22: 60–4.

Gregory, R., and V. Ho, 1985, 'Equal pay and comparable worth: what can the US learn from the Australian experience?', Discussion Paper No. 123, Centre for Economic Policy Research, ANU.

Gregory, R., and G. Woodbridge, 1993, 'Economic Rationalism and Earnings Dispersion', in S. King and P. Lloyd (eds), *Economic Rationalism: Dead End or Way Forward?*, Sydney: Allen & Unwin, pp. 220–33.

Gregory, R., A. Daly and V. Ho, 1986, 'A tale of two countries: equal pay for women in Australia and Britain', Discussion Paper No. 147, Centre for Economic Policy Research, ANU.

Gregory, R., R. Anstie and E. Klug, 1991, 'Why are lowskilled immigrants in the United States poorly paid relative to their Australian counterparts?', in J. M. Abowd and R. B. Freeman (eds), *Immigration, Trade and the Labor Market*, National Bureau of Economic Research, Washington, 1991, pp. 385–406.

Gregory, R., R. Anstie, A. Daly and V. Ho, 1989, 'Women's Pay in Australia, Great Britain and the United States: the role of laws, regulation and human capital', in R. Michael, H. Hartmann and B. O'Farrell (eds), *Pay Equity: Empirical Inquiries*, Washington DC: National Academy Press, pp. 222–42.

Gruen, D., 1995, 'Globalisation and the macroeconomy', in Economic Planning and Advisory Commission, *Globalisation*, pp. 127–54.

Gunderson, M., 1989, 'Male–female wage differentials and policy responses', *Journal of Economic Literature*, 27: 46–72.

Hamermesh, D., 1993, *Labour Demand*, Princeton NJ: Princeton University Press.

Hammond, S., and R. Harbridge, 1993, 'The impact of the Employment Contracts Act on women at work', *New Zealand Journal of Industrial Relations*, 18(1): 15–30.

Hancock, K. J., 1979, 'The first half-century of Australian wage policy' (Parts 1 and 2), *Journal of Industrial Relations*, 21: 1–19 and 129–60.

———— 1983, 'The Arbitration Tribunals and the Labour Market', in CEDA, *Wage Determination and the Market*, Melbourne: CEDA, pp. 38–52.

———— 1998, 'The needs of the low paid', *Journal of Industrial Relations*, 40: 42–62.

Hancock, K. J., C. H. Fitzgibbon and G. Polites, 1985, *Australian Industrial Relations Law and Systems: Report of the Committee of Review*, 3 vols, Canberra: AGPS.

Harding, A., 1997, 'The suffering middle: trends in income inequality in Australia 1982 to 1993–4', *Australian Economic Review*, 30(4): 341–58.

Harding, A., and J. Polette, 1995, 'The price of means-tested transfers: effective marginal tax rates in Australia in 1994', *Australian Economic Review*, July–September: 100–6.

Harding, A., and S. Richardson, 1998, 'Unemployment and Income Distribution', in Debelle and Borland (eds), *Unemployment and the Australian Labour Market*, pp. 139–64.

Haveman, R., and L. Buron, 1993, 'Escaping poverty through work – the problem of low earnings capacity in the United States, 1973–88', *Review of Income and Wealth*, 39(2): 141–58.

Hawke, A., 1993, Full- and Part-Time Work and Wages: An Application to Two Countries, unpublished PhD thesis, ANU.

Hayek, F. A., 1960, *The Constitution of Liberty*, vol. 2, Chicago: University of Chicago Press.

——— 1979, *Social Justice, Socialism and Democracy: Three Australian Lectures*, Centre for Independent Studies.

——— 1980, *1980s Unemployment and the Unions: the Distortion of Relative Prices by Monopoly in the Labour Market*, Hobart Paper No. 87, Institute of Economic Affairs.

Hilmer, F. G., and P. McLaughlin, 1990, 'The BCA Report: A Response to Frenkel and Peetz (I)', *Journal of Industrial Relations*, 32: 403–12.

Hilmer, F. G., D. Macfarlane, J. Rose and P. McLaughlin, 1989, *Enterprise-based Bargaining Units: A Better Way of Working*, Business Council of Australia.

Hilmer, F. G., P. A. McLaughlin, D. K. Macfarlane and J. Rose, 1991, *Avoiding Industrial Action: A Better Way of Working*, Business Council of Australia.

Hilmer, F. G., M. Angwin, J. E. Layt, G. Dudley, P. Barratt and P. A. McLaughlin, 1993, *Working Relations: A Fresh Start for Australian Enterprises*, The Business Library.

Hochschild, J., 1991, 'The Politics of the Estranged Poor', *Ethics*, 101: 560–78.

Horrigan, M., and R. Mincey, 1992, 'Public policy changes and the distribution of income', in S. Danziger and P. Gottschalk (eds), *Uneven Tides: Rising Inequality in America*, New York: Russell Sage Foundation, pp. 154–87.

H. R. Nicholls Society, 1997, *Mission Abandoned*, Melbourne: H. R. Nicholls Society Inc.

Hughes, B., 1973, 'The wages of the strong and the weak', *Journal of Industrial Relations*, 15: 1–24.

Hunter, B., and R. Gregory, 1996, 'The macro-economy and the growth of ghettos and urban poverty in Australia', Discussion Paper No. 325, Centre for Economic Policy Research, ANU.

Industry Commission, 1996, *The Changing of Australian Manufacturing*, Staff Information Paper, Canberra: AGPS.

——— 1997a, *Textiles, Clothing and Footware*, Draft Report, Canberra: AGPS.

——— 1997b, *Assessing Australia's Productivity Performance*, Research Paper, Canberra: AGPS.

Ingles, D., 1997, 'Low income traps for working families', Discussion Paper No. 363, Centre for Economic Policy Research, ANU.

Isaac, J., 1981, 'Equity and wage determination', *Australian Bulletin of Labour*, 7: 205–18.

——— 1982, 'Economics and industrial relations', *Journal of Industrial Relations*, 24: 495–516.

Jacques, E., 1967, *Equitable Payment: A General Theory of Work, Differential Payment and Individual Progress*, Penguin Books, UK.

Jarvie, W., and R. McKay, 1993, 'Perspectives on Department of Employment, Education and Training (DEET) Labour Market Programs', Discussion Paper No. 296, Centre for Economic Policy Research, ANU.

Jencks, C., 1989, 'What is the underclass – and is it growing?'; *Focus*, 12: 14–26.

Johnson, G. E., 1977, 'The fiscal substitution effects of alternative approaches to public service employment', *Journal of Human Resources*, 12: 3–26.

Joint Governments' Submission, 1998, to the Australian Industrial Relations Commission Review of the Safety Net.

Keating, M., 1998, 'Work, wages and welfare', mimeo, Economics Program, Research School of Social Sciences, ANU.

Keating, M., and D. Mitchell, 1999, 'Social Policy', in G. Davis, M. Keating, and P. Weller (eds), *The Future of Governance in Australia*, Sydney: Allen & Unwin, forthcoming.

Kennan, J., 1995, 'The elusive effects of minimum wages', *Journal of Economic Literature*, 33(4): 1949–65.

Killingsworth, M., 1990, *The Economics of Comparable Worth*, Kalamazoo MI: Upjohn Institute for Employment Research.

Krugman P., 1997, *Pop Internationalism*, Cambridge, Mass.: MIT Press.

Lambert, S., R. Percival, D. Schofield and S. Paul, 1994, 'An introduction to STINMOD: a static microsimulation model', Technical Paper No. 1, NATSEM, University of Canberra.

Lansbury, R., and J. Kitay, 1995, 'The Implications of Globalisation for Human Resource Management, Industrial Relations and Labour Market Policies: Australia in an international context', in Economic Planning Advisory Commission, *Globalisation*, pp. 167–82.

Lewis, P., and D. Spiers, 1990, 'Six years of the Accord: an assessment', *Journal of Industrial Relations*, 32: 237–58.

Lewis, P., 1985, 'Substitution between young and adult workers in Australia', *Australian Economic Papers*, 24: 115–26.

———— 1997, 'The economics of the minimum wage', *Australian Economic Review*, 30: 204–7.

Lewis, P., and A. Seltzer, 1996, 'Labour Demand', in K. Norris and M. Wooden (eds), *The Changing Australian Labour Market*, Canberra: AGPS, pp. 39–52.

Machin, S., and A. Manning, 1996, 'Employment and the introduction of a minimum wage in Britain', *Economic Journal*, 106(May): 667–76.

Mangan, J., and J. Johnston, 1997, 'Minimum wages, training wages and youth employment', Discussion Paper No. 229, Department of Economics, University of Queensland.

Manning, A., 1994a, 'How do we know that real wages are too high?', *Quarterly Journal of Economics*, 109: 1111–25.

———— 1994b, 'Labour markets with company wage policies', Discussion Paper No. 214, Centre for Economic Performance, London School of Economics.

———— 1996, 'The Equal Pay Act as an experiment to test theories of the labour market', *Economica*, 63: 191–212.

Marshall, A., 1930, *Principles of Economics*, 8th edn, London: Macmillan.

Martin, L., and D. Giannaros, 1990, 'Would a higher minimum wage help poor families headed by women?', *Monthly Labor Review*, 113(August): 33–7.

Martin, J., 1998, 'What Works Among Active Labour market Policies? evidence from OECD countries' experiences', in G. Debelle and J. Borland (eds), *Unemployment and the Australian Labour Market*, Conference Proceedings, Reserve Bank of Australia. Sydney, pp. 276–303.

Marx, K, 1932, *Capital*, vol. 1, Chicago: Charles Kerr & Co.

McCarthy, P., 1969, 'Justice Higgins and the Harvester Judgment', *Australian Economic History Review*, 9(1): 17–38.

McDonald, P., 1995, *Families in Australia*, Melbourne: Australian Institute for Family Studies.

McGavin, P., 1983a, 'Equal pay for women: a re-assessment of the Australian experience', *Australian Economic Papers*, 22: 48–59.

—— 1983b, 'Equal pay for women: a postscript', *Australian Economic Papers*, 22: 65–7.

Merrilees, W., 1979, 'Teenage unemployment: the role of wage rates and other factors', paper presented to 49th ANZAAS Conference, Auckland.

—— 1984, 'Do wage subsidies stimulate training? an evaluation of the CRAFT rebate scheme', *Australian Economic Papers*, 23: 235–48.

—— 1985, 'The relationship between youth wages and youth employment: estimate of the youth wage elasticity', mimeo, Bureau of Labour Market Research, Canberra.

Mincey, R., 1990, 'Raising the minimum wage: effects on family poverty', *Monthly Labor Review*, 113(August): 18–25.

Mitchell, D., 1984, 'The Australian Labour Market', in R. Caves and L. Krause (eds), *The Australian Economy: A View From the North*, Sydney: Allen & Unwin, pp. 127–94.

—— 1995, 'Women's Incomes', in A. Edwards and S. Magarey (eds), *Women in a Restructuring Australia*, Sydney: Allen & Unwin, pp. 79–94.

—— 1997, 'Family Policy', in B. Galligan, I. McAllister and J. Ravenhill (eds), *Developments in Australian Politics*, Melbourne: Macmillan, pp. 180–95.

—— 1998a, 'Life-course and Labour Market Transitions: alternatives to the breadwinner welfare state', in M. Gatens and A. MacKinnon (eds), *Gender and Institutions: Welfare, Work and Citizenship*, Cambridge: Cambridge University Press.

—— 1998b, 'Wages and Employment', in B. Caine, M. Gatens, E. Grahame, J. Larbalestier, S. Watson and E. Webby (eds), *Oxford Companion to Australian Feminism*, Melbourne: Oxford University Press.

Moorehead, A., N. Steele, M. Alexander, K. Stephen and L. Duffin, 1997, *Changes at Work: The 1995 Australian Workplace Industrial Relations Survey*, Sydney: Longman.

NATSEM, 1997, Income Distribution Report No. 7, University of Canberra.

Neumark, D., and W. Wascher, 1992, 'Employment effects of minimum and subminimum wages: panel data in state minimum wage laws', *Industrial and Labor Relations Review*, 46 (October): 55–81.

—— 1994, 'Employment effects of minimum and subminimum wages: reply to Card, Katz and Krueger', *Industrial and Labor Relations Review*, 47 (April): 497–512.

Nickell, S., and B. Bell, 1996, 'Changes in the distribution of wages and unemployment in OECD countries', *American Economic Review*, 86, Papers and Proceedings: 302–8.

Norris, K., 1980, 'Compulsory arbitration and the wage structure in Australia', *Journal of Industrial Relations*, 22: 249–63.

—— 1986, 'The wage structure: does arbitration make any difference?', in J. Niland (ed.), *Wage Fixation in Australia*, Sydney: Allen & Unwin, pp. 183–201.

OECD, 1996a, 'Labour productivity levels in OECD countries: estimates for manufacturing and selected service industries', Economics Department Working Paper No. 169, Paris: OECD.

—— 1996b, *Labour Force Statistics*, Paris: OECD.

—— 1996c, *Employment Outlook*, Paris: OECD.

Office of the Employee Ombudsman (South Australia), 1998, Annual Report 1997/98.

Pettit, P., 1997a, 'Republican political theory', mimeo, forthcoming in A. Vincent (ed.), *Political Theory: Tradition, Diversity and Ideology*, Cambridge: Cambridge University Press.

—— 1997b, *Republicanism: A Theory of Freedom and Government*, Oxford: Clarendon Press.

Piggott, J., and B. Chapman, 1995, 'Costing the Job Compact', *Economic Record*, 71(215): 313–28.

Plowman, D., 1986, 'Developments in Australian Wage Determination 1953–1983: the institutional dimension', in J. Niland (ed.), *Wage Fixation in Australia*, Sydney: Allen & Unwin, pp. 15–48.

—— 1996, 'Employer associations and bargaining structures', *British Journal of Industrial Relations*, 26: 371–96.

Preston, A., 1997, 'Where are we now with human capital theory?', *Economic Record*, 73(220): 51–78.

Rao, G. L., and F. L. Jones, 1986, 'Effectiveness of youth manpower programs', Bureau of Labour Market Research Working Paper No. 61, Canberra.

Richardson, D., 1995, 'Income inequality and trade: how to think, what to do', *Journal of Economic Perspectives*, 9(3): 33–65.

Richardson, S., 1998, 'Progress in the Workplace?', in R. Eckersley (ed.), *Measuring Progress: Is Life Getting Better?*, Melbourne: CSIRO Publishing, pp. 201–22.

—— 1999, 'Who gets minimum wages?', *Journal of Industrial Relations*, 40(4): 554–79.

Richardson, S., and A. Harding, 1998, 'Low wages and the distribution of family income in Australia', paper presented to the conference of the International Association for Research in Income and Wealth, Cambridge, UK.

Rimmer, R., and S. Rimmer, 1994, *More Brilliant Careers: The Effect of Career Breaks on Women's Employment*, Canberra: AGPS.

Rowe, L., 1982, 'Reason, force or compromise', paper presented to the 10th Conference of Economists, ANU.

Saunders, P., 1995, 'Unpacking Inequality: wage incomes, disposable incomes and living standards', in Industry Commission, *Equity, Efficiency and Welfare*, Canberra: AGPS, pp. 225–55.

Saunders, P., and J. Fritzell, 1995, 'Wage and income inequality in two welfare states: Australia and Sweden', Discussion Paper No. 60, Social Policy Research Centre, University of New South Wales.

Schultz, T. W., 1975, 'The value of the ability to deal with disequilibria', *Journal of Economic Literature*, 13(3): 827–46.

Sloan, J., and M. Wooden, 1987, 'Labour Market Programs', in J. Freebairn, M. Porter and C. Walsh (eds), *Spending and Taxing*, Sydney: Allen & Unwin, pp. 146–65.

Sloane, P., and I. Theodossiou, 1996, 'Earnings mobility, family income and low pay', *Economic Journal*, 106 (May): 657–66.

Snower, D., 1996, 'The Low-skill, Bad-job Trap', in A. Booth and D. Snower (eds), *Acquiring Skills*, Cambridge: Cambridge University Press, pp. 109–124.

Solow, R. M., 1990, *The Labour Market as a Social Institution*, Cambridge Mass.: Blackwell.

Standing, G., 1997, 'Globalization, labour flexibility and insecurity: the era of market regulation', *European Journal of Industrial Relations*, 3: 7–37.

Stiglitz, J., 1994, *Whither Socialism?*, Cambridge Mass.: MIT Press.

Stretton, A., and B. J. Chapman, 1990, 'An analysis of Australian labour market programs', Discussion Paper No. 247, Centre for Economic Policy Research, ANU.

Topel, R., 1989, 'Comment on Katz and Summers', *Brookings Papers on Economic Activity: Microeconomics 1989*, pp. 283–8.

Travers, P., and S. Richardson, 1993, *Living Decently: Material Well-being in Australia*, Melbourne: Oxford University Press.

Undy, P., H. Fosh, P. Morris, R. Smith and R. Martin, 1996, *Managing the Unions: The Impact of Legislation on Trade Unions' Behaviour*, Oxford: Clarendon Press.

Vella, F., and K. Mackay, 1986, 'The determinants of take-up of SYETP wage subsidies for youth', *Journal of Industrial Relations*, 28: 211–24.

Walzer, M., 1985, *Spheres of Justice*, Oxford: Basil Blackwell.

Wedderburn, Lord, 1991, *Employment Rights in Britain and Europe: Selected Papers in Labour Law*, London: Lawrence & Wishart.

Webb, S., M. Kemp and J. Millar, 1996, *The Changing Face of Low Pay in Britain*, Centre for the Analysis of Social Policy No. 25, University of Bath.

Wood, A., 1995, 'How trade hurts unskilled workers', *Journal of Economic Perspectives*, 9(3): 57–80.

Index

absolute cost of labour, 92
absolute wages, 19, 90
accidents, xv, 31
Accord, 19, 25, 40, 41, 42, 48, 49, 81,
   84n.2, 90–1, 121n.4, 160, 164, 170, 208
accumulated benefit superannuation
   schemes, 162
ACTU, 19, 40, 41, 42, 43, 81, 121n.4, 160
actual wage rates, 97
Additional Family Payment, 222n.8
advocates, employee, 46, 47
age
   job breaks, 173, 174
   job security, 170
   life-course events, 171–2
   low wages, 130, 149, 150, 153, 167, 168,
      173, 174
   minimum-wage workers, 134
   promotional prospects, 171, 174
   superannuation, 170, 174
   wage cuts, 148, 149, 150
   see also youth (un)employment; youth
      wages
age pension, 137
agreements
   certified, 18, 19, 42, 43, 45–6, 47, 65,
      85n.18
   collective, 20, 21, 47, 48, 65, 71, 83, 84
   consent provisions of, 19
   enterprise, 65, 70, 71
   enterprise flexibility, 43
   formal, 19, 21
   individual, 21, 22–3, 65, 71, 160
   industrial relations, 65, 71, 160
   managerial discretion, 70
   no-disadvantage test, 43, 47
   regulated forms, 89, 90

support for, 45
terms, 18–19, 40–1, 46
trade unions, 21, 45, 46, 47, 48, 70,
   71–2, 83
types, 71
wages and conditions in, 18–19, 42, 43,
   46
workplace, 22–3, 31, 46, 47–8
agriculture, 148, 149
AIRC *see* Australian Industrial Relations
   Commission
allocative efficiency, 49–62
annual leave, 45, 46, 170, 171, 173
apprentices, 112
arbitration and conciliation, 18, 19, 20,
   21, 23–4, 43, 45, 66, 67, 68, 70, 71, 72,
   73, 82, 83, 85n.24, 88, 89–90, 91, 97,
   118
Asian immigrants, 148, 149, 154
Australia
   economic underperformance, 15–16
   economy, 63, 66, 159–60, 200
   employment–population ratio, 201,
      204, 208
   enterprise focus, 62–75
   equal pay policy, 112–13
   external accounts, 63
   female pay structure, 203–4, 205, 206,
      207, 208, 209, 210, 211, 213, 215
   full employment, 200, 206
   full-time male employees, 12, 25, 103,
      105–7
   GDP per capita, 14, 15
   industrial relations, 18
   industrial relations studies, 63–75
   inflation, 15
   jobs growth, 37n.10

234